BIKING
portland

BIKING
portland

*55 Rides from the
Willamette Valley
to Vancouver*

OWEN WOZNIAK

THE MOUNTAINEERS BOOKS

To Lee

THE MOUNTAINEERS BOOKS
is the nonprofit publishing arm of The Mountaineers, an organization founded in 1906 and dedicated to the exploration, preservation, and enjoyment of outdoor and wilderness areas.

1001 SW Klickitat Way, Suite 201, Seattle, WA 98134

© 2012 by Owen Wozniak
All rights reserved
First edition, 2012

Manufactured in the United States of America

Copy Editor: Kris Fulsaas
Cover and Book Design: The Mountaineers Books
Layout: Jennifer Shontz, www.redshoedesign.com
Cartographer: Pease Press Cartography
All photographs by the author unless otherwise noted

Cover photograph: *Bicyclists on the Vera Katz Eastbank Esplanade walkway on the Willamette River, with Burnside Bridge view.* ©Anthony Pidgeon/Alamy
Frontispiece: *Midsummer cruising, Laurelhurst Park*

Library of Congress Cataloging-in-Publication Data on file

ISBN (paperback): 978-1-59485-652-5
ISBN (ebook): 978-1-59485-653-2

CONTENTS

All smiles after another neighborhood ride

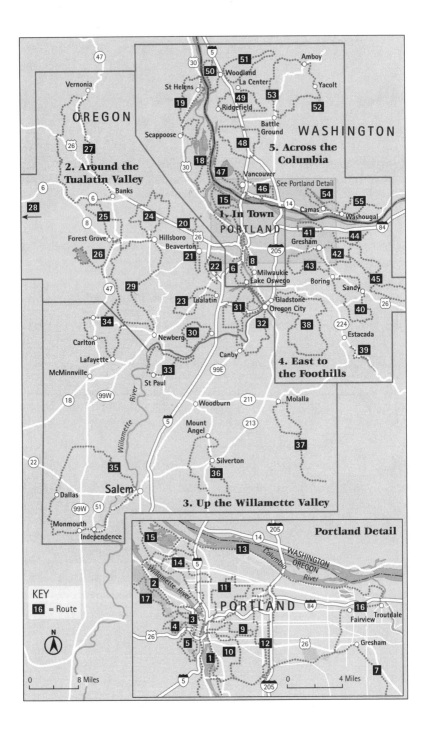

47

Vernonia

OREGON

26 27

2. Around the
Tualatin Valley

6

6

8

25

28

24

Banks

20

29

47

34

Carlton

Lafayette

McMinnville

18

99W

River

22

35

Dallas

99W 51

Monmouth

Independence

5

51 Amboy

30

50 Woodland

St Helens La Center

19 49 53

Ridgefield 52

Scappoose

48

18 Battle
Ground

30 47 Vancouver

15 46

WASHINGTON

5. Across the
Columbia

See Portland Detail

14 Camas 54 55

Washougal

84

1. In Town

PORTLAND

Forest Grove

26

Hillsboro

Beaverton

21

22 6

8

Milwaukie

Lake Oswego

205 Gresham

41

42

43 45

Boring Sandy

Tualatin

23

31

32

Gladstone

Oregon City

38

40

224

Estacada

39

Newberg

30

Canby

99E

4. East to
the Foothills

33

St Paul

Woodburn

211

Molalla

5

Mount
Angel

213

37

Silverton

36

Salem

3. Up the Willamette Valley

Willamette River

15

14

13

WASHINGTON

OREGON

Columbia River

Portland Detail

2

17

11

PORTLAND

4

3

5

26

84

16

Fairview Troutdale

9

1

10

12

26

Gresham

5

205

7

KEY

16 = Route

N

0   8 Miles

0   4 Miles

ACKNOWLEDGMENTS

My greatest thanks, and my love, go to my wife, Jen. She supported me in this project even as we began a much bigger one—having a son. Thanks also to my mother, Rachel, who graciously read nearly every word of this manuscript.

Thanks also to my ride companions: Matt Scotten, Katherine and Eric Cortes, Jon and Monica Vogel, David Miller and Nora Lehman, Michael Armstrong and Laurie Paulsen and daughters Alina and Anya.

Finally, thanks to my colleagues at the Trust for Public Land for their support and enthusiasm and to Kate Rogers, Margaret Sullivan, Janet Kimball, Kris Fulsaas, Jennifer Shontz, and Ben Pease at The Mountaineers Books for their encouragement and patience.

MAP LEGEND

———	Featured Route	·—··—··	State Boundary
- - - -	Route on Bike Path	**S**	Start and Finish
······	Option or Side Trip	**P**	Parking (if separate from start)
······	Option or Side Trip on Bike Path	**M**	MAX Station
- - - - -	Other Bike Path	**B**	Bus Stop
———	Other Route on Road	**W**	WES Station
——→	Route Direction	▪	Point of Interest
84	Interstate Highway	○	Town or City
30	US Highway	≍)(	Bridge, Underpass, or Tunnel
10	State Highway	▲	Peak
	Secondary Road	▲ ⅅ	Campground, Picnic Area
	Park/Public Land	——┼—	River or Creek, Waterfall
		⬭	Body of Water

RIDES AT-A-GLANCE

Ride No.	Route	Difficulty	Distance in Miles	Elev. Gain in Feet	Features	Transit Connections
	CHAPTER 1 IN TOWN					
1	Riverfront Loop	Easy	10.8; 2.4	175	Riverside paths, people-watching in heart of city	MAX
2	Willamette River Grand Tour	Moderate to Challenging	46.6	1600	Extended loop around the river, from city to suburbs and back	MAX
3	Downtown and Northwest	Easy to Moderate	6.8; 4.2	270	Urban cruise through Portland's cultural and commercial center	MAX
4	Washington Park	Moderate	9.6; 3.75	1450	Big climb (or not) through neighborhoods to king of Portland parks	MAX
5	Council Crest	Moderate	11.1	1200	Steep hills, parks, and city views	MAX
6	Tryon Creek	Moderate	17.4	1650	Deep woods in Portland's southwestern corner	MAX
7	Springwater Corridor	Easy	43.2	650	River views and countryside on city's premier path	MAX
8	Milwaukie and Gladstone	Easy	15	550	Historic towns, natural areas in lesser-known corner of the region	MAX
9	Southeast: Mount Tabor	Easy to Moderate	13.5	700	Vibrant neighborhoods, elegant parks, volcano-top view	MAX
10	Southeast: Woodstock and Sellwood	Easy	15.4	350	Leafy streets, river views, hidden canyon	MAX
11	Northeast	Easy	16.8	550	Diverse neighborhoods, new and old, in a rapidly changing part of the city	MAX
12	Avenue of the Roses	Easy to Moderate	21.8; 14.7	920	Quiet neighborhoods, panoramic views, cultural sites; East Portland's backbone	MAX
13	Marine Drive	Easy	19.4	75	Open riding along mighty Columbia River	MAX
14	The Peninsula	Easy	18.4	525	Willamette River history, neighborhoods in transition	MAX
15	Kelley Point	Moderate	16.6	170	Bike lane through industry and nature where Willamette and Columbia Rivers meet	MAX

Ride No.	Route	Difficulty	Distance in Miles	Elev. Gain in Feet	Features	Transit Connections
16	40-Mile Loop	Moderate	51.5; 37.8	500	Modern version of original loop path around Portland	MAX
17	Forest Park	Moderate	16.5	1900	Loop through Portland's famous urban wilderness	MAX
18	Sauvie Island	Easy to Moderate	12.1	50	Farms, fruit stands, birds, beaches on river island	TriMet bus
19	St. Helens and Scappoose	Moderate	35; 22.5; 9.8	1100	Historic towns, upland byways, floodplain farmland downriver from Portland	Columbia County bus
CHAPTER 2 AROUND THE TUALATIN VALLEY						
20	Rock Creek Greenway Trail	Easy	7.6; 9.7	400	Tualatin Valley views from wide-open greenway at edge of town	MAX
21	Westside Regional Trail	Easy	19; 16.4	1500	Beaverton views, superb nature park along greenway	MAX
22	Fanno Creek Greenway Trail	Easy	15.8; 11.5	100	Streamside path through natural areas, parks	WES or TriMet bus
23	Tualatin River	Challenging	23.5	2000	Trails, suburbs, wildlife on loop around Tualatin River	WES or TriMet bus
24	Hillsboro to Helvetia	Moderate to Challenging	28	700	Loop from Hillsboro to farm country at foot of Tualatin Mountains	MAX
25	Forest Grove	Moderate	19.2	600	Farm country, views, small-town charm in far western Tualatin Valley	MAX + TriMet bus
26	Hagg Lake	Moderate 10.4	31.8;	1450	Popular reservoir and wetlands at base of Coast Range	MAX + TriMet bus
27	Banks-Vernonia State Trail	Easy; Loop: Challenging	44.6; 57	1300; 1900	Rail-to-trail through Coast Range foothills and new state park	Tillamook County bus or MAX
28	Cape Lookout	Moderate	30.8	1600	Dramatic coastal headlands, beachfront state park	Tillamook County bus
29	Chehalem Ridge	Challenging	48.2	2000	Classic climb around and over Tualatin Valley's highest hill	MAX or Yamhill County bus

Ride No.	Route	Difficulty	Distance in Miles	Elev. Gain in Feet	Features	Transit Connections
30	Parrett Mountain	Challenging	16.2	1650	Rigorous road riding, panoramic views at metro area's southern gateway	WES
31	Stafford	Very Challenging	25.6	2200	Big hills, manicured countryside, riverside rambling at edge of suburbia	TriMet bus
CHAPTER 3 UP THE WILLAMETTE VALLEY						
32	Willamette Falls	Challenging	26.8	2000	Waterfall, historic houses, river ferry at end of Oregon Trail	MAX or TriMet bus
33	Champoeg	Easy	8.5; 16.3	650; 225	Two tours—path and road—around "Oregon's birthplace" on Willamette River	TriMet and Yamhill County bus
34	Yamhill Wine Country	Moderate to Challenging	29.5	1100	Vineyards, vistas, an abbey in Oregon's Tuscany	MAX and Yamhill County bus
35	Eola Hills	Challenging	53.5	2250	State capitol, country towns, rural roads in quiet corner of Willamette Valley	Amtrak or WES to SMART bus
36	Mount Angel and Silverton	Moderate	36.6; 22.1	1600; 425	Historic farm towns, hilltop abbey, valley views	None
37	Molalla River	Challenging	28.4; 33.9	1100; 2500	Out-and-back along one of Oregon's wildest rivers	TriMet to South Clackamas Transit District bus
CHAPTER 4 EAST TO THE FOOTHILLS						
38	Clackamas Countryside	Very Challenging	43.8; 21.8	2500	Country roads, Clackamas River views on outskirts of Oregon City	MAX or TriMet bus
39	Faraday Road	Easy	8.8	275	Car-free path by Clackamas River in Cascade foothills	TriMet bus
40	Eagle Fern Park	Very Challenging	28.5	2300	Rural byways, ancient trees in Mount Hood foothills	MAX to SAM bus
41	Gresham–Fairview Trail	Easy; Loop: Moderate	7; 18.8	110; 950	Wetlands and parks along regional trail, with optional loop to Sandy River	MAX

Ride No.	Route	Difficulty	Distance in Miles	Elev. Gain in Feet	Features	Transit Connections
42	Oxbow Regional Park	Moderate	22.4; 18.1	1300	Loop through farm country to regional park in Sandy River's secluded canyon	MAX
43	East Buttes	Moderate to Challenging	23.5	1500	Farms and forests in hills at Portland's eastern edge	MAX
44	Corbett and Crown Point	Challenging	18	1400	Rural climb to iconic Columbia Gorge vista	TriMet bus
45	Sandy River	Very Challenging	55.3; 27.8	4700	Scenic roads and long hills on flanks of Mount Hood	MAX
	CHAPTER 5 ACROSS THE COLUMBIA					
46	Fort Vancouver and Burnt Bridge Creek Greenway	Easy	23.1	750	Greenways and national historic park in heart of Vancouver	MAX
47	Vancouver Lake	Easy to Moderate	26.8	200	Easy cruise to beaches on Vancouver Lake and Columbia River	MAX
48	Salmon Creek	Easy; Loop: Moderate	6.4; 20.8	75; 1100	Stellar greenway trail along meandering creek, with rural loop to round it out	C-TRAN bus
49	Ridgefield and La Center	Moderate	23.3	1900	Two charming towns, wildlife refuge on Columbia, scenic roads along East Fork Lewis River	C-TRAN bus
50	Woodland Dike	Easy to Moderate	14.8	75	Farms and floodplain where Lewis River meets the Columbia	None
51	Cedar Creek	Challenging	27.9	2000	Back roads and historic mill near Mount St. Helens	None
52	Moulton Falls	Easy	5.2	100	Forested rail-to-trail along a very scenic river	None
53	Foothills Loop	Challenging to Very Challenging	38.8	2500	Big views, big parks on back roads of northeastern Clark County	MAX to C-TRAN bus
54	Camas and Washougal	Moderate	24.2; 11.2; 13	650; 600	Forest paths, suburban trails, country roads at gateway to Columbia Gorge	MAX to C-TRAN bus
55	Cape Horn	Challenging	18.4	1750	Country roads, spectacular view of Columbia Gorge	MAX to C-TRAN bus

Enjoying the long run down SE Gibson Road, Cape Horn

INTRODUCTION:
PORTLAND—CITY OF CYCLING

In the humble of opinion of its riders, Portland is America's premier bike city. This is a place where bicycling is not simply, or even mainly, a sport. It's a way of life.

Why? There are at least as many reasons as there are bridges in this town. Gentle topography, a mild climate, and an ever-expanding bicycling infrastructure make it easy to get around on two wheels. Respectful drivers, sporting "I share the road" bumper stickers, keep the streets (relatively) safe. Concerns about climate change motivate many Portlanders to embrace a lower-carbon lifestyle. To my mind, though, the most important answer is simply that Portlanders have woven bicycling into their civic identity, more so than in any other large city in America.

Riders of every stripe fill the streets. Spandex-clad racers zoom through the West Hills and Washington County's rolling farmland. Hipsters on fixed-gear bikes show off at downtown stoplights. Families cruise the Springwater Corridor and the city's many bike boulevards. Parents tote tots in expensive cargo bikes or ratty trailers. Specially engineered delivery bikes move truck-sized loads around town, helping businesses "green" their operations. And legions of commuters—many having ditched cars altogether—fill bike lanes and bridges year-round, creating bona fide bike rush hours. Their numbers are growing all the time.

This amounts to more than a bike scene. It's a bike culture. Decades of advocacy, an ever-expanding network of bike-related businesses (bike shops, frame builders, bike fashion houses, bike delivery businesses, and consultants of every stripe), and (mostly) strong political leadership have developed and nurtured this culture. The bike culture in turn helps attract newcomers, drawn to Portland's emerging brand of urbanism: creative, inclusive, civic-minded. Supporting it all is a system of land-use planning that's sought—with admittedly mixed results—to foster livable communities.

Portland's bike culture embraces capitalistic entrepreneurs and anarchic revolutionaries alike. Bike events cram the city's calendar, ranging from wonky "active transportation" conferences to free-spirited Naked Bike Rides. At one extreme is the mammoth Bridge Pedal, when, for one day in August, Portland's bridges close to automobiles as upward of 20,000 cyclists take over. At the other end of the spectrum are the Zoobombers, a slightly deranged, loosely affiliated crew who ride the Metropolitan Area Express (MAX) light rail up to the Oregon Zoo and then race downhill through Washington Park on kids' bikes. Between rides, they pile up their bikes into a sort of public sculpture near Powell's Books.

This bike culture is about fun, but it's also about health, economic growth, environmental sustainability, and equity. The bicycle has a role to play in all of these issues.

Community leaders have noticed. The City of Portland, as part of its effort to combat climate change and improve livability, recently adopted an ambitious bike plan. Its goal is to ensure that one out of every four trips Portlanders take by the year 2030 happens on a bike instead of in a car. With a $600 million price tag, the plan calls for hundreds of miles of new bike lanes, boulevards, trails, cycle tracks, and other improvements. The rallying cry for bike advocates is now "Build it!"

Employers, meanwhile, encourage bike commuting with subsidies and on-site bike facilities. Health-care providers use bus and billboard advertising to promote the health benefits of bicycling. The police even issue free bike lights to unlit bicyclists—though the second offense gets you a ticket! Governments, nonprofits, businesses, and community groups are working to connect and expand the network of parks, trails, and natural areas, recognizing that these are not just amenities, but vital elements of the region's economic and physical infrastructure.

THE MAKING OF A BIKE CITY

Portland developed like most American cities, driven by commerce and real estate speculation. Huge—and difficult-to-remove—trees prompted developers to build smaller city blocks to maximize more profitable corner lots and minimize tree-clearing expenses. Real estate lots were worthless without good access, though, so developers also built street-cars, which by the turn of the twentieth century crisscrossed the city.

Then the automobile ran over America. Portland dutifully joined the freeway-building boom. But then Oregonians started to question the virtue of unchecked, California-style growth. In 1973, Republican Governor Tom McCall championed innovative land-use laws to protect farmland and encourage compact urban growth.

Meanwhile, Portland's mayor, Neil Goldschmidt, threw his clout behind a neighborhood effort to block the planned Mount Hood Freeway, which would have ploughed a gash through Southeast Portland as Interstate 5 already had in North Portland. After the

Looking forward to a swim: crossing the Clackamas River on Highway 99E

freeway's defeat, Portland looked to a new paradigm for transportation: MAX light rail, buses, streetcars, and bicycling.

In the 1990s, Portlanders also woke up to climate change, adopting the first municipal global-warming action plan in the United States. It calls for reducing greenhouse gas emissions by, among other things, encouraging alternative transit and compact development. Bicycling emerged as a viable—and cheap—part of the solution to a very expensive problem.

As the millennium turned, the city built more bike lanes, bike boulevards, bike racks, and other infrastructure. The MAX network expanded. A streetcar appeared (more are on the way). A booming real estate market and growing urban sensibility transformed traditionally car-oriented neighborhoods. Soaring gas prices further encouraged people to get out of their cars. Summer weekdays on the Hawthorne Bridge witnessed a new phenomenon: bicycle traffic jams.

National media organizations have noticed the suddenly cutting-edge and urbane aura of Portland's bike-centric way of life. Bikes have become a status symbol, a badge of right-thinking and cultural belonging. The inevitable backlash is underway, with some grumbles about

A FIELD GUIDE TO PORTLAND CYCLISTS

SPECIES	HABITATS	ACTIVITIES
Spandex Superhero	Cornell Road, Sauvie Island, Helvetia, the West Hills	Century rides, hill climbs; working extra hours to pay for the bike
Eco-professional	Hawthorne Bridge, 8:30 AM	Trying to keep the hemp slacks and loafers free of chain grease for that meeting with the mayor
Bike Family	Farmers markets, Sunday Parkways, Springwater Corridor	Loading the kids into the cargo bike; gardening
Cyclocross Psycho	Mud pits at the edge of town, September through December	Lugging their bikes over hay bales and one another while grinning maniacally
Actual Bike Messenger	Downtown	Actually working for actual money; organizing "alleycat" races
Bike Messenger Look-alike	Coffee shops across Portland	Practicing track stands; checking Facebook
Grizzled Bike Purist	City Bikes Co-op, Food Not Bombs events, "Occupy" protests	Keeping it real; bartering to avoid the taint of a cash economy
Unicyclist	Hawthorne Boulevard, Last Thursday on Alberta Street	Juggling; shopping for "functional glass art"
Zoobomber	Washington Park	Racing kids' bikes downhill; visiting friends in the hospital
Freak Biker	Welding shops, Multnomah County Bike Fair, Naked Bike Ride	Building mutant bikes (tall, chopper, chariot, etc.); bike jousting; setting things on fire

money "wasted" on bike infrastructure (money which, all told, wouldn't buy even a mile of freeway). Yet ever-increasing gas prices and the collapse of the real estate bubble confirm the common-sense conclusion that bikes aren't just toys anymore.

Not toys, perhaps, but still fun. In fact, biking in Portland is more fun than ever. A countercultural anticar, anticonsumption ethos persists in some corners of Portland's bike culture, but for the most part, bicycling manages to be both mainstream and cool. This ought to keep bicycling near the top of Portland's agenda—a promising trend for people and the planet alike.

BIKE BASICS

Biking doesn't demand specialized gear or technique. That said, everyone should know a few key points. The City of Portland's "Portland by Cycle Guide to Your Ride" (www.gettingaroundportland.org) has a great overview. I've boiled it down to a few simple rules.

Be Prepared

Since the rides in this book range from short, in-town cruises to arduous loops through the boondocks, there's no one-size-fits all prescription for what to bring. That said, every ride will be safer and more enjoyable if you have the following items with you, as well as the Ten Essentials (see "The Ten Essentials for Every Ride" sidebar).

A road-ready bike. Brakes and shifters should be properly adjusted, the chain lubricated, tires properly inflated, cables intact, and bolts tightened. Fenders are a very good idea. Visit a bike shop to get a safety-check and tune-up. It's worth the investment for any cyclist, beginner or pro.

A helmet. Oregon law requires all riders under age 16 to wear a helmet, but of course riders of all ages should wear one. It should be snug but comfortable; the strap buckle should be under your chin and have no more than a finger or two's worth of slack. Replace a helmet more than five years old (the foam deteriorates with age) or after a crash.

Lights. Common sense and Oregon law require bike lights after dark. Get front (white) and rear (red) lights, make sure they're bright and flashy, and bring them every time. This is the one piece of gear you should splurge on for the high-end models.

Proper clothing. Layers are the key. Most drizzly days are humid and warmer than you might think; it's easy to overheat and then get dangerously cold when you stop to rest. A lightweight, wind-blocking, and water-resistant outer layer is ideal; bring a variety of warm layers to wear underneath. On rides in the country, I always bring a heavier layer in case of a mechanical breakdown.

The other must-have item for all but the warmest days is gloves. Padded bike shorts, protective eyewear, and shoe covers (on really cold days) are also good ideas.

Repair equipment. A mechanical problem in the middle of Portland is no big deal, but out in the country it could be highly inconvenient or worse. So always bring a tire patch kit, pump, and basic tools. Most bike shops sell cheap and lightweight multipurpose tools. I also bring zip ties and duct tape for improvised repairs. You should know how to change and patch a tire tube, reattach a slipped chain, and adjust brakes and derailleurs.

Food and water. Of course, bicycling provides an excellent means of (and excuse for) eating and drinking your way across town. If you're farther from town, carry a water bottle and a snack.

First-aid kit. I admit I sometimes leave my first-aid kit at home for in-town rides, but if you venture into the hinterlands it's a must-have.

Sunscreen and sunglasses. Yes, the sun does shine in Oregon, so protect your skin and eyes.

Lock. It's not essential, but a lock is a good idea if you plan to stop anywhere.

Map. The maps included in this book will orient you, but to find the best one for each ride, see Recommended Resources at the back of this book.

Cash and ID Card. In an emergency, make sure you have basic resources with you.

This book! Or at least bring the ride description and mileage log.

THE TEN ESSENTIALS FOR EVERY RIDE

1. Navigation: map and mileage in a waterproof, sealable bag
2. Sun protection: sunglasses and sunscreen
3. Insulation: adequate clothing layers
4. Illumination: bright white front light and red rear light
5. First-aid: a kit of emergency medical supplies
6. Fire: hand-warmer gel packs in cold weather
7. Repair kit: tools, patch kit, and pump
8. Nutrition: a snack
9. Hydration: water
10. Emergency protection: helmet plus wind- and raingear

A mid-January bike picnic on Rocky Butte, with Mount Hood beyond

Be Safe

The "Portland by Cycle Guide to Your Ride" sums it up in four basic points—to which I've added some comments:

"Ride with traffic, in a predictable manner." Take the entire road lane where you need it; the law allows this. Avoid sudden movements that could spook drivers and cause them to over-react. Use your hands to signal a turn. If you need to ride on the sidewalk, ride at pedestrian speed or, better still, walk your bike.

"Obey traffic controls (stop signs, signals, etc.)." I'd be lying if I claimed to stop at every stop sign in this town. On the other hand, just about every near-disaster I've had on a bike involved my breaking a traffic law. If you want cars to respect you, respect the laws. (On the street you're a vehicle, so a law that applies to a car also applies to a bike.)

Most traffic signals in and around Portland now have bike detectors; look for a circle on the pavement and/or a white bike icon. A number of intersections in town also have green "bike boxes" painted on the pavement. These allow bikes to move to the front of the line at a stoplight.

USE HAND SIGNALS

Hand signals tell motorists what you intend to do. For turn signals, point in the direction of your turn. Signal as a matter of courtesy and safety and as required by law.

RIDE CONSISTENTLY

Ride as close as practical to the right. Exceptions: when traveling at the normal speed of traffic, avoiding hazardous conditions, preparing to make a left turn, or using a one-way street.

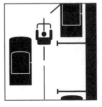

CHOOSE THE BEST WAY TO TURN LEFT

There are two ways to make a left turn: 1) Like an auto: look back, signal, move into the left lane, and turn left. 2) Like a pedestrian: ride straight to the far-side crosswalk, then walk your bike across, or queue up in the traffic lane.

USE CAUTION WHEN PASSING

Motorists may not see you on their right, so stay out of the driver's "blind spot." Be very careful when overtaking cars while in a bike lane; drivers don't always signal when turning. Some other smart things to be alert for: car doors opening and cars pulling out from sidestreets or driveways.

AVOID ROAD HAZARDS

Watch for sewer grates, slippery manhole covers, oily pavement, gravel, and ice. Cross railroad tracks at right angles. For better control as you move across bumps and other hazards, stand up on your pedals.

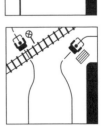

GO SLOW ON SIDEWALKS

Pedestrians have the right of way on walkways. You must give an audible warning when you pass. Cross driveways and intersections at a walker's pace and look carefully for traffic. In some communities, cycling on sidewalks is prohibited by law.

Credit: City of Portland Office of Transportation, Portland, Oregon

"Maintain control of your bicycle." Hazards likely to separate you from your bike include potholes (often lurking under puddles), railroad tracks (cross at a right angle to avoid your bike wheel getting "eaten"), road debris (especially oil, wet leaves, and gravel), sewer grates, ice, and manhole covers. If you can't avoid these hazards, slow down and try to keep cycling in a straight line. Consider stopping to walk your bike if you can safely do so.

"Be visible and aware." Being visible means staying out of drivers' blind spots, using lights and reflectors after dark, and riding where you're supposed to ride. Bright and gaudy cycling clothes are good for visibility if bad for fashion.

Being aware means riding defensively. Is there enough room between you and that parked car to avoid getting "doored"? Is that car passing you about to blindly turn to the right in front of you—and right into you (the dreaded "right hook")? Is a pedestrian about to brazenly jaywalk in front of you (a weekly occurrence on my downtown commute)? Anticipate potential problems to avoid them.

Be Comfortable

The right clothes, the right bike, and the right attitude make a huge difference:

The bike. For the pros, choosing and fitting a bicycle is supposedly an exact science necessitating lasers and other gimmicks. For the rest of us, there's really only one question: is it comfortable?

Of course, comfort involves trade-offs. Generally, bikes that put you in a more upright riding position are more comfortable on the back, wrists, shoulders, and knees. Bicycles with a racier geometry (think Tour de France) are more efficient and over longer distances are often actually *more* comfortable because they spread your weight more evenly between handlebars and saddle. They also are a lot more aerodynamic, something even a casual rider will appreciate when battling Columbia River winds on Marine Drive.

That said, for the rides in this book I recommend a bicycle on the more upright end of the spectrum. In a region like Portland's, with so many great rides and so many reasons to stop, I would trade long-distance comfort for ease of use. The bottom line, though, is that any bike can work—even that 1970s 10-speed in your dad's garage—if it's comfortable and in good working order.

If you're in the market for a bike, your options have dramatically increased in recent years. A new generation of commuter bikes, lightweight cruisers, elegant single-speed bikes, and even utility bikes designed for hauling loads (including children) are available. Many are even made locally. They sport new features like internal hub shifters, integrated racks and lights, and even (gasp!) chain guards. So go to a bike shop and talk to an expert, keeping in mind that you don't need to spend a fortune to find the right bike.

The clothes. Ventilation, rain and wind protection, and visibility are key.

The attitude. Ride with confidence, caution, and tolerance. Even here in Biketopia, drivers occasionally do scary or even mean things. There's no point in getting angry. Remember, you're almost certainly having more fun than they are!

Equally important, learn to love the rain. Your love need not be passionate, but it must be discerning. Learn the difference between a true downpour and a light drizzle. The former is rare and can be exciting or miserable, depending on your level of preparation. The latter—which is common—hardly qualifies as rain. Think of it as *refreshment*. Many seasoned riders prefer this kind of weather above all else: nothing beats cabin fever like speeding across the city in comfort, feeling the mist on your face and the breeze in your ears. And don't let all this rain talk obscure the fact that summers are mostly rain-free!

Be Oriented

You can easily get around the Portland region by bike. All it takes is a little planning:

Bring a map. Metro, the regional government covering Multnomah, Clackamas, and Washington counties, publishes a map called "Bike There," which is adequate for almost every ride in this book. See Recommended Resources at the back of this book for further suggestions.

Get familiar with bike infrastructure. In Portland, most major streets have bike lanes, which make for fast, though occasionally hairy, riding. The city has also created numerous bike boulevards: quieter, lower-traffic streets marked with giant bike symbols ("sharrows"). These boulevards discourage automobile through-traffic and concentrate bicyclists, offering some safety in numbers.

Most major suburban thoroughfares also have bike lanes, though with high-speed commuter traffic and plenty of road debris, not all are especially bike-friendly. In suburbs dating from the cul-de-sac era, bike lanes are often the only way to get from point A to point B. On the upside, the suburbs are home to excellent bike paths. These include the I-205 path (paralleling the freeway from Oregon City to

Vancouver), the I-84 path (reaching east almost to Troutdale), the Springwater Corridor (connecting Gresham with Southeast Portland), and the Fanno Greenway Trail (connecting Southwest Portland with Beaverton and Tigard). Though not always as fast as surface streets, they're definitely mellower.

Out in the countryside, it's a mixed bag. Bike lanes are virtually nonexistent, and shoulder widths vary widely. Plenty of roads have minimal traffic, though. And remember, the law gives you full use of the road lane where you need it.

Use public transit. The Portland region's several transit networks are very bike-friendly. Most useful for cyclists is MAX, the light-rail system operated by transit agency TriMet. The trains have racks inside the cars. On the rare occasion when all racks are occupied, you can generally squeeze into one of the standing areas with your bike.

In addition to MAX, the Westside Express (WES) commuter rail offers a very quick weekday north-south route from Beaverton to Wilsonville during commute hours. In Portland, two streetcar lines connect downtown neighborhoods with Inner East Portland. Amtrak trains (www.amtrak.com) depart from Union Station in the Pearl District, with stops (northbound) in Vancouver, Washington, and (southbound) in Oregon City and Salem.

Finally, there's always the bus. TriMet can get you to the start of most rides in this book; for farther-flung rides, connect from TriMet to other local providers, listed below. The "Rides At-a-Glance" chart at the beginning of the book provides information on which transit agency serves each ride.

Columbia County Rider (Scappoose and St. Helens): (503) 366-0159; www.columbiacountyrider.com.

C-TRAN (Vancouver and Clark County, Washington): (360) 695-0123; www.c-tran.com.

Sandy Area Metro (SAM) (Sandy): (503) 668-3466; www.cityof sandy.com.

South Clackamas Transportation District (Molalla): (503) 632-7000; www.southclackamastransportation.com/busroutes.htm.

South Metro Area Regional Transit (Wilsonville): (503) 682-7790; www.ridesmart.com.

Tillamook County Transportation District (Tillamook; connects to Union Station in Portland): (503) 815-8283; www.tillamookbus.com.

TriMet (Portland metropolitan area): (503) 238-7433; www.trimet.org.

Yamhill County Transit Area (Newberg, Dundee, and McMinnville): (503) 472-0457; www.yctransitarea.org.

A GUIDE FOR EXPLORATION

This book is for everyone interested in exploring the Portland region on two wheels. The rides range from beginner outings on car-free paths to demanding tours on isolated rural highways, with most somewhere in between. You'll find close-to-home rides to do after work on a summer evening, farther-flung adventures to fill a Saturday, family-friendly rides, and rides to explore the region—whether you're visiting for a few hours or have lived here your entire life.

This book reflects my biases. I'm an urbanite who rides mostly for transportation, not fitness (I don't even own any spandex). When I ride for fun, I poke along, stopping often to visit parks, restaurants, neighborhoods, historic sites, and oddities. I also ride to reduce my carbon footprint and liberate myself from automobiles. (That said, I do own a car and am no bike purist—especially not by Portland standards!)

The more urban routes in this book especially emphasize exploration, providing plenty of reasons to get off the bike. For rides at the region's edges, I've searched out scenic routes that offer some kind of destination and options for shortening or extending the ride. All of the rides stick to lower-traffic roads wherever possible, and I've called out the few spots where traffic is especially vexing. All of the rides are suitable for any time of year—though keep in mind that in winter, rain in downtown Portland can sometimes mean snow (and ice) in the hills.

Finally, I've connected as many of the rides as possible to Portland's extensive light-rail network (MAX) or other public transit options (see the preceding section). With only a little bit of effort, you can reach most of these rides without a car. Aside from being virtuous, it offers you the freedom to conveniently do one-way rides or otherwise make your own way. Try it!

HOW TO USE THIS BOOK

At the front of the book you'll find the "Rides At-a-Glance" chart. Start here when choosing a ride to suit your time and ambition. Note that many ride descriptions have potential shortcuts and extensions.

I've grouped the rides into five regions: in town, around the Tualatin Valley (west of the Tualatin Mountains, aka West Hills), up the Willamette Valley to Salem, east to the Cascade foothills, and across the Columbia around Vancouver, Washington. Within each of these regions, the rides are grouped around the primary acess route—usually a freeway or major highway—working from this point out toward the suburbs and countryside.

Once you've found a ride in the chart, read the full description for more information. Each ride features an information block with some basic information plus additional elements to help you select the ideal ride and find your way.

Difficulty rating: Each ride is rated Easy, Moderate, Challenging, or Very Challenging. But this is a subjective measure. Though the difficulty ratings take into account each ride's distance and elevation gain, the real focus is on the "intangibles." These include exposure to traffic (do you have to pedal on a busy highway?), isolation (is bailing out and catching a bus not an option?), sustained climbing (are the hills long lung-busters?), and rural hazards (are you riding past a six-foot ditch on deteriorating pavement?). Plenty of the "easy" rides entail significant mileage and/or climbing, but if a ride is rated "easy," you shouldn't experience any "white knuckle" moments.

Distance: The ride's mileage is always round-trip (even for out-and-back rides) and doesn't include any of the suggested side trips. Note that many rides have alternative options described in the text and included in the "Rides At-a-Glance" chart and mileage logs.

Elevation Gain: This cumulative measure of all the climbing you'll do is given in feet. These are estimates, generally accurate to within 50 feet (for totals under 1000 feet) or 100 feet (for totals over 1000 feet).

Getting There: Here you'll find directions to the start of the ride, both by car and by public transit and/or bicycle.

Route Description: This sets the context and hits the ride's major points. Most descriptions also include plenty of digressions.

Route Map: Each map shows the starting point, highlights along the way, and most major roads.

Elevation Profile: These visual overviews show where and how much you'll climb, with landmarks noted.

Valley fog below, winter sun above: December on Parrett Mountain

Mileage Log: Refer to the log for turn-by-turn directions and occasional notes. Read the mileage log completely and compare it to the map before starting your ride to minimize confusion en route. You might want to keep the mileage log in a weatherproof map case attached to your handlebars for easy reference.

Now, let's ride!

A NOTE ABOUT SAFETY

Safety is an important concern in all outdoor activities. No guidebook can alert you to every hazard or anticipate the limitations of every reader. Therefore, the descriptions of roads, paths, routes, and natural features in this book are not representations that a particular place or excursion will be safe for your party. When you follow any of the routes described in this book, you assume responsibility for your own safety. Under normal conditions, such excursions require the usual attention to traffic, road conditions, weather, terrain, the capabilities of your party, and other factors. Keeping informed on current conditions and exercising common sense are the keys to a safe, enjoyable outing.

—*The Mountaineers Books*

IN TOWN

These rides cover the City of Portland and close-in suburbs. They're mostly urban in character, full of historical and cultural offerings. The last two—Sauvie Island (Ride 18) and St. Helens and Scappoose (Ride 19) venture farther down the Willamette and Columbia Rivers to visit countryside just beyond the city's working waterfront—hardly "in town," but not really so far out either.

1 Riverfront Loop

DIFFICULTY: Easy
DISTANCE: 10.8-mile loop; option: 2.4-mile loop
ELEVATION GAIN: 175 feet

Getting There: From I-5 southbound, take exit 300B, Morrison Street–City Center. From bridge, follow right-hand off-ramp toward SW Naito Pkwy. and follow it south several blocks to Salmon St. Springs. Tom McCall Waterfront Park is at left; park on street or in Smart Park garage at SW Fourth Ave. and SW Taylor St.

Transit: Take MAX Red or Blue Line to SW Oak St. and SW First Ave.; go east a block and cross SW Naito into the park, then bike south a few blocks to Salmon St. Springs.

There's no better introduction to Portland bicycling than this lap around the Willamette River, following scenic and busy riverfront paths. This is where the city comes to celebrate its connection to the river.

Begin at the Salmon Street Springs fountain in Tom McCall Waterfront Park. Mobbed by kids in summer, the fountain shoots erratic blasts of water from jets built into the pavement. It routinely soaks unsuspecting out-of-towners blithely enjoying their lunch on nearby benches—always a fun sight.

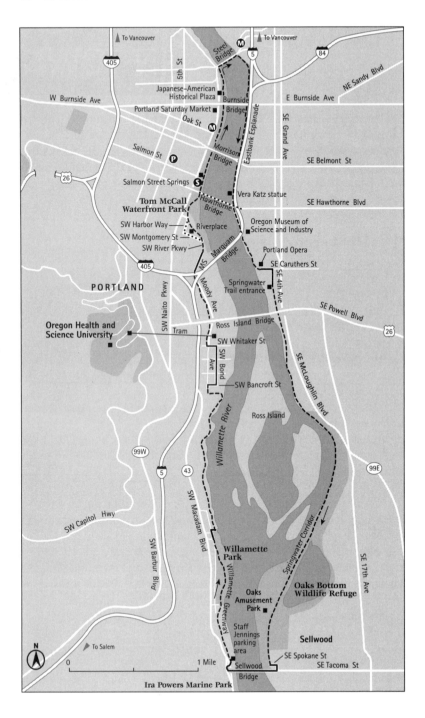

To Vancouver
To Vancouver
405
5th St
Steel Bridge
M
5
84
W Burnside Ave
Japanese–American Historical Plaza
Portland Saturday Market
Oak St
Burnside Bridge
E Burnside Ave
NE Sandy Blvd
Eastbank Esplanade
SE Grand Ave
Salmon St
M
Morrison Bridge
SE Belmont St
26
P
Salmon Street Springs
S
Vera Katz statue
SE Hawthorne Blvd
Tom McCall Waterfront Park
Hawthorne Bridge
SW Harbor Way
Riverplace
Oregon Museum of Science and Industry
SW Montgomery St
SW River Pkwy
SW Marquam Bridge
Portland Opera
SE Caruthers St
405
SW Moody Ave
Springwater Trail entrance
SE 4th Ave
PORTLAND
SW Naito Pkwy
SE Powell Blvd
26
Oregon Health and Science University
Tram
Ross Island Bridge
SW Whitaker St
SW Bond Ave
SW Bancroft St
SE McLoughlin Blvd
99W
Willamette River
Ross Island
5
43
99E
SW Capitol Hwy
SW Macadam Blvd
Willamette Park
Springwater Corridor
SE 17th Ave
SW Barbur Blvd
Willamette Greenway
Oaks Amusement Park
Oaks Bottom Wildlife Refuge
Staff Jennings parking area
Sellwood
To Salem
N
0   1 Mile
Sellwood Bridge
SE Spokane St
SE Tacoma St
Ira Powers Marine Park

From the fountain, head north along the seawall beneath the Morrison Bridge. Beyond, a new plaza hosts the famed Portland Saturday Market, where kitschy souvenirs and exquisite crafts have mingled underneath the Burnside Bridge for decades. Just beyond the bridge, the Japanese-American Historical Plaza, a quiet counterpart to the market's bustle, memorializes Oregon's Nikkei community and the mistreatment they endured during the Second World War.

Waterfront Park ends at the hulking Steel Bridge, built in 1912. The lower deck can rise independently of the upper deck to allow small boats passage. It's the only bridge in the world, according to the state of Oregon, with this ability. It's also the world's second-oldest vertical-lift bridge, after the nearby Hawthorne. Cycle across the bridge's lower pedestrian deck, which affords a unique close-up on the Willamette.

On the far shore, follow the lower path to loop back upstream on the Eastbank Esplanade, which clings to the fringe of East Portland riverfront not destroyed by Interstate 5. The Esplanade's champion, former mayor Vera Katz, is honored in bronze at the Esplanade's south end near the Hawthorne Bridge. Here you can recross the Willamette to shorten the loop to 2.4 miles; the main route continues south under the bridge to the Oregon Museum of Science and Industry (watch out for kids!) and the Portland Opera, where the path dumps you onto SE Caruthers Street.

After a few blocks of quiet riding among warehouses, you reach the official entrance of the Springwater Corridor, Portland's best-known multi-use path. (This stretch is officially called Springwater on the Willamette.) As you enter the trail, the noise and smell of busy SE McLoughlin Boulevard disappear above a high bluff, replaced by the croaking of great blue herons. The path hugs the Willamette's wooded shore alongside Holgate Channel, separated from the main river channel by Ross Island. Though a shadow of its former self after a century of gravel mining, Ross Island remains a sanctuary for birds and paddlers alike.

In such an idyllic place you should expect crowds. On a nice day, the path can get so clogged with joggers, slow caravans of novice riders, and distracted birders that you might have to walk your bike. If you want to ride fast, ride elsewhere.

Approximately halfway down the path, an exit ramp leads to several worthy side trips. Go left (through the underpass) to visit Oaks Bottom Wildlife Refuge. When the city proposed in the 1970s to fill this wetland for urban uses, a ragtag group of citizens mobilized in opposition, more or less launching Portland's modern green spaces movement. In 1988 it was designated the city's first urban wildlife refuge.

At right is Oaks Amusement Park, where time appears to have stopped around 1960. A live pipe organ provides the soundtrack at the vintage roller rink, while charmingly low-tech carnival rides keep kids busy outside. At the back of the park, an inconspicuous staircase leads down to the river and (at low water) a quiet beach.

In Sellwood you bid farewell to the Springwater Corridor to cross the Sellwood Bridge and return north via the Willamette Greenway. At the far end of the bridge, consider a detour to visit Ira Powers Marine Park. Here you can venture south along a gravel path—or, when the water is low, a sandy beach—and quickly leave civilization behind. It's a great place for a secluded picnic.

The Willamette Greenway ensures public access to the river at intervals along its entire length. (The several days' paddle from Eugene to Portland—languid in summer and amazingly secluded—is one of Oregon's best-kept secrets.) Portland's stretch of the greenway has a bike path, which briefly parallels SW Macadam Boulevard (OR 43) before entering the woods en route to busy Willamette Park. This wide and shallow river reach is a good place to watch for racing sailboats.

After another mile, the scene changes abruptly as you pass through the swanky South Waterfront neighborhood. A decade ago, this place was weeds and derelict barge yards. Then visionary developers, a city government eager to promote urban density, and the great real estate boom conspired to cut a city out of whole cloth. It's almost painfully shiny and far too empty. The Great Recession dealt the half-built neighborhood a near-mortal blow, forcing the auction of million-dollar condos at cut rates.

The neighborhood's north end is anchored by Portland's iconic aerial tram. Built by the city to connect the Oregon Health and Science University (OHSU) campus atop Marquam Hill to a planned biotech center along the river, the fabulously expensive tram has stirred fierce debate over its value as public transportation—especially as long as the promised job-creating biotech patents fail to materialize. Still, the view from the tram is great.

Mere feet from the tram's base, the Zidell Marine Corporation continues to crank out cargo barges that have plied the Columbia River for more than a century. On the massive vacant lot beyond, OHSU intends to build another campus. Thus will the brave new high-tech Portland surround and eventually extinguish the gritty old river city. See it now while you still can.

SW Moody Avenue continues north from the tram. The street has just been rebuilt, complete with a cycle track, in anticipation of the new

Eastbank Esplanade with Hawthorne Bridge

bridge that will carry MAX, pedestrians, and bicyclists across the river. The track leads under the hulking Marquam Bridge to the RiverPlace condominium development. In the warm months, RiverPlace's waterfront promenade is too crowded to ride. Walk your bike or follow the bike route along SW Montgomery Street and SW Harbor Way. Waterfront Park, the Hawthorne Bridge, and the Salmon Street Springs lie just beyond.

MILEAGE LOG

0.0 Begin at Salmon St. Springs fountain in Tom McCall Waterfront Park.

0.9 Go right onto Steel Bridge lower deck, then right onto Eastbank Esplanade (lower path).

2.1 Vera Katz statue; continue straight under Hawthorne Bridge. (**Option:** To shorten the ride to a 2.4-mile loop, follow signs at left to cross bridge, then follow exit ramp at right to return to Salmon St. Springs.)

2.7 Path ends at Portland Opera; continue east on SE Caruthers St.

2.8 Right onto SE 4th Ave.

3.0 Enter Springwater Corridor at SE Ivon St.

4.8 At path to Oaks Bottom Wildlife Refuge, continue south on trail.

5.5 At path to Oaks Amusement Park, continue south on trail.

5.9 Left onto SE Spokane St., immediate right, then right again onto Sellwood Bridge sidewalk.

6.4 Right at end of bridge onto bicycle-pedestrian ramp (walk bike).
Continue north through Staff Jennings parking area to rejoin
path along SW Macadam Blvd. (**Side trip:** To visit Ira Powers
Marine Park, in Staff Jennings parking area, continue downhill
to boat launch.)

6.7 Go right at path's end (look for Macadam Bay sign), down short
hill, then left to resume path.

7.0 Enter Willamette Park.

7.3 Cross boat ramp via crosswalk and continue north on path to
exit park.

7.6 Path enters condominium property through narrow opening in
fence (caution).

8.7 Path makes sharp left to leave river, then sharp right to parallel
trolley tracks.

8.9 Right onto SW Bancroft St. at end of path, then left onto SW Bond Ave.

9.3 Left onto SW Whitaker St.; cross SW Moody Ave. and go right onto
cycle track. Continue north on SW Moody at end of cycle track.

10.0 Right onto SW River Pkwy., then left to resume bike path.

10.3 Enter Tom McCall Waterfront Park.

10.8 End at Salmon St. Springs fountain.

2 Willamette River Grand Tour

DIFFICULTY: Moderate to Challenging
DISTANCE: 46.6-mile loop
ELEVATION GAIN: 1600 feet

Getting There: See Ride 1's directions to Salmon St. Springs.

From thundering Willamette Falls to the Willamette River's confluence
with the Columbia, the lower Willamette knits the Portland region
together. This ride laps the whole thing, showcasing the River City—
or, rather, the River Cities. You'll pass through chic neighborhoods,

industrial zones, historic downtowns, and forested parks, leaving and returning to the river several times.

Begin at Salmon Street Springs fountain in Tom McCall Waterfront Park and head north (see Ride 1). Near the Steel Bridge, look for a path leading past the Friendship Circle, two 20-foot towers celebrating Portland's relationship to sister city Sapporo, Japan. Follow the path under the Steel Bridge and across some rail tracks, then continue on SW Naito Parkway. (If you'd prefer a more scenic, but winding, route, go right just across the tracks to follow a riverfront path along condominiums; it returns to Naito in about 1 mile.)

Under the Fremont Bridge's immense arch, turn left onto NW 15th Avenue and continue on NW Thurman Street, along the edge of elevated US Highway 30. Follow bike signs along NW Wilson Street

Elizabeth Caruthers Park in South Waterfront

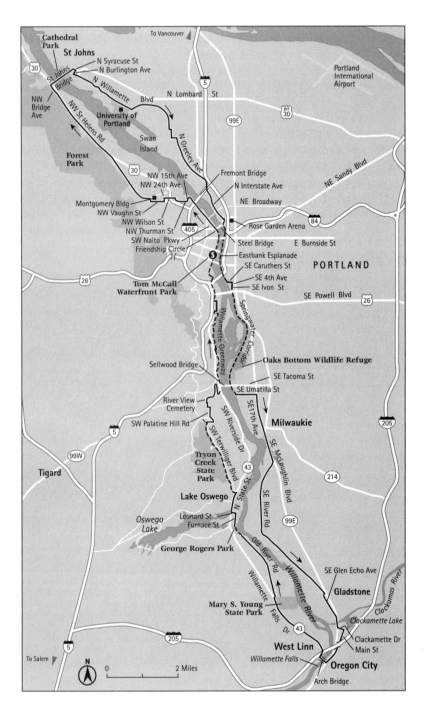

Cathedral Park
St Johns
N Syracuse St
N Burlington Ave
To Vancouver
Portland International Airport
30
St Johns Bridge
N Willamette
N Lombard   St
Blvd
5
99E
BY 30
NW Bridge Ave
NW St Helens Rd
University of Portland
Swan Island
N Greeley Ave
NE Sandy Blvd
Forest Park
30
NW 15th Ave
NW 24th Ave
Fremont Bridge
N Interstate Ave
NE Broadway
Montgomery Bldg
NW Vaughn St
NW Wilson St
NW Thurman St
SW Naito Pkwy
Friendship Circle
405
84
Rose Garden Arena
Steel Bridge   E Burnside St
Eastbank Esplanade
SE Caruthers St
PORTLAND
26
Tom McCall Waterfront Park
SE 4th Ave
SE Ivon St
SE Powell Blvd
26
Willamette Greenway
Springwater Corridor
Oaks Bottom Wildlife Refuge
Sellwood Bridge
SE Tacoma St
SE Umatilla St
River View Cemetery
SW Palatine Hill Rd
5
SW Riverside Dr
SW Terwilliger Blvd
SE 17th Ave
Milwaukie
205
99W
Tryon Creek State Park
43
SE McLoughlin Blvd
214
Tigard
Lake Oswego
N State St
SE River Rd
Oswego Lake
Leonard St
Furnace St
99E
George Rogers Park
Old River Rd
Willamette River
SE Glen Echo Ave
Clackamas River
Gladstone
Mary S. Young State Park
Willamette Falls
Clackamette Lake
43
Clackamette Dr
West Linn
Main St
To Salem
5
N
0   2 Miles
205
Willamette Falls
Oregon City
Arch Bridge

and NW 24th Avenue to reach NW Vaughn Street, which divides the upscale neighborhoods of Northwest Portland from the gritty industrial riverfront. Continue past the Montgomery Building (worth a stop to see its immense atrium) and down to NW Nicolai Avenue and NW St. Helens Road.

Here the distractions fade and the road opens. Steep, wooded ravines of Forest Park (see Ride 17) rise to the left, opposite tank farms and Superfund sites lining the river. After several miles, a left turn leads you up NW Bridge Avenue to the St. Johns Bridge.

Every Portland bridge has great views, but this one may be the best: the green wall of Forest Park behind you, the distant downtown skyline to your right, the port on your left, and tidy St. Johns sloping down to Cathedral Park directly in front of you. These scenes sum up Portland—a river city rooted in commerce and nature, balancing as best it can an ambitious urbanism with neighborhood-scale quality of life.

Down from the bridge in St. Johns, the route turns upstream to follow N. Willamette Boulevard. Beyond the University of Portland, it runs along Mocks Crest in a long arc above Swan Island. The industrial district sprawls below you (Ride 14 has some background on Portland's industrial history).

At N. Greeley Avenue, you begin a long and fast descent to N. Interstate Avenue and the historic Albina neighborhood along N. Russell Street, where grain elevators, rail yards, and a brewery maintain links to the neighborhood's beginnings. Beyond the Broadway Bridge, you'll pass the Rose Garden Arena, likely festooned with oversize portraits of Portland Trailblazer stars. This area is frenzied during the home games of Portland's biggest (and until very recently only) professional sports team. The rest of the time it's pretty dead. City leaders are perpetually pondering ways to revitalize it.

Past the maze of MAX tracks and bus routes, a bike signal beckons you diagonally across NE Oregon Street to a plaza, whence a pedestrian bridge leads down to the Eastbank Esplanade. Cruise the Esplanade beyond the Hawthorne Bridge and continue south on the Springwater Corridor through its beautiful and busy stretch past Ross Island and Oaks Bottom Wildlife Refuge.

Continue south from Sellwood, where SE 17th Avenue descends gently to Milwaukie and the newly restored mouth of Johnson Creek. (See all those logs? That salmon habitat didn't get there by accident.) Here you pick up a beautified stretch of SE McLoughlin Boulevard. About 0.25 mile later, a right turn on SE 22nd Avenue shoots you uphill to SE River Road.

Several leafy, rolling miles later, you return to SE McLoughlin Boulevard. It's not charming, but also not long: you soon cross the Clackamas River immediately upstream from its confluence with the Willamette, then bail from McLoughlin down to Clackamette Drive.

Past Clackamette Cove—an old quarry—Clackamette Drive becomes Main Street. It ducks under Interstate 205 and into Oregon City's historic downtown, nestled at the foot of bluffs and booming Willamette Falls. Oregon City has a lot to explore (see Ride 32).

Now head north and cross the Arch Bridge to West Linn. (Note: this bridge is closed until early 2013; until then, a shuttle carries bicyclists on a detour—see www.archrehab.com for details.) Willamette Falls Drive's ample bike lane shoots you through West Linn's meager downtown.

〜〜〜〜〜〜〜〜〜〜〜〜〜〜〜〜〜〜〜〜〜〜

BRIDGE CITY

With a dozen major bridges, Portland has earned its "Bridgetown" nickname. Here's a bit of trivia about these landmarks.

Before the bridges: Portlanders reached their friends across the river, in the wilderness towns of East Portland, Albina, and Milwaukie, via the Stark Street Ferry.

First: the Morrison (1887—but the current structure dates from 1958).

Oldest: the Hawthorne (1910).

Scariest: the Sellwood. This rickety span, built in 1925 and seemingly held together with chewing gum, has been threatening to collapse for decades. As of this writing, it rates a terrifying 2 (out of 100!) on the National Bridge Inventory's sufficiency scale. By the time you read this, a replacement should be on the way.

Newcomer: scheduled to open in 2015, a sleek new span will connect the Oregon Museum of Science and Industry in Southeast Portland to the South Waterfront neighborhood and Portland State University downtown. The first new bridge in 35 years, it will serve cyclists, pedestrians, and transit—*but not cars.* Score another point for livability!

Most Beautiful: the Fremont. Who would have thought the 1970s would produce such an icon?

Biggest Headache: the Interstate 5 (aka Columbia River Bridge). A key bottleneck on I-5, it needs to be modernized. But how? State transportation planners call for a freeway monster with as many as 14 lanes. Skeptics point to the multibillion-dollar price tag and greenhouse gas emissions it will create. Political gridlock looks set to ensure traffic gridlock for the foreseeable future.

〜〜〜〜〜〜〜〜〜〜〜〜〜〜〜〜〜〜〜〜〜〜

About 2 miles down the road, a forest at right interrupts the subdivisions—this is Mary S. Young State Park. Consider a side trip to the park to wander the wooded riverbank. If you're here in summer, park your bike where pavement ends and continue on foot over a seasonal bridge to Cedar Island, where long beaches and a lagoon invite swimming.

From Willamette Falls Drive (Oregon Route 43), continue to Old River Road, a quiet neighborhood lane. Just before the road curves sharply left to climb, look for a paved trail veering off to the right. This carries you along the river to George Rogers Park and another beach.

Now you pass through Lake Oswego, first through "Old Town" (with very little old left in it), then the swank, newish downtown centered on SW A Avenue. At the north edge of town, look for a path on the opposite side of N. State Street; this leads up into Tryon Creek State Park, where a dense forest canopy casts evergreen shade on the relentlessly climbing trail. Two and a half forested miles and 350 feet of elevation gain later, you'll return to civilization at the Lewis and Clark Law School.

From the path, go left onto SW Terwilliger Boulevard, right at the traffic circle, and left onto SW Palatine Hill Road to pass the River View Forest and enter River View Cemetery. Now enjoy a long descent past manicured graves, but please ride courteously and show consideration to the cemetery's visitors. Nothing disturbs the paying of respects like getting grazed by a speeding cyclist.

Cross OR 43 at the cemetery's lower gate to pick up the Willamette Greenway Trail at the base of the Sellwood Bridge. This carries you north along the river, through Willamette Park, past low-slung older condos in Johns Landing, and into the new high-rise mini-city known as South Waterfront. The greenway is a work in progress here; for now, follow the cycle track along SW Moody Avenue and cut through the RiverPlace development to return to Tom McCall Waterfront Park.

MILEAGE LOG

0.0 Begin at Salmon St. Springs fountain in Tom McCall Waterfront Park.

0.9 Go left at Friendship Circle onto path leading under Steel Bridge. Cross tracks, go left onto path, and continue onto SW Naito Pkwy. (**Option:** For slower but more scenic route, go right across tracks onto Willamette Greenway, which returns to SW Naito Pkwy. in approximately 1 mile. Portions of this route are on wood boardwalks; use caution when wet.)

2.9   Left onto NW 15th Ave., which curves right to become
      NW Thurman St.

3.1   Cross NW 19th Ave. and continue onto frontage road paralleling
      (elevated) US 30.

3.3   Curve right to exit frontage road onto NW 21st Ave., then go left
      onto NW Wilson St. Cross highway on overpass.

3.6   Left onto NW 24th Ave.

3.7   Right onto NW Vaughn St. Montgomery Bldg. at right.

4.3   Left at bottom of hill onto NW Nicolai St., which curves right to
      become NW St. Helens Rd. (US 30).

5.9   Left at stoplight to stay on NW St. Helens Rd.

8.0   Left at stoplight onto NW Bridge Ave.

8.6   Right onto St. Johns Bridge.

9.3   Right at end of bridge onto N. Syracuse St., then right onto
      N. Burlington Ave., and left onto N. Willamette Blvd.

11.4 N. Willamette Blvd. curves left at Waud Bluff.

12.6 Right to stay on N. Willamette Blvd. at far end of bluff.

13.3 Right onto N. Greeley Ave.

14.8 Right onto N. Interstate Ave. (caution: bike lane shifts across
      exit lane on Greeley).

15.4 Stay left to remain on N. Interstate Ave. Pass Memorial
      Coliseum and Rose Garden Arena at left.

16.2 Right into plaza immediately past intersection with NE Oregon
      St. Follow path down ramp and over railroad tracks.

16.5 Sharp left at bottom of ramp onto Eastbank Esplanade.

18.1 Path ends. Continue east on SE Caruthers St.

18.2 Right onto SE 4th Ave.

18.4 Enter Springwater Corridor at SE Ivon St.

21.3 Cross SE Spokane St. and continue on Springwater.

21.5 Left at trail's end onto SE Umatilla St. (Note: Trail to be extended
      in 2013)

22.2 Right onto SE 17th Ave.

23.4 Right onto SE McLoughlin Blvd (OR 99E).

23.8 Right onto SE 22nd Ave (one way). Curves left onto SE Sparrow
      St., then right onto SE River Rd.

28.4 Right onto SE Glen Echo Ave. Follow main road as it curves left
      to become SE River Rd.

29.2 Right onto SE McLoughlin Blvd. (OR 99E). Cross Clackamas River.

29.7 First right across bridge onto Dunes Dr. (unmarked; look for
      bikeway sign), then right onto Clackamette Dr. Follow it (now
      called Main St.) under I-205 and into downtown Oregon City.

31.3 Right onto 7th St. to cross Arch Bridge over Willamette River. Continue on Willamette Falls Dr. (OR 43) under I-205.

33.6 Mary S. Young State Park entrance at right. (**Side trip:** Go right here to reach Cedar Island.)

33.9 Bear right onto path (at gap in guardrail) to Old River Rd.

35.7 Right onto paved path (just before Old River Rd. curves sharply left and uphill to become Glenmorrie Dr.).

36.5 From George Rogers Park lower parking area, go right onto Furnace St.

36.8 Left onto Leonard St., then right onto S. State St. (OR 43) through downtown Lake Oswego.

37.3 Left at SW E Ave., then immediate right onto path paralleling OR 43. Path leads uphill, now paralleling SE Terwilliger Blvd., into Tryon Creek State Park.

39.7 Right at side path (steep uphill) to exit park. Left onto SW Terwilliger Blvd. Go right at traffic circle onto SW Palater Rd., then immediate left onto SW Palatine Hill Rd. River View Forest at right.

40.6 Right to enter River View Cemetery. Take second right in cemetery to go downhill. Take downhill turn at all intersections.

42.2 Cross OR 43 at stoplight to exit River View Cemetery, then immediately go left onto path between OR 43 and Sellwood Bridge off-ramp. (See map for Ride 1 for details of rest of route.)

42.3 Continue north through Staff Jennings parking area to join Willamette Greenway path along SW Macadam Blvd.

42.5 Go right at path's end (look for Macadam Bay sign), down short hill, then left to resume path.

42.8 Enter Willamette Park.

43.1 Cross boat ramp via crosswalk and continue on path to exit park.

43.4 Path enters condominium property through narrow opening in fence (caution).

44.5 Path makes sharp left to leave river, then sharp right to parallel trolley tracks.

44.7 Right onto SW Bancroft St. at end of path, then left onto SW Bond Ave.

45.1 Left onto SW Whitaker St., then right onto SW Moody Ave. After one block, cross Moody to continue on cycle track. Continue on SW Moody at end of cycle track.

45.8 Right onto SW River Pkwy., then left to resume bike path.

46.1 Path enters Tom McCall Waterfront Park.

46.6 End at Salmon St. Springs fountain.

3   Downtown and Northwest

DIFFICULTY: Easy to Moderate
DISTANCE: 6.8-mile loop; option: 4.2-mile loop
ELEVATION GAIN: 270 feet

Getting There: From I-5 southbound, take exit 300B, Morrison Street–City Center, and cross bridge west a few blocks to Pioneer Courthouse Square, bounded by Broadway, Sixth, Yamhill, and Morrison. From I-405 northbound, take exit 1C, Sixth Ave., and drive north a few blocks to Pioneer Courthouse Square. Metered street parking available; Smart Park Garage at 10th and Morrison.

Transit: Take any MAX line to Pioneer Courthouse Square station.

Downtown Portland is bike-friendly, with generally low traffic speeds and adequate bike lanes. Still, it's a bustling place with the usual urban hazards: unpredictable pedestrians, distracted drivers, car doors flying open, and light rail and streetcar tracks waiting to eat your front wheel. Don't fear; just be alert and ride with caution.

The ride visits downtown, the Pearl District, Northwest Portland, and Old Town. It follows streets with bike lanes and/or low traffic—but you can, of course, make your own route. The street grid makes it easy to find your way.

Begin at Pioneer Courthouse Square. This storied block was once home to the Portland Hotel, built in 1890 to welcome arrivals on the recently completed transcontinental Northern Pacific railroad. The ornate eight-story building served as Portland's social hub for a generation. That era ended definitively with the Second World War, after which the automobile conquered cities across America. As money moved higher up the hills and into the suburbs, the hotel declined. It was demolished in 1951 and replaced by a parking lot for the nearby department store.

For some reason, though, Portland—long a conservative town—rediscovered the virtues of urbanism a little sooner than the rest of the nation. When the city proposed building a massive parking structure

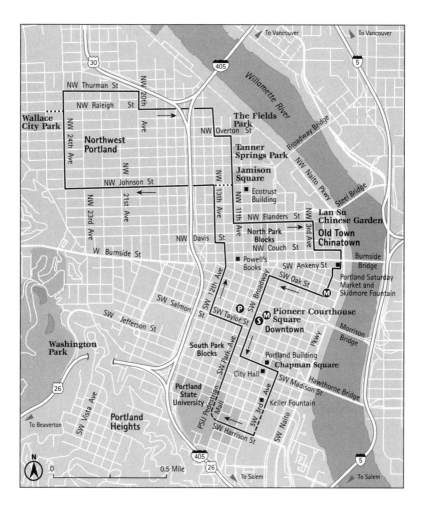

on the site in 1969, citizens revolted. After years of debate, delay, and fund-raising, the city opened Pioneer Courthouse Square in 1984. It's been "Portland's living room" ever since, complete with leaky fountain and grungy street kids.

From the square, Broadway and Madison lead you south and east past City Hall and the Portland Building. The latter, built in 1982, is a major American landmark in postmodern architecture. With small windows and an ornamented exterior—if you think "wedding cake" you won't be alone—it rejects the steel-and-glass functionalism that has long dominated modern architecture. But like so much from the '80s, it looks a bit regrettable now. The city bureaucrats laboring in its dim

Sunday Parkways in the Pearl District (Jonathan Maus/*Bike Portland*)

offices must sometimes wonder if the architect, Michael Graves, ever spent a winter in Portland.

Behind the Portland Building is elegant Chapman Square, the civic heart of late 19th-century Portland and in 2012 the scene of Occupy protests. A statue in the park commemorates the 150th anniversary of the Oregon Trail.

Go right at SW Third Avenue to reach the Keller Fountain. Designed by Angela Danadjieva and Lawrence Halprin and built in 1970, the fountain's jumble of concrete slabs, pillars, pools, and waterfalls somehow manages to unite Portland's most urbane civic virtues with the raw power of the surrounding natural landscape.

Cross SW Market Street and continue south on a pedestrian path. Walk your bike here if there are crowds—they provide a good excuse to linger at Pettygrove City Park, tucked like a sanctuary among the surrounding high-rises. The path ends at SW Harrison Street, which leads you west to Portland State University. The pedestrian-oriented campus stretches down the South Park Blocks. On summer Saturdays, it hosts Portland's largest farmers market. A visit to this market is one of the city's most enjoyable, if crowded, culinary experiences.

The campus ends at SW Market Street. Continue north on SW Park Avenue along the Park Blocks to Salmon Street, where the exclusive Arlington Club offers lunch to Portland's elite. You might consider lunching a block farther at Director Park, a popular urban plaza that opened in 2010. Beyond the park, continue to downtown's west end along SW 12th Avenue and across W. Burnside Street.

As recently as the mid-1990s, the area north of Burnside was a land of warehouses, auto body shops, and vacant lots. Thanks to the dark magic of tax incentives and a real estate bubble, it transformed almost overnight into the Pearl District: art galleries, chic restaurants, and hitherto unimaginably expensive condominiums. Anchoring the whole thing is venerable Powell's Books at 10th and Burnside, purportedly the world's largest independent bookstore.

VANPORT AND PSU

Few universities have such humble origins as Portland State. It opened in 1946 as the Vanport Extension Center, serving the residents of Oregon's temporary city, Vanport, during World War II.

The Housing Authority of Portland erected the city of Vanport ("Vancouver" plus "Portland"—get it?) in 1943 on the Columbia River's floodplain in North Portland. The thousands of quickly built, shoddy houses absorbed a flood of workers streaming into the nearby Kaiser Shipyards, where a sizable chunk of America's World War II fleet was being built. For several years, the instant city boomed.

At war's end, Vanport began a steady decline as residents sought jobs and better housing elsewhere. The poorer and older residents remained. So did many of the town's recently arrived African Americans, their alternatives limited by the city's informal but rigid segregation, enforced by real estate agents and mortgage lenders. By 1948, Vanport was home to Portland's most vulnerable citizens.

In May of that year, unusually high river levels threatened the levees protecting Vanport. The morning of Memorial Day, Portland officials assured residents the levees were safe. Many were thus unprepared to evacuate when, later that day, a levee suddenly and catastrophically failed. Many of the town's 18,000 residents were away for the holiday, but those who stayed mostly lacked vehicles or access to public transportation. They had nowhere to flee. Amazingly, only 15 people died—but thousands lost homes and all their possessions. Many were never compensated or effectively rehoused, left to struggle on or simply disappear. It was Portland's Hurricane Katrina.

Despite tragedy and neglect, Vanport Extension Center refused to close. After a fierce political struggle, it found a new home and reinvented itself as Portland State College (later University). It's now Oregon's largest public institution of higher education.

Crossing under I-405, you trade the Pearl District's hip sheen for Northwest Portland's leafy avenues and staid, graceful brick apartments. (Alternatively, go right at NW Johnson St. to shorten the tour to a 4.2-mile loop that skips Northwest Portland.) NW 21st and 23rd Avenues are the neighborhood's main drags, intimate streets bustling with shops and restaurants. These streets are better explored on foot, so consider locking up somewhere and strolling awhile.

Back in the saddle, cruise down NW 24th Avenue to NW Thurman Street. If it happens to be an autumn evening, detour one block west to Wallace City Park, where at dusk a flock of Vaux's swifts nest in the chimney at neighboring Chapman Elementary School. The spectacle of swifts swarming and disappearing into a smokestack by the thousands, often while avoiding a peregrine falcon seeking dinner, is magical. Hundreds of spectators gather every evening throughout September.

The route visits Northwest's quiet north side before looping back to the Pearl District at NW 11th Avenue. For the next few blocks, you visit three new parks: the Fields, Tanner Springs, and Jamison Square. Kitty-corner to Jamison Square is the Ecotrust Building, a former warehouse creatively recycled into a hub for all things green in Portland. You can take a self-guided tour of the building's eco-friendly features and eat great pizza to boot.

The North Park Blocks divide the Pearl District from Portland's historic Chinatown. Not much is left, gentrification having driven most of the former residents out to East 82nd Avenue. (To explore that area, Portland's most ethnically diverse, see Ride 12.) One sight not to be missed, though, is the Lan Su Chinese Garden at NW Flanders Street and NW Third Avenue. Behind the white walls circling this block hides an enchanting miniature landscape of pools, sculpted trees, and exquisite woodwork. A traditional teahouse offers ceremonies and the occasional musical performance.

The route now passes under the west end of the Burnside Bridge to reach Skidmore Fountain and the heart of Old Town. Here, in 1843, William Overton and Asa Lovejoy staked a clearing in the deep, silent woods along the canoe route from Oregon City to Fort Vancouver. A decade later mercantile houses, ship companies, and banks crowded the area, turning Portland into the commercial capital of the Pacific Northwest.

By the fountain's dedication in 1888, however, centers of trade were shifting east and north. Old Town earned a new name—Skid Road— and entered a century of ill repute. Not until the 1970s did it begin to revive, spurred in part by a National Historic Landmark designation.

Recent arrivals, including the University of Oregon and the humanitarian group Mercy Corps, have renovated historic buildings, helping to revitalize the area. Mercy Corps' Action Center, next to the fountain, invites visitors to learn about humanitarian needs and opportunities around the world. And, of course, hawkers at the Portland Saturday Market beckon with elephant ears and handmade crafts.

There's a lot to see in Old Town. Stop and wander—just keep an eye on your bike. When you're done, Pioneer Courthouse Square and the loop's end are just a few minutes away.

MILEAGE LOG

0.0 Begin at Pioneer Courthouse Square; ride south (uphill) on SW Broadway.

0.2 Left onto SW Madison St. Portland Building and Chapman Square on left; City Hall at right.

0.4 Right onto SW 3rd Ave. Keller Fountain on right. Enter pedestrian path (walk bike up stairs) across SW Market St. Pettygrove Park at left.

0.8 Right onto SW Harrison St. Enter Portland State University campus across SW Broadway and go right into South Park Blocks. Continue north on SW Park Ave.

1.6 Left onto SW Taylor St. Director Park on right. Right onto SW 12th Ave.

2.0 Cross SW Burnside St. Powell's Books one block away at right. Left onto NW Davis St., then right onto NW 13th Ave.

2.3 Left onto NW Johnson St. (**Option:** Go right here to shortcut to North Park Blocks for a 4.2-mile loop.)

3.2 Right onto NW 24th Ave. (**Side trip:** Go one block west to visit Wallace City Park.)

3.7 Right onto NW Thurman St. (**Option:** Connect here with Ride 17, Forest Park.)

4.1 NW Thurman St. curves right to become NW 20th Ave.

4.2 Left onto NW Raleigh St.

4.6 Right onto NW 13th Ave.

4.7 Left onto NW Overton St.

4.8 Right onto NW 11th Ave. Fields, Tanner Springs, and Jamison parks at left.

5.3 Left onto NW Flanders St.

5.7 Right onto NW 3rd Ave. Lan Su Chinese Garden at left.

5.8 Left onto NW Couch St.

6.0 Right onto NW Naito Pkwy. Pass under Burnside Bridge.

6.1 Right onto SW Ankeny St. (at crosswalk with pillars). Skidmore Fountain and Mercy Corps Action Center at right. Left onto SW 1st Ave.

6.4 Right onto SW Oak St.

6.6 Left onto SW Broadway.

6.8 End at Pioneer Courthouse Square.

4 Washington Park

DIFFICULTY: Moderate
DISTANCE: 9.6-mile loop; option: 3.75 miles one way
ELEVATION GAIN: 1450 feet

Getting There: See Ride 3's directions to Pioneer Courthouse Square MAX station.

If you're visiting Portland for the first time, go to Washington Park. If you've lived here all your life ... go to Washington Park. It's one of Portland's oldest and most beautiful places, with panoramic views and days' worth of cultural sites to explore.

The only problem with bicycling in the park is gravity: there's a lot to overcome here. You can address this challenge in two ways: combine a workout with the sightseeing, or use MAX to facilitate a one-way trip downhill. I describe the entire loop here, so take your choice.

The route begins at Pioneer Courthouse Square and heads up to the Northwest neighborhood. Here you leave the street grid behind and enter the Hillside neighborhood, aka Kings Heights. Every street curves and every home positively luxuriates on its lot, enjoying the fine views and immaculate landscaping. The streets constantly change names, but if you keep heading uphill, you'll stay on track. At NW Monte Vista Terrace, don't be fooled by the "dead end" sign: a chain-link fence blocks cars but admits pedestrians and bikes. The empty road beyond leads a few hundred yards to Pittock Mansion.

Newspaper magnate Henry Pittock, who rose from destitute typesetter to owner, publisher, and lord of the *Oregonian,* built this 22-room palace in 1914. He was a prototypical westerner, a self-made man who unflinchingly crushed his opponents. He was a plutocrat with stakes in ranching, mining, logging, milling, and, that most western of pursuits, real estate. He also was a member of the first party to ascend Mount

Pittock Mansion

Hood, in 1857. Pittock died in 1919. His heirs remained in the mansion until 1958, when the City of Portland bought it.

While you're visiting Pittock Mansion, consider hiking a short distance on the Wildwood Trail. It leads north into Macleay and Forest Parks, an urban wilderness covering 5000-plus acres (see Ride 17). A short descent from Pittock Mansion precedes a long climb up NW Barnes Road, parts of which are terribly potholed. Ride with caution—not that you'll be speeding too quickly up this punishing hill. At the top is SW Skyline Boulevard.

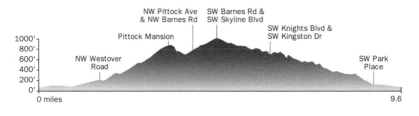

The geographically inclined can detour briefly here to Willamette Stone State Park where, tucked in the trees behind Mount Calvary Cemetery, lies the reference point for all land surveying in the Pacific Northwest. Back on Skyline, continue downhill to Washington Park, where the World Forestry Center, Oregon Zoo, Vietnam Veterans Memorial, Children's Museum, Hoyt Arboretum, Japanese Garden, and International Rose Test Garden all vie for your time and attention.

Those of you who opt to skip the climb should start at the Washington Park MAX station, which is 0.25 mile down SW Knights Boulevard from its intersection with SW Kingston Drive. Join the route here. From this intersection, Kingston drops to the Japanese and Rose gardens. The descent continues past several reservoirs filled with Bull Run water (see Ride 45). All along, Washington Park's magnificent forest and landscaping beg you to slow down and enjoy the view, while gravity urges you on faster. The downhill continues all the way back to Pioneer Courthouse Square.

Lest you feel bad about skipping the climb, know that you're in good company: ride on a Sunday evening and you'll probably encounter a pack of hipsters—the Zoobombers—speeding down this hill on kids' bikes. Occasional bloody wipeouts add an undercurrent of danger to the revelry. If you hear them hootin' and hollerin' up above you, get out of the way!

One more argument in favor of MAX: you get to visit the deepest transit station in North America, 260 feet underground. Something about the cool, humid wind blowing across the platform communicates depth. You can really tell you're in the earth—a sense made manifest by the core sample displayed along the platform wall. The elevator ride to the surface will make your ears pop!

MILEAGE LOG

0.0 Begin at Pioneer Courthouse Square. Go left onto SW Morrison St.

0.5 Right onto SW 18th Ave. Cross W. Burnside St.

0.9 Left onto NW Flanders St.

1.5 Bear right onto NW Westover Rd.

2.0 Right to stay on NW Westover Rd.

2.3 Left onto NW Cumberland Rd.

2.7 Left onto NW Ariel Ter., right onto NW Alpine Ter., right onto NW Macleay Blvd., left onto NW Hermosa Blvd., right onto NW Monte Vista Ter.

3.5 Continue past gate to Pittock Acres Park. Mansion and parking area ahead at right.

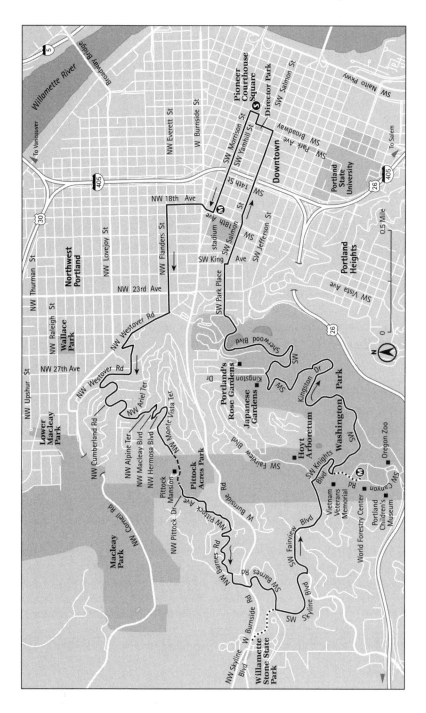

3.6 Straight ahead to continue downhill from Pittock Mansion on NW Pittock Dr.

3.9 Left onto NW Pittock Ave.

4.1 Right onto NW Barnes Rd.

4.4 Right to stay on SW Barnes Rd.

4.9 Left onto SW Skyline Blvd. (**Side trip:** Go right here to visit Willamette Stone State Park.)

5.3 Left onto SW Fairview Blvd.

5.9 Right onto SW Knights Blvd. (no street sign—signs point toward Washington Park).

6.1 Left onto SW Kingston Dr. in Washington Park. (**Option:** MAX users ride SW Knights Blvd. 0.25 mile uphill to join route at this intersection.)

7.7 Right (at Rose Garden) onto SW Sherwood Blvd.

8.4 Right at stop sign onto SW Sacajawea–Washington Way (no sign).

8.6 Right onto SW Park Pl. to exit Washington Park.

8.9 Right onto SW King Ave., then immediate dogleg left onto SW Salmon St.

9.4 Left onto SW Park Ave., then right onto SW Yamhill St.

9.6 End at Pioneer Courthouse Square.

5   Council Crest

DIFFICULTY: Moderate
DISTANCE: 11.1-mile loop
ELEVATION GAIN: 1200 feet

Getting There: See Ride 3's directions to Pioneer Courthouse Square MAX station.

A friend of mine who grew up in the West Hills confesses she's always found East Portland drearily flat and barren. As an Eastsider, I couldn't disagree more, but every visit to the West Hills reminds me why someone could feel that way. Outsize homes, many of them elevated precariously on stilts, crowd narrow streets winding relentlessly uphill. Dense forest drips with rain and moss. On a misty winter day, when fog shrouds the hills, you could as well be somewhere near road's end in the Coast Range.

Big hill, big views: Council Crest

The West Hills (aka the Tualatin Mountains) are a world apart in other ways, too. Most obviously, they're the abode of the rich. You'll find a modest home here and there, though if it's for sale, don't expect a modest price. Mini-palaces are the rule. Many are beautiful, from turn-of-the-20th-century manses to midcentury experiments in modernism, with a few eco-contemporary palaces thrown in.

You'll have trouble admiring the homes, though, if your lungs and legs are exploding—which leads us to yet another fact setting the West Hills apart. Many of the streets are so steep that casual cruising is out of the question. You're here to climb. Your reward is a dizzying view from the highest point in the city: Council Crest.

Begin at Pioneer Courthouse Square and proceed south through downtown to SW Terwilliger Boulevard. This long, green ribbon through Marquam Nature Park is a classic parkway, like something shipped around the Horn a century ago from New York or Philadelphia. It's got a good bike lane and lots of pullouts with benches for taking in the views.

Near the top, tiny SW Westwood Drive, marked with a bike icon, leads you up into airy neighborhoods. Some of these homes are wedged into the hill at crazy angles, above one-lane streets with hairpin turns. It makes for great views and great bicycling, but where do they go for a gallon of milk?

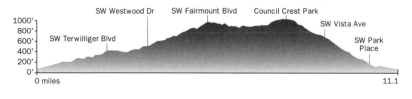

Several tricky turns later, you arrive at SW Fairmount Boulevard, a mostly level street that winds below Council Crest. The forest canopy parts in places to reveal huge views over the Tualatin Valley. The route curves around Council Crest's west, north, and east slopes before finally reaching the very top, 1073 feet above sea level.

In the early 1900s, Council Crest was home to an amusement park. Portlanders thronged here on fine weekends, riding a streetcar from downtown that climbed a gargantuan wooden trestle. No road led here then, but it was a much busier place than the quiet park you'll find today, where a radio tower and some water tanks preside over the city.

From Council Crest it's downhill all the way. The street grid reappears in Portland Heights. If you like, detour from SW Vista Avenue to poke around side streets in this elegant neighborhood.

At the north end of Portland Heights, SW Vista Avenue drops through curves to cross the Canyon Road viaduct into Goose Hollow. Turn right at SW Park Place and continue east onto SW Salmon Street, past the Multnomah Athletic Club—where Portland's High Society works out—and the stadium. Cross over the freeway into downtown. Pioneer Courthouse Square is just a few blocks farther.

MILEAGE LOG

0.0   Begin at Pioneer Courthouse Square. Go left onto SW Broadway.

0.8   Cross I-405 and bear left to stay on SW Broadway (caution), then bear right onto SW 6th Ave., which becomes SW Terwilliger Blvd.

1.3   Left at stoplight to stay on SW Terwilliger Blvd.

3.4   Bear right onto SW Westwood Dr.

4.0   Right at T intersection (no sign) to continue uphill on Westwood.

5.0   Westwood curves left to becomes SW Mitchell St.

5.3   Left onto SW Fairmount Blvd.

6.9   Sharp right onto SW Talbot Ter. (the upper road), then merge right onto SW Greenway Ave.

7.3   Right onto SW Council Crest Dr.

7.5   Right onto one-way loop at Council Crest Park.

7.7   Right at end of loop back onto SW Council Crest Dr., then left onto SW Greenway Ave. at stop sign.

8.5   Right onto SW Patton Rd., then immediate left onto SW Vista Ave.

10.0   Right onto SW Park Pl., right onto SW King Ave., then immediate left onto SW Salmon St. (dogleg).

10.9   Left onto SW Park Ave., then right onto SW Yamhill St.

11.1   End at Pioneer Courthouse Square.

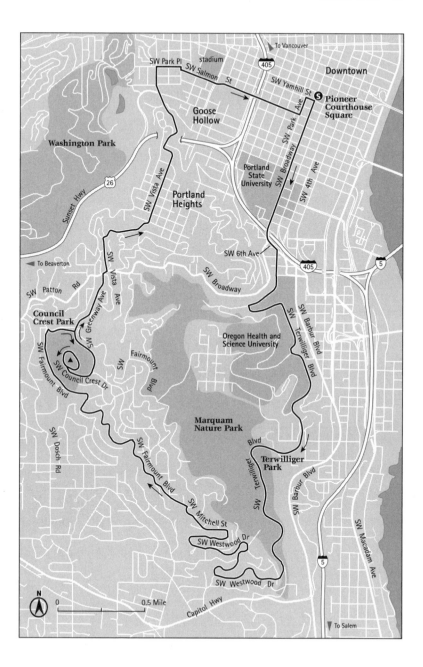

6   Tryon Creek

DIFFICULTY: Moderate
DISTANCE: 17.4-mile loop
ELEVATION GAIN: 1650 feet

Getting There: From I-5 northbound, take exit 298, Corbett Ave., and go right onto SW Corbett, left onto SW Richardson, then right onto SW Macadam Ave. (Oregon Rte. 43) to Willamette Park. From I-5 southbound, take exit 299A for OR 43 S; stay right when crossing under freeway to join SW Macadam Ave.; go left onto SW Nebraska St. to enter park.

Transit: Take MAX Red or Blue Line to SW Oak and SW First Ave. and bicycle Willamette Greenway Trail (see Ride 1) south to the park.

This meandering loop visits deep woods and quiet streets in one of Portland's leafier corners. Other than some long hills and lots of turns, it's a relaxed ride.

The route begins at Willamette Park in Johns Landing and follows the Willamette Greenway south to the Sellwood Bridge (see Ride 1). It then turns in to the River View Cemetery. If you're not sure of where to go, follow the college kids huffing uphill toward Lewis and Clark College.

Among the topiaries and headstones, you won't fail to notice how exquisitely landscaped this cemetery is. When it was established in 1882, River View brought to Portland a new way of death. For centuries, cemeteries had been utilitarian places. Built on marginal land at a healthy distance from the living, they were modest, unadorned spaces designed to efficiently house the dead. They treated death as an egalitarian event. In early Portland, at cemeteries like the Lone Fir (see Ride 9), patriarchs crowded alongside prostitutes, captains of industry next to petty criminals.

Not so at River View. In late 19th-century America, with improved medicine and rising living standards, a more sentimental—even

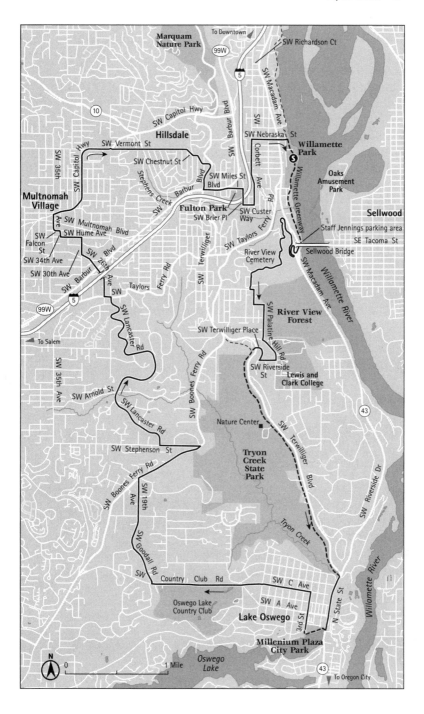

romantic—view of death spread. Cemeteries, in turn, became more than mere burying grounds. Meticulously landscaped, they became places to enjoy. Such elegant, "designed" places also made possible the extension of this world's pecking order into the afterlife. At River View, Portland's elite could be buried as they had lived: high on a hill behind gates and far from the riffraff.

To accommodate this more expansive way of death, River View amassed a huge chunk of land. Almost 150 years later, much of it remains undeveloped. With more Americans opting for cremation, and the future of death looking correspondingly less land-intensive, the River View Cemetery Association recently sold most of its excess land. After more than a century of waiting in vain to house the dead, the 150-acre forest south of the cemetery is a new park—the biggest addition to the city's natural heritage in a generation.

Cruising the Headlee Walkway along Oswego Lake

The cemetery, however, is private property—as is the road through it. Bicyclists are allowed, but cemetery management struggles with the occasional disrespectful rider bombing downhill through a funeral party. Please, keep your voice and speed down.

Beyond the cemetery and forest, you pass Lewis and Clark College, set on a former estate. Routinely ranked among the nation's most beautiful, the campus is worth a side trip before you cruise downhill through Tryon Creek State Park. The only Oregon state park in a major urban area, Tryon Creek was a working forest until the 1970s, feeding the Oregon Iron Company furnace in Lake Oswego. That's right: tony Lake Oswego started as an industrial town, aspiring to be the "Pittsburgh of the West." Its iron furnace—in what is now George Rogers Park—was the West Coast's first.

Halfway down the paved bike path through Tryon Creek is the Nature Center (restroom), where the Friends of Tryon Creek State Park offer guided hikes, summer camps, and volunteer events.

The bike path continues south through forest to emerge onto busy Oregon Route 43 (State Street) in Lake Oswego. Oswego is a natural lake, but keeping it pleasant (free of foul-smelling algae) requires perpetual dredging.

After a brief cruise along the shore, the route passes through L.O.'s historic neighborhoods to Country Club Road. Beyond the golf course are the comparatively modest neighborhoods of Southwest Portland. Get ready: all that elevation you gained through River View, then lost through Tryon Creek, you're now about to gain again.

After a long climb through the wooded expanse of Southwest Portland, the route crosses under Interstate 5 and reaches the top of Tryon Creek's watershed in Multnomah Village. The village's main drag has cafes, restaurants, galleries, an independent bookstore, and a bike shop. It's an island of urbanity in this suburban forest, and a great place to stop for brunch now that the climbing's done.

From the village, the route follows SW Capitol Highway into Hillsdale, then begins a long descent down the Stephens Creek watershed. Mount Hood dominates the skyline as you race down the steep streets of Johns Landing. Willamette Park lies just across SW Macadam Avenue.

MILEAGE LOG

0.0 Begin at Willamette Park. Proceed south on Willamette Greenway.

0.7 At path's end, continue into driveway for Staff Jennings boat launch. Partway down the driveway, path resumes on the right and passes under a roadway. Beyond, veer left off paved path onto unpaved trail, which ends at SW Macadam Ave (OR 43). Cross Macadam at stoplight and continue uphill through gates into River View Cemetery.

2.4   Left out of cemetery onto SW Palatine Hill Rd.

3.0   Left at T intersection to stay on SW Palatine Hill Rd. Lewis and Clark College at left.

3.2   Right onto SW Riverside St., then right onto SW Terwilliger Pl.

3.5   Cross SW Terwilliger Blvd and continue onto path in Tryon Creek State Park (caution on steep downhill). Go left at first junction.

4.3   Tryon Creek Nature Center (restroom) at right.

5.9   Path ends at OR 43 (N. State St.) in Lake Oswego.

6.3   Right at Foothills Rd. stoplight into plaza, then go left onto Headlee Walkway (gravel path) following lakeshore.

6.4   Right to cross tracks and exit path onto 3rd St.

6.7   Left onto SW C Ave., which becomes Country Club Rd.

8.2   Right onto SW Goodall Rd., which becomes SW 19th Ave.

9.2   Right onto SW Boones Ferry Rd. (caution).

9.8   Left onto SW Stephenson St.

10.1   Right onto SW Lancaster Rd.

10.8   Cross SW Arnold St. (caution) and continue uphill on SW Lancaster Rd.

12.3   Left onto SW Taylors Ferry Rd., then immediate right onto SW 26th Ave. Pass under I-5.

12.9   Right onto SW 30th Ave.

13.0   Left onto SW Hume St.

13.2   Right onto SW 34th Ave., which curves left to become SW Falcon St., then right to become SW 35th Ave.

13.5   Right onto SW Capitol Hwy. in Multnomah Village.

14.3   Continue straight (main road curves left) onto SW Vermont St., then SW Chestnut St.

15.3   Right onto SW Terwilliger Blvd.

15.6   Left onto SW Barbur Blvd. at stoplight, then right onto SW Miles St.

16.0   Right onto SW Brier Pl., which becomes SW Custer Way across I-5. Take second left, onto SW Corbett Ave.

17.0   Right onto SW Nebraska Street. Cross SW Macadam Ave. (OR 43) and rail tracks and continue south on Willamette Greenway.

17.4   End at Willamette Park.

7 Springwater Corridor

DIFFICULTY: Easy
DISTANCE: 43.2 miles
ELEVATION GAIN: 650 feet

Getting There: From I-5 northbound, take exit 300 toward I-84, then go right off the ramp for Central Eastside Industrial District. Go right onto SE Water Ave., which becomes SE Fourth Ave., to official trailhead at SE Ivon St. From I-5 southbound, take exit 300B, then stay left for Oregon City. Bear right onto SE Martin Luther King Jr. Blvd. at the base of the off-ramp. Go right onto SE Clay St. and left onto SE Water Ave., then follow preceding directions to trailhead. Parking available.

Transit: Take MAX Red or Blue Line to SW Oak and SW First Ave. stop; continue by bike over Hawthorne Bridge and then south on Eastbank Esplanade to SE Fourth Ave. and SE Ivon St. (see Ride 1).

The Springwater Corridor parallels the Willamette River and Johnson Creek from inner Southeast Portland to Gresham and beyond. It's Portland's best-loved multi-use path, a classic ride welcoming cyclists of all abilities.

On the boardwalk at Tideman Johnson Park

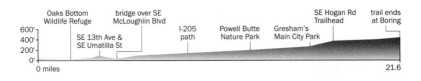

The idea of a recreation trail along Johnson Creek has floated around for almost a century. The Olmsted brothers—sons of famed landscape architect Frederick Law Olmsted—included it in their 1903 proposal for a 40-Mile Loop (see Ride 16). Like much of that proposal, the idea went nowhere and a rail line was built instead. For 50 years it carried produce to the city and, on weekends, carloads of fun seekers to Oaks Bottom Amusement Park, built by the Portland Railway Light and Power Company to boost business.

As it did to so many local rail lines, the automobile killed the Springwater. Passenger service ended in 1958, and freight service went into a terminal decline. By the 1980s, the line was abandoned. Trail advocates pounced. By 1990 the right-of-way was in public ownership and segments of trail were opening. It's still a work in progress—someday the trail might reach Estacada and even Mount Hood—but for now it offers an almost uninterrupted route from the Willamette to the southeastern edge of the metro area.

One of the trail's many virtues is its scenic variety, from surprisingly wild creekside stretches to industrial, suburban, and eventually rural sections. In between are some excellent parks and natural areas. For the sake of description, think of the trail as three sections: Springwater on the Willamette, Sellwood to Gresham, and Gresham to Boring.

The first section runs south along the Willamette River to the Sellwood neighborhood. See Ride 1 for details on this very popular stretch.

A gap in the trail sends you through Sellwood on city streets—not such a bad thing as this is one of Portland's most charming neighborhoods. (Consider a side trip to visit the shops and cafes along SE Tacoma Street and SE 13th and 17th Avenues.)

The second section begins at the southern edge of town, crossing SE McLoughlin Boulevard on a high bridge before turning east to follow Johnson Creek. The trail now enters a tight ravine. A moment ago you were soaring over an industrial landscape; now you could be lost somewhere in the Coast Range, hemmed in by walls of green. Halfway through this pocket of wilderness is Tideman Johnson Nature Park, where the city has "engineered" salmon habitat with dead trees carefully placed in the stream.

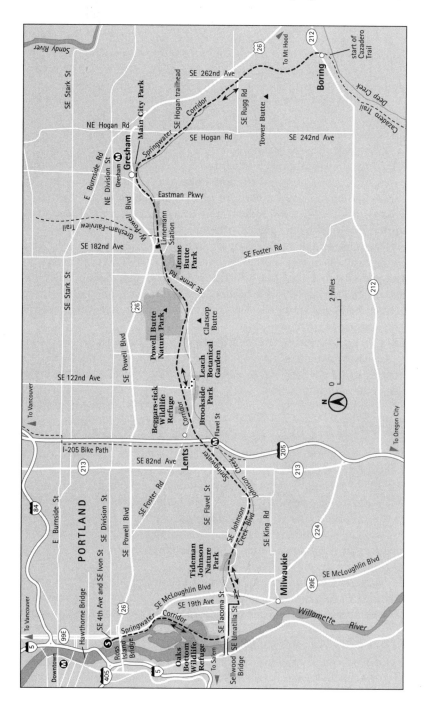

Emerging from the woods, you now cross SE Johnson Creek Boulevard and continue past a mix of homes, warehouses, and light industrial buildings. Many of them back right up to the trail. This continues to the Lents neighborhood, where you might consider a stop at the Beggars-tick Wildlife Refuge, a wetland rich in wildlife despite the massive junkyard next door. (The refuge's namesake, by the way, is a plant, not a bug.)

After Lents the route turns more residential. At SE 122nd Avenue, a quick side trip southward leads to one of Portland's lesser-known treasures, the Leach Botanical Garden. John and Lilla Leach bought this reach of Johnson Creek riverfront in 1931 and spent decades growing a horticultural collection several thousand species strong. The City of Portland now owns the garden, which is run by a nonprofit.

The Springwater continues east to the base of Powell Butte, where hiking trails lead to panoramic views atop this 612-acre nature park. Beyond Powell Butte, the trail skirts Jenne Butte, another patch of urban wilderness, to reach Linnemann Station (restrooms), the lone remaining station from the trail's previous life. Johnson Creek meanders through a widening floodplain nearby. Just beyond the station, the Gresham–Fairview Trail heads north to the Columbia (see Ride 41).

Gresham is 2 miles farther. If you've never poked around Gresham's charming old downtown, consider a quick side trip 0.25 mile up Main Street at Main City Park.

Beyond the park, suburbia ends and the trail's rural third stretch begins. You're not really out of town, but it sure feels like it. Forested Tower Butte looms to the west above scattered farms and mini-estates. Don't be surprised to cross paths with a deer or even a coyote.

As of this writing, the path turns to gravel around mile 19, rideable for all but the skinniest tires. It's scheduled to be paved sometime in 2012. After a few bucolic miles, the trail ends at a brand-new trailhead in Boring. With due respect to the good people of Boring, this little crossroads is well named. Someday that may change if long-standing plans to ram a freeway through here ever come to life.

Ambitious riders could continue across Oregon Route 212 to pick up the Cazadero Trail, currently a dirt track leading down the secluded canyon of Deep Creek to OR 224 and the Clackamas River. The rest of us will be content to idle awhile in Boring before the long pedal home.

MILEAGE LOG

Note: Trail mileposts don't match actual route mileage, shown here.

0.0 Begin at Springwater Corridor entrance, SE 4th Ave. and SE Ivon St.

1.8 At path to Oaks Bottom Wildlife Refuge, continue south on trail.

2.5 At path to Oaks Bottom Amusement Park, continue south on trail.

3.1 Path ends at SE Umatilla St (Note: Trail is scheduled to be extended farther south in 2013.) Continue east on Umatilla.

3.9 Right onto SE 19th Ave.

4.2 Continue past barrier; sharp left onto Springwater Corridor.

4.5 Cross SE McLoughlin Blvd. on high bridge.

5.3 Tideman Johnson Nature Park.

5.7 At Johnson Creek Blvd. trailhead, cross SE Johnson Creek Blvd.

8.7 At intersection with I-205 path, continue straight on Springwater Corridor.

9.7 Beggars-tick Wildlife Refuge at left.

10.3 Cross SE 122nd Ave. (**Side trip:** Go right onto SE 122nd Ave. 0.3 mile to Leach Botanical Garden.)

11.6 Powell Butte Nature Park at left.

13.9 Linnemann Station trailhead (restrooms) at left.

15.9 S. Main St. and Main City Park, Gresham. (**Side trip:** Go left 0.2 mile and cross W. Powell Blvd. to visit downtown Gresham.)

17.3 SE Hogan Rd. trailhead.

19.3 Pavement ends beyond SE Rugg Rd.

21.6 Ends at Boring trailhead. Retrace route to return.

8 Milwaukie and Gladstone

DIFFICULTY: Easy
DISTANCE: 15-mile loop
ELEVATION GAIN: 550 feet

Getting There: From I-5 southbound, take exit 300B for Oregon City, or from I-5 northbound take exit 300 for Central Eastside. Turn right onto SE Martin Luther King Jr. Blvd. (becomes SE Grand Ave., then SE McLoughlin Blvd.) and continue approximately 5 miles. Turn left onto SE Harrison St. in Milwaukie, go two blocks, and turn left onto SE 21st Ave. to Scott Park.

Transit: Take MAX Green Line to Clackamas Town Center Transit Center. Bicycle west to Milwaukie via Sunnyside, Harmony, and Lake Rds., approximately 4 miles.

Bicycle: Ride from Portland to Milwaukie (see Ride 2) via Springwater Corridor and SE McLoughlin Blvd., approximately 5 miles.

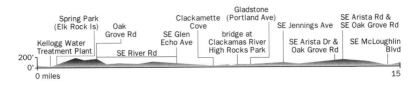

Milwaukie and Gladstone—to many Portlanders, these are just places to speed past on SE McLoughlin Boulevard, aka Oregon Route 99E. Yet tucked behind the big-box stores and car dealerships hide quaint Main Streets, all but swallowed up by Portland's growth. This ride visits both towns, plus a few equally underappreciated natural areas.

Begin in downtown Milwaukie at Scott Park. From the park, follow 21st Avenue to Harrison Street, then right to cross SE McLoughlin Boulevard. A path leads left, bringing you to the Jefferson Boat Ramp and Kellogg Creek Wastewater Treatment Plant. The path continues behind the parking lot, leading to the Island Station neighborhood and Spring Park, gateway to Elk Rock Island.

If you have time for only one side trip on this ride, visit this fantastic nature area. Lock your bike at Spring Park and walk down to the river. In late summer and fall when the water is low, you can walk across a dry channel to the "island," a mass of basalt deflecting the river westward. Meadows and secluded coves ring the island. In the center, a forest of oak, cottonwood, and ash forms a miniature wilderness. You'll hardly believe you're in the middle of a city.

Back on the route, ride up a short but steep hill on SE Sparrow Street to SE River Road. The next several miles roll through a fascinating neighborhood, where mansions mingle with ramshackle ranch houses and questionable-looking commercial establishments. Traffic is moderate, the bike lane generous, and the tree canopy immense.

After you cross Oak Grove Boulevard, SE River Road plunges downhill. Several miles later, it emerges from the trees at SE McLoughlin Boulevard, which carries you across the Clackamas River. Take your first right across the river to escape McLoughlin's exhaust and noise, circling back to the Clackamas on Clackamette Drive. It leads you past Clackamette Cove, a scenic if not exactly pristine lake. (A wetland once sustained fish and wildlife here, but the gravel underneath it proved too desirable.) Just beyond the lake, look for a path, the Clackamas River Trail, leading left.

The path leads upriver to a bridge back over the Clackamas at High Rocks Park. Here, local daredevils, fueled by testosterone and astoundingly poor judgment, leap from low basalt cliffs into the seemingly

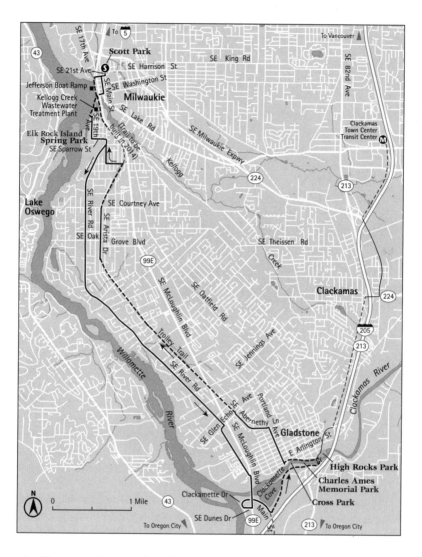

placid river. Submerged rocks and spooky currents periodically claim jumpers' lives. Still, it's a beautiful stretch of river, and by all accounts the fly-fishing is superb.

From High Rocks, head back downstream through Cross Park to Portland Avenue, where the route turns north toward Gladstone's main drag. Though you're mere blocks from busy McLoughlin, you could just as easily be lost somewhere deep in the Willamette Valley country-side. A flashing stoplight, a hardware store, a tavern, and a post office:

Taking a break on the Clackamas River Trail near High Rocks

that's about it, except of course for the excellent coffee shop. This *is* Portland, after all.

If Milwaukie once had grand economic pretensions, Gladstone's were cultural. Home to Oregon's first state fair, Gladstone for a time also hosted the third-largest permanent Chautauqua in America. Chautauquas were a sort of adult summer camp, mixing education, entertainment, and worship. Part serious educational institution and part party, Chautauquas helped alleviate the isolation and loneliness of rural life in 19th-century America.

Launched in 1894, Gladstone's Chautauqua drew visitors by the tens of thousands to hear performances by John Philip Sousa, sermons by Billy Sunday, and speeches from the likes of Theodore Roosevelt and William Jennings Bryan. For a time it was arguably the biggest cultural event in the Pacific Northwest. But by the 1920s, Gladstone's Chautauqua was losing out to the racier vaudeville shows popular in Portland. In 1929 the Chautauqua grounds were sold to the Seventh-day Adventist Church, which to this day holds annual camp meetings around Chautauqua Lake.

From Portland Avenue in Gladstone, go left onto Abernethy Lane, and cross Glen Echo Avenue to the brand-new Trolley Trail, built on the old streetcar route that once connected Oregon City, Gladstone,

Oak Grove, and Milwaukie to Portland. The line opened in 1893, sparking a boom among these previously isolated river villages. But just as the trolley shaped these places, the automobile effaced them, obscuring their unique identities behind the sprawling strip of Oregon Route 99E (aka McLoughlin Boulevard). Perhaps the Trolley Trail will help swing the pendulum back in the other direction. Imagine a future day when the trail, not soot-choked OR 99E, is the "main drag."

The Trolley Trail runs a few blocks past backyards to SE McLoughlin Boulevard. It's a good idea to cross on foot at this tricky intersection; the trail resumes 100 feet or so down (and on the opposite side of) McLoughlin. It continues gradually uphill to Oak Grove, paralleling SE Arista Drive. A block beyond SE Creighton Avenue, the trail joins Arista and travels on streets through what's left of "downtown" Oak Grove, established in 1890. The path resumes after SE Courtney Avenue, gradually descends back to SE McLoughlin Boulevard, and parallels for the final mile back to Milwaukie.

MILEAGE LOG

0.0 Begin at Scott Park. Go south on SE 21st Ave.; right onto SE Harrison St.

0.2 Cross SE McLoughlin Boulevard at stoplight and go left onto path paralleling road.

0.4 Right at SE Washington St. into Kellogg Creek Wastewater Treatment Plant. Path continues at back end of parking lot.

0.7 Path ends at SE Eagle St. in Island Station. Continue straight on SE 19th Ave.

1.0 Street curves left to become SE Sparrow St. (**Side trip:** Go right into Spring Park; lock bike and continue on foot trail down to Elk Rock Island.)

1.2 SE Sparrow St. curves right to become SE River Rd.

2.5 Cross Oak Grove Blvd.

5.5 Right onto SE Glen Echo Ave.

6.2 Right on SE McLoughlin Blvd.

6.7 Right onto SE Dunes Dr., across Clackamas River Bridge, then right onto Clackamette Dr. Continue under SE McLoughlin Blvd.

7.2 Left onto Clackamas River Trail.

8.2 Left at path's end onto S. Washington St. Cross Clackamas River at High Rocks Park bridge.

8.4 Left onto path through Cross Park. Continue on E. Clackamas Blvd. and resume path in Charles Ames Memorial Park.

8.8 Right onto Portland Ave. into downtown Gladstone.

9.3 Left onto Trolley Trail just before SE Abernethy Lane.

10.3 Cross SE McLoughlin Blvd. at SE Jennings Ave.

12.3 Right onto SE Arista Dr. in Oak Grove.

13.0 Trolley Trail resumes beyond SE Courtney Ave.

13.6 Left at trail's end onto SE Park Ave. (Trail to be extended in 2014.)

13.8 Right onto SE 23rd Ave. Continue straight onto SE River Rd.

14.3 Left to resume Trolley Trail.

14.7 Right to cross SE McLoughlin Blvd. at SE Washington St. in Milwaukie, then left onto SE Main St.

15.0 End at Scott Park.

9 Southeast: Mount Tabor

DIFFICULTY: Easy to Moderate
DISTANCE: 13.5-mile loop
ELEVATION GAIN: 700 feet

Getting There: See Ride 1's directions to Salmon St. Springs.

Inner Southeast Portland is the city's bohemian heartland, heir to the Sixties counterculture. Hawthorne Boulevard is the main drag, a string of independent businesses, restaurants, and bars stretching from the river to Mount Tabor's flank. Old homes line the quiet side streets, replete with chicken coops, gardens, and other emblems of Portland-style urban homesteading. Inner Southeast abounds with self-conscious (and at times, self-congratulating) displays of community spirit. But unlike other, more recently hip areas, it retains an eclectic and unpretentious vibe.

Begin at Salmon Street Springs fountain in Tom McCall Waterfront Park. Cross the Hawthorne Bridge and loop down to SE Clay Street, a quiet bike boulevard paralleling SE Hawthorne Boulevard.

Continue on Clay across SE 12th Avenue to enter the Ladd's Addition neighborhood. William S. Ladd, former mayor of Portland, platted it in the 1890s. Determined to outdo the competition, Ladd copied the

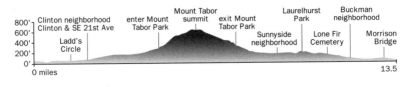

famous diagonal street grid of Washington, DC, with streets radiating in spokes from a traffic circle. It's nearly impossible to navigate your way through Ladd's without getting lost, but if ever there was a neighborhood worth getting lost in, this is it—big trees, beautiful homes, and rose gardens invite exploration.

HOW TO WIN FRIENDS AND RUIN YOUR KNEES

Stubby handlebars, top tube pad, maybe a card in the spokes, no gears—and no brakes. You've seen them around, piloted by the young and beautiful. Designed for velodrome racing, fixed-gear bikes have long been the ride of choice for bike messengers, who prize their simplicity, weight, and—one suspects—macho allure.

At some point the kids decided bike messengers were really cool, or at least that fixed-gear bikes were fun to ride. And they are. With no freewheel, the pedals spin whenever the bike moves, in either direction. This allows for sexy "track stands"—wherein fixie riders pose motionless on their bikes at stoplights, seeming to defy gravity. This also means that on a downhill, the only way to stop is to resist the force of the turning pedals with your leg muscles, or put your foot directly against the front wheel like you did on that dirt bike when you were 10. Neither technique is easy.

Fixie fans insist the bikes aren't technically "brakeless"—you're the brake. Still, it's not a sport for the faint of heart. Cranking uphill in that one gear can strain your knees. And forget about stopping on a dime.

But man, you'll look *great*.

From Ladd's, cross SE Division Street to the Clinton neighborhood, centered on SE Clinton Street at 21st and 26th Avenues. Consider a stop to fortify yourself at one of the area's many fine bars, cafes, or restaurants, because soon you'll be climbing a volcano.

Things start gently enough on SE Clinton Street. You might notice tiny Piccolo Park at SE 27th Avenue. It owes its existence to a freeway planned to connect downtown to outer Southeast neighborhoods. It would have demolished this entire area and replaced charming Clinton Street with an elevated expressway. With construction imminent, the state started buying up homes along the proposed route.

But this was the late 1960s, and something was changing in Portland. Local grassroots freeway opponents gained citywide support as Portlanders began to think differently about questions of livability and transit. Mounting opposition forced the state to cancel the project,

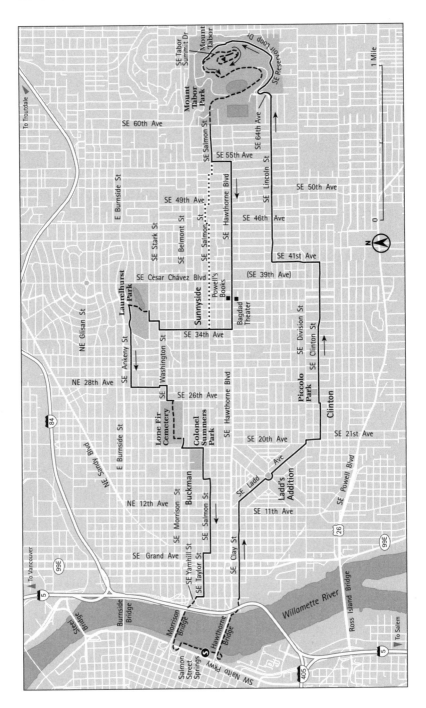

Mount Tabor

SE Tabor Summit Dr

Mount Tabor

SE Tabor Summit Dr

Golf Loop Dr

SE Reservoir

Mount Tabor Park

To Troutdale

SE 60th Ave

SE Salmon St

SE 55th Ave

SE 64th Ave

E Burnside St

SE 49th Ave

SE Lincoln St

SE 50th Ave

SE Stark St

SE Belmont St

SE Salmon St

SE Salmon St

SE Hawthorne Blvd

SE 46th Ave

Laurelhurst Park

SE César Chávez Blvd

Powell's Books

SE 41st Ave

NE Glisan St

Sunnyside

(SE 39th Ave)

SE Ankeny St

Bagdad Theater

SE Division St

SE Clinton St

NE 28th Ave

SE Washington St

SE 34th Ave

Piccolo Park

SE 26th Ave

Lone Fir Cemetery

Colonel Summers Park

SE Hawthorne Blvd

Clinton

SE 20th Ave

SE 21st Ave

E Burnside St

NE Sandy Blvd

84

Buckman

NE 12th Ave

SE Morrison St

SE Salmon St

SE Ladd Ave

Ladd's Addition

SE 11th Ave

SE Powell Blvd

26

To Vancouver

99E

SE Grand Ave

SE Yamhill St

SE Taylor St

SE Clay St

99E

5

Steel Bridge

Burnside Bridge

Morrison Bridge

Hawthorne Bridge

Willamette River

Ross Island Bridge

Salmon Street Springs

SW Naito Pkwy

405

To Salem

5

N

0   1 Mile

which more or less ended freeway building in Portland. (Interstate 205, already in the works, was scaled back but ultimately completed.) The state was left holding some property along Clinton Street—now Piccolo Park. What better monument to the triumph of people over cars than a neighborhood park full of kids?

The climbing ratchets up a notch as you continue east. Across SE 60th Avenue, a bike-friendly road leads to the top of Mount Tabor. (Dormant now, it really was once an active volcano; the park's builders quarried cinder atop the hill for roads.) The view across Southeast from the summit more than justifies the climb. Busy SE Hawthorne Boulevard stretches westward toward downtown skyscrapers, which gleam brilliantly in the evening light. The scowling figure in bronze atop the park is Harvey Scott, former editor of the *Oregonian* and tireless Portland promoter. Sculptor Gutzon Borglum created Scott's monument during a break from his main project, a quartet of presidents he was carving from the side of a South Dakota mountain.

From Tabor's wooded summit, continue downhill on a loop passing the park's reservoirs, which store drinking water from the Bull Run watershed on Mount Hood. These reservoirs have become controversial in recent years. Post–September 11, 2001, security concerns prompted the city to propose covering them. Neighbors revolted and the city backed down. But then the US Environmental Protection Agency decreed that all of Portland's open reservoirs must be covered or replaced. Though the political wrangling continues, the eminently practical and elegant reservoirs appear destined to be disconnected from the water system.

Coasting downhill among giant old Craftsman homes, you arrive at SE Hawthorne Boulevard, Southeast Portland's heart and soul. (West of SE 50th Avenue Hawthorne becomes a busy commercial street; if you're not comfortable riding here, detour a few blocks north to the bike boulevard along SE Salmon Street.) Tucked among the head shops, antique stores, cafes, and general cultural ferment is Nobel Laureate Linus Pauling's boyhood home, at 3945 SE Hawthorne Boulevard. Beyond the busy intersection with SE César Chávez Boulevard (aka SE 39th Avenue), you pass a branch of Powell's Books and the historic Bagdad Theater.

Having sampled Hawthorne, now turn right onto SE 34th Avenue and cruise through the Sunnyside neighborhood, centered on 34th Avenue and SE Belmont Street.

A few turns of the crank farther is Laurelhurst Park, the most beautiful park in all of Portland. (It's my neighborhood park, so I might be a little biased. It *does* own the distinction of being the first city park ever listed on the National Register of Historic Places, though.) Cross through the park, past the great concert lawn and Firwood Lake, to exit near the restrooms on SE Ankeny Street.

Ankeny leads you west past a few grandiose old mansions and then down to SE 28th Avenue, home to one of the city's great restaurant rows. Between here and NE Glisan Street, you could spend a week eating out and not do justice to the culinary offerings. Turn left instead and continue to the Lone Fir Cemetery, Portland's oldest extant burial ground. When it was founded in 1855, there really was only *one* fir in it—the immense trees have all grown up since.

Until the River View Cemetery opened in 1882 (see Ride 6), this was Portland's only cemetery. Portland's founder, Asa Lovejoy, is buried here, as are several mayors. So too are criminals, inmates of the "Insane Asylum" formerly at SE 12th and Hawthorne, and members of the demimonde. (One of the more prominent headstones honors a famed 19th-century prostitute, erected by a group of her bereaved clients.)

Follow paths to the cemetery's southwest corner, where you exit onto SE Morrison Street past a vacant lot. For decades this lot was home to a county office building. In 2004, the county moved to sell it for development. Before the sale went through, though, someone discovered human remains. Further investigation revealed that dozens of 19th-century Chinese laborers were buried here in unmarked graves. Now the site is slated to become a memorial to them and the largely unacknowledged role they played in building the city. (This is just one of many stories in the cemetery—join one of the monthly walking tours to hear more: www.friendsoflonefircemetery.org.)

Down Morrison to SE 20th Avenue, you pass Colonel Summers Park, a stronghold of Portland bike hipsterism. The park has hosted the Multnomah County Bike Fair—think bike polo, jousting, and track stand (see "How to Win Friends and Ruin Your Knees" sidebar) contests—and is a gathering spot for the young, tattooed, and beautiful bike set.

The final stretch follows the bike boulevard on SE Salmon Street, through the bohemian heart of the Buckman neighborhood. At SE 11th Avenue, cross back into the industrial blocks. At the base of SE Taylor Street, go right onto SE Water Avenue and left onto the Morrison Bridge's luxurious new bike path. It loops down to SW Naito Parkway and Waterfront Park, your end point.

Among the departed, Lone Fir Cemetery

MILEAGE LOG

0.0 Begin at Salmon Street Springs fountain in Tom McCall Waterfront Park. Cross Hawthorne Bridge and exit onto Eastbank
Esplanade path (first right across the bridge). Take first left from
the path, through Portland Boathouse parking area. Cross
SE Water Ave. and continue east on SE Clay St.

1.4 Cross SE 12th Ave. and bear right onto SE Ladd Ave. Continue
around through Ladd Circle to stay on SE Ladd Ave.

2.1 Cross SE Division St. at stoplight. Continue south on SE 21st Ave.
to stop sign, then left onto SE Clinton St. Piccolo Park at left.

3.3 Left onto SE 41st Ave.

3.6 Right onto SE Lincoln St.

4.7 Left at SE 64th Ave. to enter Mount Tabor Park. Continue uphill
on unsigned street, staying left (uphill) where road forks.

5.6 Sharp left at parking area to continue uphill on SE Tabor
Summit Dr. (closed to cars). Continue around summit loop,
return to parking area, and continue past gate onto SE Reservoir
Loop Dr. to go downhill.

7.6 Cross SE 60th Ave. and continue on SE Salmon St.

7.9 Left onto SE 55th Ave., then right onto SE Hawthorne Blvd.
(**Option:** To avoid Hawthorne, go right at SE 55th Ave. and
follow bike signs downhill to SE 34th Ave.)

9.1 Right onto SE 34th Ave.

9.6 Right onto SE Stark St, then left onto SE 35th Ave.

9.8 Right onto SE Oak St., then left into Laurelhurst Park. Follow
path downhill through park. Exit near restrooms, left onto
SE Ankeny St.

10.6 Left onto SE 28th Ave. Continue through stoplight at SE Stark St.
and go right onto SE Washington St.

10.9 Left onto SE 26th Ave. and immediate right into Lone Fir
Cemetery. Left at T intersection in cemetery to exit.

11.3 Right onto SE Morrison St., then left at stoplight onto SE 20th Ave.

11.5 Right onto SE Taylor St. Colonel Summers Park at right.

11.7 Left onto SE 16th Ave., then right onto SE Salmon St.

12.3 Right onto SE 6th Ave., then left on to SE Taylor St. Cross
SE Grand Ave. and SE Martin Luther King Jr. Blvd. at stoplight.

12.6 Right onto SE Water Ave. Continue through stop sign at SE Yamhill St. and go left onto Morrison Bridge bike-pedestrian lane.

13.3 At base of bridge, cross SW Naito Pkwy. into Tom McCall Waterfront Park and go right on path.

13.5 End at Salmon Street Springs fountain.

10 Southeast: Woodstock and Sellwood

DIFFICULTY: Easy
DISTANCE: 15.4-mile loop
ELEVATION GAIN: 350 feet

Getting There: See Ride 1's directions to Salmon St. Springs.

Ride 9 visits some of Southeast Portland's hot spots. This ride takes a quieter path, looping through the slightly farther-flung neighborhoods of Woodstock and Sellwood.

Like the preceding ride, this one begins at Salmon Street Springs fountain in Tom McCall Waterfront Park and crosses the Hawthorne Bridge to Ladd's Addition. Here the two routes part ways: this one continues up SE Harrison Street through the Colonial Heights neighborhood. Climb steadily up to SE 30th Avenue, just enough elevation gain to afford a good view back across the sea of trees in Ladd's.

The route turns south here to ramble through the Richmond neighborhood. The bustle of SE Division Street gives way to quiet along SE Franklin Street. At SE Powell Boulevard, a tricky crossing and steep path lead you to Creston Park, where giant Douglas firs surround an outdoor pool. This is kid central in summer.

After Creston's winding paths and rolling topography, continue on a steady, subtle climb southward through block after block of appealing neighborhood streets—the leafy, quiet places just about everyone wishes they grew up in. Just when you think you might be entering suburbia, though, you reach SE Woodstock Boulevard, a neighborhood center lined with restaurants and stores.

Now the ride turns west and back downhill. Beyond SE César Chávez Boulevard (SE 39th Avenue), Woodstock divides the red brick and open lawns of Reed College from the prestigious homes of Eastmoreland. The route goes left at SE Reed College Place to follow the Reed College Parkway, a linear park fronted by graceful homes.

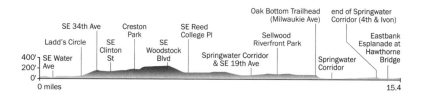

Winter sun on SE Sellwood Boulevard, with Oaks Bottom and downtown beyond

First, though, consider a quick side trip looping through the campus. Follow the entrance drive north to Eliot Hall. Behind it hides a natural area unknown to many Portlanders: Reed Canyon. Though not very deep, it is indeed canyonlike: a steep, lake-filled gully ringed with forest and crossed by a high bridge. The scene is surprisingly dramatic. For decades the lake was an algal swamp, but recent restoration efforts have cooled the water, removed the smell, and improved habitat for native species, including salmon.

On the north side of the canyon, skirt dormitories and a sports field and recross the canyon, then pass the Crystal Springs Rhododendron Garden. Consider a stop here, especially if it's springtime, before continuing on the route.

The parkway along Reed College Place ends at SE Crystal Springs Boulevard, which follows a bluff above Johnson Creek. At SE 37th Avenue, a short, steep, and unpaved street breaches the bluff to reach the Springwater Corridor. Follow the Springwater west (see Ride 7 for details); where it ends at SE 19th Avenue, turn right to enter Sellwood.

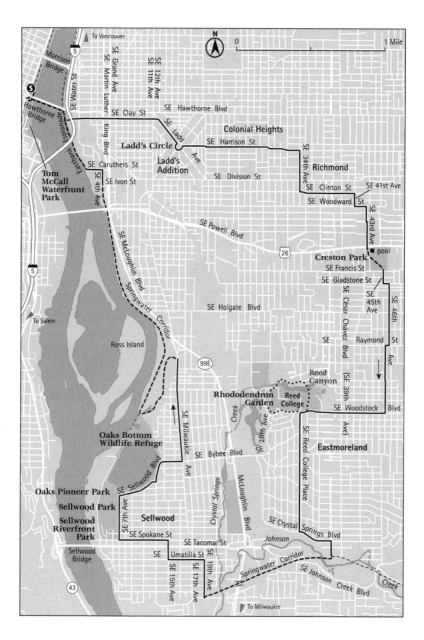

More genteel than Woodstock and more urban than Eastmoreland, Sellwood is many Portlanders' idea of a perfect neighborhood. A small-town feel reigns along SE 17th and 13th Avenues, the twin main streets. Modest homes cluster around Westmoreland Park while bigger ones command views on the bluffs above Oaks Bottom Wildlife Refuge. Yuppie amenities (day spas, baby boutiques) mix with older working-class institutions (hardware store, second-run movie theater, dive bars).

Linger in Sellwood, especially if you like antiques. When it's time to go, follow SE Milwaukie Boulevard north to the Oaks Bottom trailhead, just before the McLoughlin Boulevard overpass. A paved trail leads downhill and back to the Springwater Corridor, where after several miles of riverfront riding you return to the Hawthorne Bridge and Waterfront Park.

MILEAGE LOG

0.0 Begin at Salmon Street Springs fountain in Tom McCall Waterfront Park. Cross Hawthorne Bridge and exit onto Eastbank Esplanade path (first right across the bridge). Take first left from the path, through Portland Boathouse parking area.

0.8 Cross SE Water Ave. and continue east on SE Clay St.

1.4 Cross SE 12th Ave. and go right onto SE Ladd Ave.

1.7 At Ladd Circle, go three-quarters of the way around and then right onto SE Harrison St.

2.7 Right onto SE 34th Ave.

3.0 Left onto SE Clinton St.

3.4 Right onto SE 41st Ave., left onto SE Woodward St., then right onto SE 43rd Ave.

4.0 Cross SE Powell Blvd., go left briefly along Powell's sidewalk, then right onto path entering Creston Park. Pass pool at left, then go left to pass central lawn, then right to exit park straight onto SE 45th Ave.

4.6 Left onto SE Gladstone St., then immediately right onto SE 46th Ave., which jogs to right at SE Raymond St.

5.6 Right onto SE Woodstock Blvd.

6.3 Left onto SE Reed College Place. (**Side trip:** Go right to loop through campus. Behind Eliot Hall, continue across Reed Canyon on bridge; head up small rise and go left onto path skirting sports field; left again in several hundred yards to recross canyon on second bridge, then right onto SE Botsford Dr. by athletic center; left onto SE 28th Ave., past Crystal Springs Rhododendron Garden at right; left onto SE Woodstock Blvd. and right onto SE Reed College Pl. to rejoin route.)

7.4 Left onto SE Crystal Spring Blvd.

7.7 Right onto SE 37th Ave. Continue down short, steep hill and go right onto Springwater Corridor.

9.0 Sharp right onto SE 19th Ave. at end of trail.

9.2 Left onto SE Umatilla St., then right onto SE 15th Ave. Cross SE Tacoma St. and go left onto SE Spokane St.

10.0 Right onto SE 7th Ave. Sellwood Park at left. Road curves right to become SE Sellwood Blvd., overlooking Oaks Bottom Wildlife Refuge.

10.6 Left onto SE 13th Ave., which curves right to become SE Bybee Blvd.

10.9 Left onto SE Milwaukie Ave.

11.8 Left (caution) into Oaks Bottom trailhead parking area. Continue downhill on paved path.

12.2 Right onto Springwater Corridor.

14.2 Left onto SE Caruthers St. at trail's end. Continue west onto Eastbank Esplanade.

14.9 Right onto path leading up to Hawthorne Bridge. Cross bridge.

15.4 End at Salmon Street Springs fountain in Tom McCall Waterfront Park.

11 Northeast Portland

DIFFICULTY: Easy
DISTANCE: 16.8-mile loop
ELEVATION GAIN: 550 feet

Getting There: See Ride 1's directions to Salmon St. Springs.

Northeast Portland is without a doubt the most diverse quadrant of the city. This ride ranges across the spectrum.

Begin at Tom McCall Waterfront Park and follow the Burnside Bridge east across the Willamette. Once a no-go zone for bikes, lower E. Burnside Street now has a generous bike lane—perfect for cruising this newly hip district's nightclubs and bars.

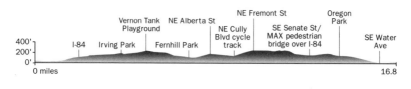

The route turns north at NE 12th Avenue and crosses Interstate 84 into the Lloyd District, still in search of an identity after 1950s-era urban renewal. Parking-lot wastelands surround isolated high-rises. Fast-food chains ring the Lloyd Center shopping mall. Here the city serves cars, not the other way around. Still, this is Portland—there are bike lanes!

Across NE Broadway the scene changes abruptly at Irvington, one of Portland's classic streetcar neighborhoods. Continue north up NE 15th Avenue to NE Knott Street, where a left turn leads you down a wide, quiet boulevard of mammoth trees. A right at NE Ninth Avenue leads north to Irving Park.

Captain William Irving acquired all of this land as a 635-acre claim, stretching west to the river, in 1851. Forty years later, Portland annexed the villages along the east riverbank. Within a few years, streetcar lines extended across the river and north toward Irving's land. Captain Irving himself had long since headed north to pilot steamships on Canada's Fraser River, building a fortune in British Columbia's gold rush, but his family stayed on in Portland and made a pile in real estate.

From the beginning, Irvington was designed to be elite, with large house lots. Prosperous merchants and lumbermen built spacious mansions, many of which still stand. Most of Irvington has remained the abode of the comfortable ever since.

Immediately west and north lie the historic neighborhoods of King, Sabin, and Eliot, long home to Portland's ethnic immigrant communities. Irving Park straddles the boundary. Enter the park's south side from NE Ninth Avenue. Continue up and over the hill, past soccer fields, to exit the park and cross NE Fremont Street.

Now you're in the Sabin neighborhood, where several old African-American churches attest to Portland's historic segregation (enforced by postwar real estate agents and lenders), now fading under the rush of gentrification. Clues to the neighborhood's even older Polish and Scandinavian populations are scattered about.

From NE Ninth, head right up NE Skidmore Street, where a short climb ends at the Vernon Tank Playground, where water towers loom over a park and community garden. Go left onto NE 20th Avenue and continue a few blocks to Alberta Street. Long a center of the African-American community, Alberta started drawing white Portlanders priced out of Southeast in the late 1990s. Now Alberta outdoes SE Hawthorne Boulevard for the sheer concentration of yoga studios, "artisanal" food shops, art galleries, bars, restaurants, and all the wonderful things *Portlandia* has taught America about our city.

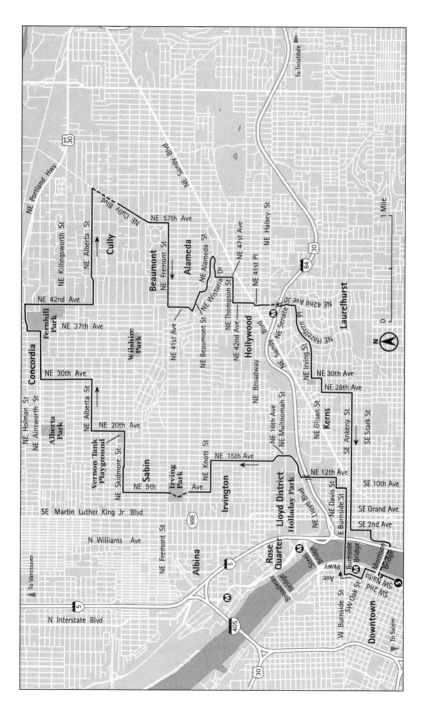

Plenty of reasons to get off the bike on NE Alberta Street

The change is clearly not to everyone's liking, most obviously the older inhabitants being forced or induced to leave by rising rents and home prices. Even some of the newer residents would like to slow the pace of change, as evinced by recent controversy over the now (in)famous Last Thursday event. Conceived as a freewheeling counterpoint to the Pearl District's somewhat stuffy monthly art opening, it's morphed into Portland's most raucous street fair. It's great fun to visit, but you might not want to live through it on a monthly basis.

Riding on Alberta Street is easy enough, but all the action demands vigilance. Feel free to bail to a side street or walk your bike to better enjoy the street's many diversions. At NE 30th, head left. The land slopes gently northward toward the Columbia Slough, speeding your way to Fernhill Park in the Concordia neighborhood.

Here you enter a very different Northeast Portland: the Cully neighborhood, a patchwork of convenience stores, low-rent apartment complexes, ranch homes on oversize lots, and the occasional "green" in-fill development. This is probably not the place to find single-origin coffees or imported Japanese small-batch sea salt, but there is plenty worth exploring: Buddhist temples, Asian and Mexican groceries, even the odd holdout farm.

Cully also has an attraction other Portland neighborhoods can only envy: the city's first true cycle track. From NE Killingsworth to NE Prescott Street, a slightly raised concrete path parallels the road, offering cyclists a route entirely separated from both pedestrians and traffic. For a few blocks you can pretend you're in Amsterdam—the ultimate Portland dream. (Cully's cycle track has since been upstaged by the newer one in the South Waterfront neighborhood.)

The boring old bike lane resumes after Prescott, then disappears altogether on NE Fremont Street. Welcome to the Beaumont neighborhood, a solidly upper-middle-class district of tidy yards and abundant gardens. A left turn onto NE 41st Avenue brings you to the top of the socioeconomic ladder at Alameda, perched on the edge of Alameda Ridge. Like Irvington, Alameda was built at the turn of the 20th century for streetcar-commuting professionals. Unlike Irvington, it never experienced the racial and class tumult of the 1960s. It retains a distinctly patrician vibe, evidenced by the palaces along Alameda Street.

Just before the ridge peters out, turn sharply onto NE Wistaria Drive to descend into the Hollywood neighborhood, centered on NE Sandy Boulevard. At NE 42nd and NE Halsey you'll reach the Hollywood MAX station, where you cross I-84 into the Laurelhurst neighborhood.

Like Ladd's Addition, Laurelhurst was created from William S. Ladd's 486-acre Hazelfern Farm, which once covered much of inner East Portland. Like Irvington, it was designed to be upscale: no alcohol-serving establishments, no apartments, and no ethnic minorities allowed. Among the immense trees and fine Craftsman homes, an air of exclusivity persists. (This is not a neighborhood where you can let your lawn grow too long.) As in Ladd's Addition, you could spend happy hours here getting lost and found again among the curving streets.

The street grid returns at Oregon Park: two blocks of forest faced by homes and apartments. It's a gateway of sorts to the Kerns neighborhood, centered along NE 28th Avenue. Follow this busy street past one of Portland's great restaurant rows, then cross Burnside and continue west down SE Ankeny Street all the way to its end at SE Second Avenue. Here you might consider a quick detour one block north, to the skate park underneath the Burnside Bridge. Near-pros ride alongside kids in a scene that's vaguely intimidating and always interesting. From here, continue south down to SE Water Avenue and over the Morrison Bridge to return to the Waterfront Park.

MILEAGE LOG

0.0 Begin at Salmon Street Springs fountain in Tom McCall Waterfront Park. Proceed north on SW Naito Pkwy.

0.4 Left onto SW Oak St., then right onto SW 2nd Ave.

0.8 Right onto W. Burnside St. to cross Burnside Bridge.

1.7 Left onto NE 10th Ave., right onto NE Davis St., and left onto NE 12th Ave. to cross over I-84.

2.1 Right onto NE Lloyd Blvd. Stay right to join NE 16th Ave. and continue north on NE 15th Ave.

3.3 Left onto NE Knott St.

3.6 Right onto NE 9th Ave.

3.9 Enter Irving Park. Continue straight through park, cross NE Fremont St., and continue north on NE 9th Ave.

4.5 Right onto NE Skidmore St. Vernon Tank Playground and Sabin Garden at NE 19th Ave.

5.1 Left onto NE 20th Ave.

5.4 Right onto NE Alberta St.

6.0 Left onto NE 30th Ave.

6.4 Right onto NE Ainsworth St.

6.9 Left onto NE 37th Ave. Fernhill Park straight ahead. Then right onto NE Holman St. and right again onto NE 42nd Ave. to circle the park.

8.0 Left onto NE Alberta St.

9.1 Sharp right onto NE Cully Blvd. cycle track.

9.9 Right onto NE Fremont St.

10.7 Left onto NE 41st Ave.

10.9 Left onto NE Beaumont St., which becomes NE Alameda St.

11.5 Sharp right onto NE Wistaria Dr.

11.7 Left onto NE 47th Ave.

11.9 Right onto NE Thompson St.

12.1 Left onto NE 42nd Ave.

12.6 Cross freeway at Hollywood MAX station pedestrian overpass. Sharp right at bottom of ramp onto NE Senate St., then left to continue south on NE 42nd Ave.

12.9 Right onto NE Hazelfern Pl. Cross NE César Chávez Blvd. (SE 39th Ave.).

13.3 Bear right onto NE Irving St.

13.7 Left at Oregon Park onto NE 30th Ave., then right onto NE Glisan St. and left at stoplight onto NE 28th Ave.

14.2 Right onto SE Ankeny St.

15.4 Left onto SE 2nd Ave. (**Option:** go right one block to visit Burnside Skate Park.)

15.7 Right onto SE Stark St., which curves left to become SE Water Ave.

15.9 Right onto Morrison Bridge bike-pedestrian lane.

16.6 At base of bridge, cross SW Naito Pkwy. to Tom McCall Waterfront Park.

16.8 End at Salmon Street Springs fountain.

12 Avenue of the Roses

DIFFICULTY: Easy to Moderate
DISTANCE: 21.8-mile loop; option: 14.7 miles one way
ELEVATION GAIN: 920 feet

Getting There: From I-205 northbound take exit 23A, NE Sandy Blvd., and go left at first stoplight into MAX Parkrose/Sumner station parking area.
Transit: Ride MAX Red Line to Parkrose/Sumner station.

NE 82nd Avenue, aka the Avenue of the Roses, might seem like a strange choice for a bike tour. True, the old thoroughfare is famous for its used-car dealerships, prostitution, and "adventurous" pedestrian and bike conditions. But look past the broken glass and skinny sidewalks, and you'll find incredible cultural diversity, unmatched anywhere in Oregon.

Since 82nd Avenue is no place to ride a bike, the route instead parallels the old thoroughfare through some of East Portland's underappreciated neighborhoods. It crosses 82nd several times at intersections strategically located near several of the street's many excellent Vietnamese restaurants. (There's also no shortage of other cuisines, but a guidebook has only so much room!) You'll be ready for a meal after climbing up Rocky Butte, with views from St. Helens to Hood and beyond.

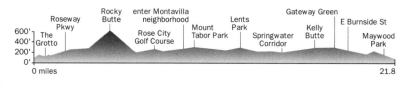

High up in the Grotto

Start at the Parkrose/Sumner MAX station. After crossing over Interstate 205 on NE Sandy Boulevard, you'll soon reach the first of several potential stops: the National Sanctuary of Our Sorrowful Mother, or simply the Grotto.

Here, in 1923, Father Ambrose Mayer of the Catholic Servite Order turned an old quarry into an outdoor cathedral of sorts. A full-scale replica of Michelangelo's *Pieta* stands in an immense cave of black basalt, carved from the face of a cliff. Towering firs guard the entrance, where worshippers from across the globe light candles and offer their respects. You don't need religion to appreciate the sanctity of this place. You do need four dollars, though, to ride the elevator up to an intimate botanical garden hiding atop the cliff. It's a bargain. Budget some time for the Grotto—if you've never been there, you might be surprised.

From here, the route heads across 82nd to the Roseway Parkway, an elegant stretch of NE 72nd Avenue that leads directly to Annie's Donuts, another institution. Fuel up here for the climb to Rocky Butte, which looms to the east.

Two routes lead up the butte to Joseph Wood Hill Park. Elevated on a basalt rampart ringed with a stone parapet, it commands 360-degree views over Mount Hood, the Columbia River and Gorge, downtown Portland, the Tualatin Hills, Northeast and North Portland, and Mount St. Helens beyond. It's probably the best vista anywhere in East Portland.

The return trip down Rocky Butte is a blast—but watch your speed on the turns! Back on the flats just west of the butte, note the sharp dip in NE Fremont Drive—evidence of the massive floods that scoured Rocky Butte (and all of Portland) millennia ago (see "The Floods" sidebar in Ride 43). The Rose City Golf Course across 82nd fills an extension of this flood-cut channel.

South of the golf course and across I-84 lies Montavilla, a late 19th-century rural crossroads that suddenly boomed when a railroad reached it from Portland. A century later, the neighborhood's on the move again. Hip restaurants, coffee shops, boutiques, and a renovated movie theater have taken their places alongside the lumberyard and vacuum store, slowly but surely transforming this formerly blue-collar community.

The route now skirts the base of Mount Tabor and loops back to 82nd. If Portland's many Asian communities can be said to have a center, you're about to see it: the massive Fubonn Market, where an entire grocery aisle is dedicated to different varieties of soy sauce. You owe it to yourself to stop at one or more of the many eateries in the immediate vicinity.

Onward to Lents; like Montavilla, it began as a country town linked to distant Portland by a rutted, lonely old highway called Foster Road. In 1983, Lents suffered the indignity of being sundered in two by I-205. Its civic fabric grievously torn, Lents went into a decline from which it is only now, tenuously, emerging. The old nickname of "Felony Flats" is fading as homes get fixed up, the farmers market attracts ever-larger crowds, and the Eastern European immigrant community expands. Best of all is Lents Park, where residents of every origin come to play (soccer, mostly) among the trees.

South of Lents, sleepy residential streets lead to the Springwater Corridor and the I-205 path, your speedway back north to the Parkrose/ Sumner MAX station. (Alternatively, you can catch the MAX Green Line at SE Flavel Street to shorten the ride to 14.7 miles.) While the I-205 path is generally more useful than enjoyable, the stretch around Rocky Butte is an exception. It leads through an island of open space surrounded by freeways, which community activists dream of one day turning into a proper park, to be called Gateway Green.

Beyond is Maywood Park, a tiny city entirely surrounded by Portland. It incorporated as a separate town in 1968 to fight the construction of I-205. Citizens failed to stop the freeway but did manage, unlike Lents, to get it routed around the center of their community.

The stretch of path through Maywood Park also features a linear

arboretum. Some of the more vigorous specimens have sent roots under the asphalt, creating some nasty bumps. So slow down—maybe you'll learn a new tree while you're at it. The Parkrose/Sumner MAX station is just beyond.

MILEAGE LOG

0.0 Begin at Parkrose/Sumner MAX station. Cross bridge to parking lot and go right onto I-205 multi-use path.

0.1 Veer left onto path to NE Sandy Blvd. Cross over I-205.

0.3 Left onto NE 92nd Ave.

0.5 Right onto NE Skidmore St. Entrance to the Grotto at left.

0.9 Right onto NE 85th Ave. Cross NE Sandy Blvd. at crosswalk.

1.0 Left onto NE Prescott St.

1.7 Left onto NE 72nd Ave. (Roseway Pkwy.).

2.2 Left onto NE Fremont St. Cross SE 82nd Ave.

3.2 Left onto NE 91st Ave., which becomes NE Rocky Butte Rd.

4.6 Enter Joseph Wood Hill Park at top of Rocky Butte; continue south on NE Rocky Butte Rd. to descend.

6.0 Proceed straight at NE 92nd Ave. onto NE Russell St., then right onto NE Fremont Dr.

6.4 Left onto NE Siskyou St. Cross SE 82nd Ave.

7.1 Left onto NE 72nd Ave.

7.3 Right onto NE Sacramento St., then immediate left onto NE 72nd Dr. through Rose City Golf Course.

7.8 Left onto NE Tillamook St.

7.9 Right onto NE 74th Ave. and overpass across I-84.

9.0 Left onto E. Burnside St.

9.2 Right onto SE 80th Ave. Cross SE Stark St. into Montavilla neighborhood.

9.7 Right onto SE Yamhill St.

9.9 Left onto SE 76th Ave. Mount Tabor Park at right.

10.6 Cross SE Division St. (caution) to continue south on SE 75th Ave.

10.9 Left onto SE Woodward St.

11.2 Cross SE 82nd Ave. at stoplight. (**Side trip:** Fubonn Market straight ahead.) Follow SE 82nd Ave. sidewalk one block south, then go left onto SE Brooklyn St.

11.6 Right onto SE 87th Ave.

11.8 Right onto SE Powell Blvd. Cross Powell at first stoplight, to SE 86th Ave., then left onto SE Lafayette St.

12.2 Right onto SE 92nd Ave.

12.6 Cross SE Holgate Blvd. Lents Park at right.

13.3 Right onto SE Foster Rd. in Lents. (**Side trip:** Lents International Farmers Market at SE 92nd and Foster.)

13.6 Left onto SE 87th Ave.

14.7 Left onto SE Flavel St. (**Option:** End here at Flavel St. MAX station.)

14.8 Left onto Springwater Corridor.

15.2 Left onto I-205 path. Kelly Butte at right near US 26.

18.7 Cross I-205 at E. Burnside St. to continue on I-205 path.

20.8 Pass through Maywood Park.

21.8 End at Parkrose/Sumner MAX station.

13 Marine Drive

DIFFICULTY: Easy
DISTANCE: 19.4 miles
ELEVATION GAIN: 75 feet

Getting There: From I-5 northbound, take exit 305B for Marine Dr. NE. At bottom of ramp, take right fork, then go left at **T** intersection, following signs for NE Marine Dr. Continue approximately 3.1 miles to M. James Gleason Memorial Boat Ramp.

Transit: Ride MAX Yellow Line to Expo Center station. Bicycle the path north to Marine Dr. W., turn right, cross Marine Dr., and continue on path under I-5. Take second left, onto path paralleling NE Marine Dr. At path's end, continue east on Marine Dr. Go right onto NE 33rd Dr., then immediately left onto Marine Drive path (adds approximately 4 miles one way).

This ride follows the Columbia River upstream on a fabulously scenic—and often windy—bike path. NE Marine Drive follows the Columbia atop a levee; sandwiched between road and river is a path. It's flat, mostly straight, and rarely interrupted by road crossings—and a great place to ride full throttle, unless you're there on a sunny weekend, in which case expect crowds.

The wind is legendary here, too. On summer afternoons, a cool breeze often blows upstream, drawn by hotter air rising east of the Cascades. On a really hot day, Marine Drive can be a full 10 degrees Fahrenheit cooler than places 0.25 mile inland. In winter, sinking cold air often flows down the Columbia Gorge, scouring Troutdale and

200'
0'
0 miles

path   path
ends resumes

path   Blue Lake
ends   Regional Park

9.6

Gresham before slowing at the river's broad floodplain. Sometimes this winter wind is downright frigid. Bottom line: be prepared for stiff head winds and interesting microclimates. It only adds to the uniqueness of riding along one of the continent's great waterways.

Marine Drive stretches east from Kelley Point to Troutdale. This ride focuses on the section between NE 33rd Drive and Blue Lake Regional Park, a portion suitable for all riders. To judge from the number of kids out there, it's a great family ride. Two notes of caution, though. First, bike traffic can be heavy—and plenty of riders are training, so do them a favor and pull off the path if you choose to stop. Second, the path is interrupted at two places, necessitating brief stretches of road riding on NE Marine Drive. The bike lane is generous, but the speeding traffic demands vigilance.

Family-friendly: an Indian summer ride on the Marine Drive path

Begin at the M. James Gleason Memorial Boat Ramp at NE 33rd Drive and NE Marine Drive. If you park in the main lot, pick up the path at the lot's southeast corner. If you park in the gravel lot on the south side of NE Marine Drive, cross at the crosswalk and head right onto the path. There's a great beach here, so expect lots of pedestrian traffic—including distracted people lugging enormous coolers and grills down to the water.

The first few miles set the tone: huge views of Mount Hood, close-up views of the planes landing at Portland International Airport, and—if the weather is warm—boaters buzzing around on the Columbia. Farther east, Government Island splits the river into two channels. This island, owned by the state of Oregon, is a hybrid of state park and working ranch. The interior is off-limits, a mix of protected habitat and cattle-grazed fields. The island's many miles of shoreline are open to anyone with a boat and the courage to take it on the Columbia. Completely surrounded by a metropolis and cut through by a freeway, the island is surprisingly wild nonetheless.

Just before the path crosses under Interstate 205 it abruptly ends, forcing you across NE Marine Drive at a signaled crosswalk. The path resumes after NE 122nd Avenue, now on the inland side of NE Marine Drive. It crosses the road 0.75 mile later at an unmarked crosswalk—cross with care here. More miles of scenic riverfront riding ensue, with the Columbia's channel narrowed further by McGuire Island.

The path ends again near NE 185th Avenue; a path continues a short distance on the inland side of NE Marine Drive, but at this point you're better off continuing on the road itself. A mile and half later, follow a path leading downhill to NE Blue Lake Road and continue 0.25 mile to the park's entrance.

Blue Lake Regional Park is a sprawling, busy place. Huge shelters host crowds of picnickers among the trees. Armies of Little Leaguers compete on a half dozen sports fields. Kids swarm the play structures and the swimming beach. Anglers work the lake from the fishing pier. This is mass recreation in the best sense, a democratic kind of park that's offered something for everyone since the 1920s. Pack a picnic or grab a bite at the food stands.

Retrace your route from the park entrance. (Alternatively, you can follow the path west through the park, past the swimming beach, toward a wetland. The path turns to dirt and then exits the park through a gated fence onto NE Interlachen Lane; head right 0.25 mile up the road to Marine Drive and go left—cross with caution!—to rejoin the route back to your starting point.)

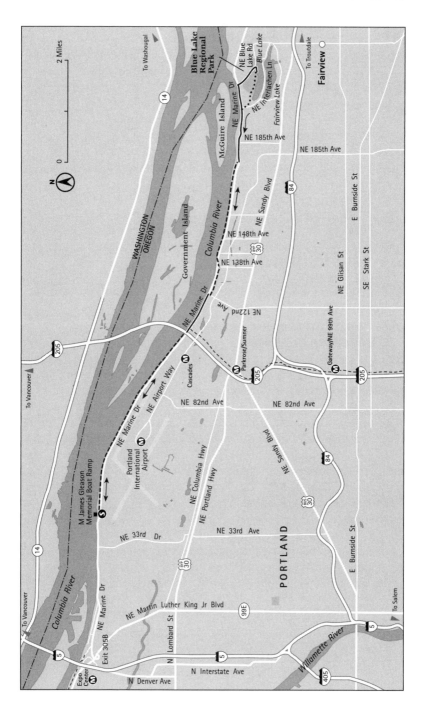

MILEAGE LOG

0.0 Begin at M. James Gleason Memorial Boat Ramp parking area. Cross NE Marine Dr. via crosswalk and go right onto Marine Drive path.

4.2 Path ends. Cross NE Marine Dr. at crosswalk and continue in bike lane.

5.0 Path resumes past NE 122nd Ave.

5.7 Path crosses NE Marine Dr. and continues along river.

7.7 Path ends. Cross NE Marine Dr. at crosswalk and continue in bike lane.

9.3 Right onto path along NE Blue Lake Rd.

9.7 Right to enter Blue Lake Regional Park. Retrace route to return.

14 The Peninsula

DIFFICULTY: Easy
DISTANCE: 18.4-mile loop
ELEVATION GAIN: 525 feet

Getting There: From I-5 northbound, take exit 302A, Weidler St., toward Rose Quarter–Broadway; go left onto N. Broadway Ave. From I-5 southbound, take exit 302A, Rose Quarter–City Center, and turn right onto N. Broadway. From Broadway, turn right onto N. Larrabee Ave. immediately before Broadway Bridge. Larrabee becomes N. Interstate Ave. after intersection with N. Tillamook St. Continue four blocks farther to MAX station at N. Russell St. Park on street.

Transit: Take MAX Yellow Line to Albina/Mississippi station on N. Interstate Ave. at N. Albina Ave.

North Portland, that "peninsula" of land wedged between the Willamette and Columbia Rivers, has always been a place apart. Blame it on Interstate 5, which sundered it from the rest of the city in the 1960s. Or credit the fiercely loyal residents, many of them born and raised here.

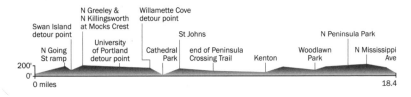

The St. Johns Bridge soars above Cathedral Park

Or chalk it up to neglect from city leaders downtown, as many North Portlanders do. Whatever the cause, the peninsula exists in something of a time warp. (This is a place, after all, where manufacturing jobs still exist and homes are still relatively affordable.) But change is coming.

This ride investigates those changes via a rambling loop full of potential stops and detours. You could spend a whole day at it or breeze through in two hours.

Begin at the Albina/Mississippi MAX Station, where a little cluster of brick buildings along the Union Pacific tracks marks Albina's early days as a railroad company town. From here you climb up N. Interstate Avenue, ascending the class ladder to arrive among the tidy homes of the Overlook neighborhood. From N. Melrose Drive you get a great view over the sprawling rail yards.

Cross N. Going Street on a tricky spiral pedestrian ramp and follow Going downhill. The main route now turns up N. Greeley Avenue—but if you have time, consider a detour through Swan Island (see "Exploring Swan Island" sidebar).

On the main route, the ride up N. Greeley Street takes you past Adidas's swanky North American headquarters. N. Greeley Street leads to N. Willamette Boulevard and views from Mocks Crest over Swan Island and Mocks Bottom. The latter, immediately below you, was once a vast wetland like Oaks Bottom (see Ride 1).

At the bluff's north end is the University of Portland. It's worth a detour to admire this attractive campus perched high above the river. In 1806 Captain William Clark poked up the Willamette to this point on his return from the Pacific. Satisfied it didn't lead anywhere he wanted to go, Clark turned around and continued up the Columbia River. A heroic, if somewhat implausible, monument on campus commemorates the event.

The riverbank far below played a major role in Portland's economic development. Wild in Clark's day, by the 1860s it buzzed with ironworks, lumber mills, and shipyards. The Willamette was truly a working river then, to which Portland owes much of its early prosperity. Now our debts to nature are coming due; much of this land and the river fronting it are polluted with a century's worth of toxic sediments. It will cost billions to clean up, costs that—environmental laws notwithstanding—will mostly be borne by taxpayers like you and me.

A small community garden at the end of N. Warren Street, just north of campus, offers a vantage over the old harbor's remains. Below you lies the former Riedel shipyard, recently purchased by the university, and the site of the former McCormick and Baxter creosote plant, long

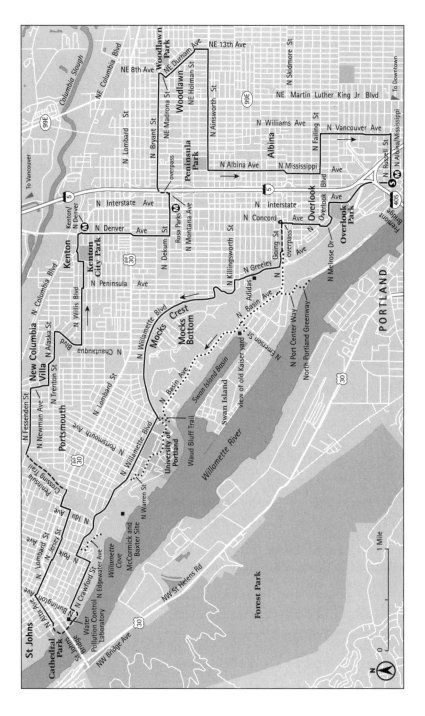

since demolished but until recently still oozing toxic black muck into the river. Beyond the rail tracks is Willamette Cove, another industrial ruin now owned by Metro.

Someday the North Portland Greenway will cross these tainted lands. For now, you can explore them on foot from N. Edgewater Avenue off N. Willamette Boulevard. Lock up your bike near the gate and hike down the crumbling road to explore Willamette Cove, where forest slowly closes in around ghost parking lots and the foundations of long-disappeared buildings. Venturing farther south under the railroad trestle may or may not invite trespassing charges.

Back on N. Willamette Boulevard, the route heads north and then back to the river to pick up another section of the North Portland Greenway. Check out the rain gardens at the city's Water Pollution Control Laboratory and then head next door to glorious Cathedral Park, where the St. Johns Bridge soars overhead. This is without a doubt one of Portland's most beautiful parks.

Continue on paths that climb steeply through the park to downtown St. Johns, where cafes, restaurants, and shops line N. Lombard Street. Laid out in 1865, St. Johns once vied with Portland for supremacy on the Willamette. Portland annexed St. Johns in 1915.

You now loop east through the Portsmouth neighborhood and New Columbia Villa, an experiment in contemporary public housing that opened in 2005. It replaced the old Columbia Villa, built—like ill-fated Vanport on the floodplain below (see "Vanport and PSU" sidebar in Ride 3)—during World War II as temporary housing for shipyard workers but later converted to public housing.

Living conditions at Columbia Villa, always rustic at best, grew deplorable as the neighborhood aged. By the 1990s, it was isolated, crumbling, and plagued by drugs and gangs. In a controversial modern-day "slum clearance" action, the city demolished the villa's entire 82 acres and built, from scratch, a modern mixed-use community. Life at New Columbia is still far from idyllic, but few residents miss the old days. A small history exhibit at the New Columbia Community Education Center (at 4625 N. Trenton St.) tells more of this fascinating and too-little-known story.

From Portsmouth you're off to Kenton, yet another old settlement gobbled up by Portland. Now known mainly for its outsize Paul Bunyan statue at the intersection of N. Interstate Avenue and N. Denver Avenue, Kenton once enjoyed widespread fame for meat. Yes, meat! In 1908, the Swift Company built massive stockyards and a livestock exchange (now the Expo Center) on the flats below Kenton. It quickly became the biggest livestock market in the Northwest, drawing crowds to the annual Pacific International Livestock Exposition. Out-of-town traders stayed at the elegant Kenton Hotel, awaiting cattle drives up N. Greeley Avenue from the Albina rail yards. Swift Company executives lived in handsome concrete homes—the hot new building material of its day—along N. Denver Avenue. Many of these distinctive houses remain.

EXPLORING SWAN ISLAND

Yes, it was once an island. The Port of Portland filled Swan Island in the 1920s to create Portland's first airport. Now the "island" is an industrial zone full of intriguing sites.

An optional detour on Ride 14 takes you onto the island. From N. Going Street, cross the Union Pacific tracks and turn left onto N. Port Center Way. Be alert for trucks around here. After a short distance, go right onto a paved path toward the river. This is a section of the planned North Portland Greenway. Someday, hopefully, it will run the length of the river from the Eastside Esplanade to Kelley Point. For now, it leads only to a secluded beach perfect for a picnic.

From here, backtrack to N. Going Street and head north on N. Basin Avenue. A left turn at N. Emerson Street leads to a boat ramp and a great view of the island's last shipyard. Between 1942 and 1945, the Kaiser Company constructed warships here at a record-setting pace, employing thousands of the new arrivals housed at Vanport (see "Vanport and PSU" sidebar in Ride 3). Now the Cascade General Company operates what it bills as the largest ship-repair facility on the West Coast—big enough, but a mere shadow of the former Kaiser yard. The Coast Guard has recently moved in as well.

Continue northwest on N. Basin Avenue, which dead-ends at the tracks below Waud Bluff. The new Waud Bluff Trail continues at road's end, leading up some stairs to cross the railroad tracks and then climbing steeply to N. Willamette Boulevard where it rejoins the main route. Alternatively, you can backtrack to N. Going Street to rejoin the route there.

Kenton declined after the war. The meatpacking industry moved out of town. The Livestock Exposition held its last fair in the 1960s. The Kenton Hotel was abandoned (it only recently avoided demolition to become an apartment building). Kenton spent the last decades of the 20th century as a nearly forgotten working-class neighborhood. But like so many other places in Portland, signs of a revival are everywhere, if temporarily obscured by the current recession.

Your final stretch laps through the Woodlawn neighborhood, technically outside North Portland but cut from the same cloth. New bars and shops have opened along once-moribund N. Dekum Street and NE Durham Avenue. Rambling Woodlawn Park—formerly a gang hot spot—again beckons visitors.

Now head west along tree-lined NE Ainsworth Street, past the rose gardens of Peninsula Park. This brings you to the "upper" section of Albina, most dramatically transformed of all North Portland's neighborhoods. Beginning in the 1960s, downtown politicians and bureaucrats decided to "renew" Albina's "blighted" areas with bulldozers. Residents fought back, with mixed success. The decades-old vacant lots along N. Vancouver and N. Williams Avenues, cleared by the city in anticipation of redevelopment that never came, bear witness to the struggle.

Not until the early 1990s, after decades of community pressure, did the city finally embrace the idea of supporting rather than demolishing Albina. Soon after—coincidentally?—"urban pioneers" in search of affordable homes flooded the neighborhood. Now, as high-end boutiques and trendy restaurants replace African-American businesses and churches along Williams, Vancouver, Albina, and above all Mississippi Avenues, Portlanders wring hands about gentrification.

The most recent neighborhood controversy involves—you guessed it—bicycling. Bike traffic on North Williams Avenue has quadrupled in recent years. Encouraged by the trend, in 2011 the city proposed improvements to the bike lane. Some longstanding residents were miffed by city's responsiveness to the newly arrived bicycle advocates—mostly white, mostly professional—after decades of perceived neglect. The city's proposed improvements are likely to benefit all users of the road, but that fact, unfortunately, does little to alter the perception that bicycling and gentrification go hand in hand. Well-meaning folks disagree about what to do—but residents old and new agree that history is happening here, right now.

A quick descent down N. Russell Street brings you back to your starting place and the Widmer Brewery, where a post-ride beer awaits.

MILEAGE LOG

0.0 Begin at Albina/Mississippi MAX Station. Proceed north on N. Interstate Ave.

0.9 Left onto N. Overlook Blvd., then first left onto N. Melrose Dr. in Overlook neighborhood.

1.2 Right onto N. Failing St., then immediate left onto N. Concord Ave.

1.5 Cross N. Going St. on spiral ramp and continue west (downhill) on Going St. bike path.

1.8 Right onto N. Going Ct. (**Side trip:** Continue straight on bike path to tour Swan Island—see "Exploring Swan Island" sidebar.)

2.0 Right onto N. Greeley Ave.

2.4 Left onto N. Killingsworth St., then right onto N. Willamette Blvd. Mocks Crest at left.

4.3 At N. Harvard St., Waud Bluff Trail is on left (Swan Island detour rejoins route here). Continue west on N. Willamette. (**Side trip:** Left to tour University of Portland campus.)

5.8 N. Edgewater Ave. on left. (**Side trip:** Descend N. Edgewater— rough road—and cross tracks to visit Willamette Cove.)

5.9 Left onto N. Polk Ave.

6.0 Right onto N. Crawford St.

6.4 Left onto N. Burlington Ave. Cross tracks to reach path. Continue on path past Water Pollution Control Laboratory and cross to Cathedral Park. Go right to continue uphill through park.

7.1 At north end of park, continue northeast on N. Alta Ave.

7.4 Right onto N. Lombard St. ("downtown" St. Johns). At N. Jersey St., continue straight onto N. Jersey.

8.3 Left onto N. Ida Ave., then first right, back onto N. Lombard St. Cross tracks on bridge and take immediate left onto Peninsula Crossing Trail.

9.1 Right onto N. Fessenden St.

9.7 Right onto N. Newman Ave. in New Columbia Villa.

9.8 Left onto N. Trenton St.

10.0 Right onto N. Alaska St.

10.4 Right onto N. Chautauqua Blvd.

10.7 Left onto N. Willis Blvd.

11.5 Left onto N. Delaware Ave. at Kenton City Park, then first right, onto N. Argyle St. Immediate right to stay on N. Argyle.

11.8 Right onto N. Interstate Ave., then immediate right onto N. Denver Ave. in Kenton.

12.7 Left onto N. Dekum St.

13.1 Left onto N. Montana Ave.; immediate right onto N. Saratoga St. Cross I-5 on path at end of N. Saratoga. Continue on N. Bryant St. across freeway.

14.2 Right onto NE 8th Ave.; immediate right onto NE Madrona St.; immediate left onto NE Durham Ave. ("downtown" Woodlawn).

14.7 Left onto NE Holman St.; immediate right onto NE 13th Ave.; first right onto NE Ainsworth St.

16.0 Left onto N. Albina Ave. at Peninsula Park. Albina becomes
      N. Mississippi Ave. right before intersection with N. Skidmore St.
17.0 Left onto N. Failing St.
17.4 Right onto N. Vancouver Ave.
18.0 Right onto N. Russell St.
18.4 Left on N. Mississippi Ave. to end at Albina-Missippi MAX station.

15 Kelley Point

DIFFICULTY: Easy to Moderate
DISTANCE: 16.6-mile loop
ELEVATION GAIN: 170 feet

Getting There: From I-5 northbound take exit 306B, Expo Center.
Go left onto N. Victory Blvd., follow it under freeway, then right onto
N. Expo Rd. MAX Delta Park station is immediately at right.
   Transit: Ride MAX Yellow Line to Delta Park station.

This is one of my favorite rides, an easy loop around the sloughs and
wetlands tucked among North Portland's sprawling port facilities. At
the loop's midpoint, between Port Terminals 5 (a grain elevator) and
6 (container ships), sits a little wilderness: Kelley Point Park. Here
at the tip of the North Portland peninsula, you can watch the great
rivers meet.
   Portland's industrial northern edge is terra incognita to many
residents. The nearest house is miles away. Port terminals line the
Columbia and Willamette, their colossal cranes hoisting containers
from Asian ships onto immense parking lots and awaiting trucks.
Anonymous warehouses, supersized descendants of the depots that
once lined Front Street downtown, absorb and distribute the foreign
treasure. Monumental grain elevators disgorge the Pacific Northwest's
harvest into westbound freighters. The region's economic metabolism
is on display, in all its dingy glory.

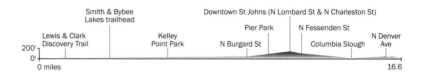

Rest stop along the Columbia River, Kelley Point Park

The ride begins at the Delta Park MAX station and traverses wetlands northward to the Columbia River, then west on the Lewis and Clark Discovery Trail. Houseboats and the half-empty Jantzen Beach shopping center line Hayden Island across the channel.

Where the path crosses under the rail bridge, you get a good view of west Hayden Island, 831 acres of forest and riverfront owned by the Port of Portland. The island is a flashpoint in debates about our economic future. Should it be paved over with port terminals, like the river's south bank? So contends the camp wringing its hands about Portland's supposed shortage of industrial land (and therefore, the argument goes, industrial jobs). Or should the island's extensive habitat be protected and restored? The city has punted on this question for decades. But with "jobs" currently on the lips of every politician, another fight is brewing.

From the river it's a quick pedal to Smith and Bybee Wetlands. This 2000-acre wetland is the surviving remnant after a century of land filling. The entire industrial area once looked like this—a vast waterscape of sloughs and marshes through which the Willamette and Columbia meandered and met. You can't ride your bike in the wetlands, but a short walk down to the Smith Lake canoe launch gives a good flavor for the place. A wildlife sighting is virtually guaranteed.

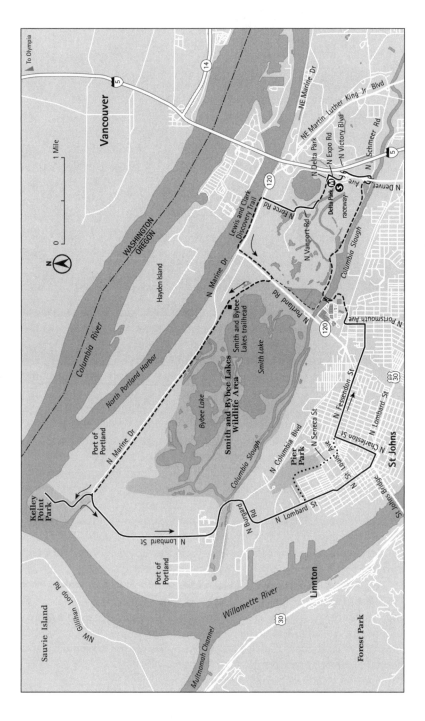

From Smith and Bybee, the path continues alongside N. Marine Drive. Look for Kelley Point Park's entrance across the road, just beyond the ocean of asphalt at Terminal 6. Despite my repeated visits, Kelley Point still feels to me like a secret and improbable place. From the entrance drive you disappear into deep forest, suddenly cut off from the industrial din. A paved path leads from the north parking area through black cottonwoods, ash, and maples to a meadow and beach, where container ships pass within hailing distance. Sometimes you can actually see the two rivers come together, blending their hues, Cascade and Coast Range water greeting Rocky Mountain runoff.

Beautiful as this place is, Kelley Point hasn't actually been a *point* for all that long. Until the Port of Portland started filling in the area, sloughs and wetlands separated it from the mainland. Pearcy Island, as it was then known, was a fairly remote and swampy place.

It nevertheless captured the imagination of Oregon's original booster, a Massachusetts schoolteacher named Hall Jackson Kelley. Like many of his generation, Kelley read the recently published journals of Lewis and Clark with intense interest. Unlike most, Kelley also dreamed of colonizing the Oregon Territory himself. In 1828, a time when the few Americans roaming the Pacific Northwest still focused on fur trading, Kelley began promoting settlement schemes.

After a failed effort for Puget Sound, Kelley turned his attention to Pearcy Island. Given that he'd never been within a few thousand miles of the place, Kelley didn't realize it was frequently underwater. But facts of nature rarely deter boosters, and Kelley avidly promoted his colony to anyone who would listen, including the US Congress.

Kelley finally made it to Oregon six years later. Delirious with malaria and nearly broken by the rigors of his journey, he spent the winter as an unwelcome guest at Fort Vancouver and caught a ship home the following spring. Back in Massachusetts, an undaunted Kelley continued churning out pamphlets and books extolling the territory he hardly knew.

His misadventures notwithstanding, Kelley inspired his contemporaries. When the Oregon Trail opened in the 1840s, many early migrants carried Kelley's compelling—if not always accurate—writings with them. To honor his service to Oregon, in 1926 a group of Portlanders petitioned the federal government to name the site of Kelley's would-be metropolis after him.

From Kelley Point, the ride crosses the Columbia Slough and heads south past shipping terminals and the former St. Johns landfill, now an unlikely bird haven. Be careful here. Not all of the area's many trucks are interested in sharing the road, and even the friendly ones can't always see you, especially when they're turning.

N. Lombard Street leads you out of the port area and into St. Johns. Consider a detour through Pier Park, where towering Douglas firs offer shady sanctuary on even the hottest days; you'll share the woods with disc golfers, dead serious in pursuit of their quarry despite the beer in hand. Otherwise, stay on the main route past Pier Park on N. Lombard into downtown St. Johns.

Continue east, then cross N. Columbia Boulevard to reach a quiet path along the languid Columbia Slough. Willows trail in the slow current; great blue herons alight on half-submerged logs. The wastewater treatment plant and junkyards lie just out of sight. Stand still for a moment, and you can imagine an earlier world of water, grass, and sky.

Too soon, the path ends and the sounds of a heavy civilization return. A final loop under N. Denver Avenue returns you to the MAX station.

MILEAGE LOG

0.0 Begin at Delta Park MAX station. Proceed north on N. Expo Dr. and go immediately left onto W. Delta Park–N. Broadacre Rd. Continue past gate barring cars.

0.5 Right onto N. Vanport Rd.

0.8 Right onto N. Force Ave.

1.2 At stoplight, cross N. Marine Dr. and turn left onto Lewis and Clark Discovery Trail.

1.9 Path crosses back over N. Marine Dr. to continue south between N. Portland Rd. and railroad tracks.

2.4 At a crosswalk, cross N. Portland Rd.; continue west past barrier.

3.1 Smith and Bybee Lakes trailhead and parking area at left. Continue west, paralleling N. Marine Dr.

5.8 Exit path left onto N. Marine Dr. Immediate right to enter Kelley Point Park. Beware killer potholes on park road!

6.5 Kelley Point Park parking area. Path continues to confluence. Retrace route to N. Marine Dr.

7.2 Right onto N. Lombard St. Watch for trucks here.

9.5 Right onto N. Burgard Rd., which curves left to become N. Lombard St. again.

10.5 Entrance to Pier Park on left (detour: follow trails through the park—walk your bike—to N. Seneca St. and N. St. Louis Ave. to rejoin main route at N. Fessenden St.).

11.5 Left onto N. Charleston St. (downtown St. Johns).

12.0 Right onto N. Fessenden St.

13.4 Left onto N. Portsmouth Ave. At stoplight, cross N. Columbia
      Blvd., then go right onto N. Columbia Court. Continue straight
      onto bike path and across rail tracks.

14.3 Cross Columbia Slough and go right.

15.9 Path merges onto N. Schmeer Rd. Follow it under N. Denver Ave.
      and make a sharp left at stop sign to merge onto N. Denver
      Ave. northbound. Follow bike lane as it exits N. Denver.

16.4 Left at stop sign onto N. Victory Blvd. Pass under N. Denver
      Ave. and go right onto N. Expo Rd.

16.6 Right to end at Delta Park MAX station.

16 The 40-Mile Loop

DIFFICULTY: Moderate
DISTANCE: 51.5-mile loop; option: 37.8-mile loop
ELEVATION GAIN: 500 feet

Getting There: See Ride 1's directions to Salmon St. Springs.

It's not 40 miles and it's not really a loop. But read on. (For the impatient: the ride is a 51.5-mile lap around East Portland linking Marine Drive, the Gresham–Fairview Trail, and the Springwater Corridor.)

In 1905 Portland staged the Lewis and Clark Centennial Exposition and World's Fair. City leaders aimed to establish the Rose City as a peer to Chicago, which had recently staged the most famous fair of all, the 1893 World's Columbian Exposition. To spiff Portland up ahead of its turn in the spotlight, city fathers called on John and Charles Olmsted—sons of Frederick Law Olmsted, famed designer of New York's Central Park and Boston's Fenway Park.

The Olmsted Brothers proposed that Portland create a system of parks and parkways circling the city in a loop approximately 40 miles long. This ambitious vision called for preserving vast meadows and

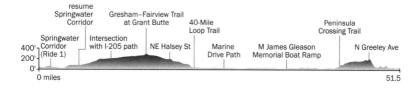

wetlands on the Columbia Slough, protecting Ross Island, and turning Guild's Lake, site of the World's Fair, into a park.

No such luck. After the fair, Guild's Lake was paved over for warehouses. Much of the Columbia Slough suffered the same fate. Ross Island largely disappeared, shovelful by shovelful of quarried gravel. Most of the planned parkways morphed into utilitarian, traffic-clogged thoroughfares.

The *idea* of a loop never died, though. To the contrary: civic leaders have spent the century since building a network of trails and paths. To date, it far exceeds 40 miles. But the city's failure to act on the Olmsted vision when it was new created consequences we're still grappling with—namely, a fragmented system full of gaps. As a result, it's not really possible to travel "the" 40-Mile Loop, but you can link plenty of its constituent parts.

This ride does just that, connecting the major eastside paths in a big loop. (The original 40-Mile Loop included Forest and Washington Parks but excluded Gresham, practically a wilderness at the time.) It mostly covers terrain described elsewhere in the book; see the other ride descriptions referenced below for additional details.

The ride begins at Tom McCall Waterfront Park and follows the Springwater Corridor (see Ride 7) to Linnemann Station in Gresham where the Gresham–Fairview Trail cuts north to NE Halsey. Several miles down Halsey, you'll pass the former Multnomah County Poor Farm. "Pauper farms" were a common feature in 19th-century America, offering the destitute a place to live (usually in conditions barely better than prison) in exchange for work. This farm opened in 1911 and gradually added land, a hospital, jail, and dormitories. During the Great Depression more than 600 people called it home.

"Work relief" acquired a bad name after the war, prompting the county to curtail farming and eventually convert the hospital into a nursing home. It closed in the 1980s. The county tried to demolish the entire site to make way for redevelopment, but historically minded citizens resisted. They petitioned, successfully, to have the farm added to the National Register of Historic Places. Then, in 1990, the McMenamin brothers bought the buildings to add to their brewpub empire. They've creatively recycled the farm—rechristened The Edgefield—into a hotel, brewery, and concert venue. The county still owns some surrounding land; a few years ago it quietly resumed farming, this time with community volunteers.

From Halsey, turn left onto NE Graham Road just before Troutdale's Old Town to traverse a no-man's land along the outlet mall and

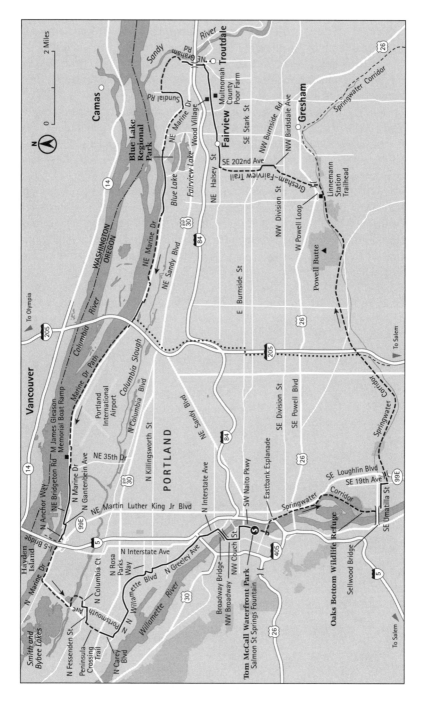

Interstate 84. Beyond the freeway appears, as if by magic, an orphaned 1.5-mile stretch of the 40-Mile Loop, passing through a secluded mosaic of wetlands and forest along the Sandy River. If you have time, follow any of the trails (on foot) to the right. They quickly lead to the Sandy's gravel bars and sloughs.

The path ends all too soon at Sundial Road. Head left, past the massive FedEx distribution center and a hinterland of warehouses, to join the path paralleling NE Marine Drive. At Blue Lake Regional Park in Fairview, the path reaches the Columbia and begins a long, glorious riverfront cruise (see Ride 13).

At NE 33rd Drive the path ends again, forcing you to continue on NE Marine Drive to I-5. A path reappears underneath the freeway. Follow it west along the river opposite Janzten Beach's houseboats and semiderelict shopping centers, much of which will be destroyed by the Columbia River Crossing—a supersized freeway project masquerading as a bridge replacement—if it ever gets built.

Quiet riding along the Sandy River near Troutdale

At N. Portland Road, head inland along the Peninsula Crossing Trail. It parallels the Union Pacific tracks past Smith Lake, across the Columbia Slough, and through St. Johns. This quick succession of natural, industrial, and residential environs is part of what makes North Portland such a fascinating place to ride (see Ride 15).

The loop now turns southeast on N. Willamette Boulevard, passing the University of Portland to trace a long and scenic arc along Mocks Crest. The final leg descends N. Greeley and N. Interstate Avenues to the Union Pacific Railroad's Albina Yard (see Ride 14); it then crosses the Broadway Bridge to return to Waterfront Park via Chinatown.

You've now seen most of urban Multnomah County. Congratulations.

Along the way, you've probably noted the loop trail's many gaps. It will be a long time before they're all closed, but enough is in place to imagine the loop whole. The City of Portland reckons it's acquired about 25 of the Olmsteds' original 36 proposed park sites. The nonprofit 40-Mile Loop Land Trust (www.40mileloop.org) is diligently working on the missing parts. The work set out for Portland by the Olmsteds continues.

MILEAGE LOG

0.0 Begin at Salmon Street Springs fountain in Tom McCall Waterfront Park. Ride waterfront path south, then cross Hawthorne Bridge and take first right to go south on Eastbank Esplanade.

1.2 Esplanade path ends at SE Caruthers St. Continue on street and go right onto SE 4th Ave.

1.4 Enter Springwater Corridor at SE Ivon St.

4.5 Path ends at SE Umatilla St. (Note: Trail is scheduled to be extended farther south in 2013.) Continue on Umatilla.

5.3 Right onto SE 19th Ave.

5.6 At end of 19th, continue past barrier and make sharp left onto Springwater Corridor.

10.2 Intersection with I-205 path. (**Option:** Go left here to shorten loop by 13.7 miles.)

15.2 Linnemann Station at left.

15.4 Sharp left onto Gresham–Fairview Trail.

17.3 Left at path's end onto NW Birdsdale Ave. Cross tracks, go left onto E Burnside St., and right onto continuation of path.

18.7 At path's end, right onto NE Halsey St. Multnomah County Poor Farm at mile 21.

22.0 Left onto NE Graham Rd. (**Side trip:** Continue straight to visit Troutdale's historic downtown.) Pass under I-84 and cross N. Frontage Rd.

22.8 Right onto 40-Mile Loop Trail (near end of Troutdale Airport runway).

24.3 Left at end of path onto Sundial Rd.

25.6 Cross NE Marine Dr. and go right onto path paralleling road.

26.9 Path crosses Blue Lake Regional Park entrance road, goes briefly uphill, and ends at Marine Dr. Go left to continue on Marine Dr. (caution).

28.4 Go right onto Marine Dr. path.

30.3 Cross NE Marine Dr. on path.

31.0 Path ends at NE 122nd Ave. Cross NE Marine Dr. and continue in bike lane. Path resumes beyond I-205. (**Option:** Shorter loop rejoins route here.)

35.8 At M. James Gleason Memorial Boat Ramp, cross NE Marine Dr. to continue on path.

36.8 Right at path's end onto NE 33rd Dr., then left onto NE Marine Dr.

37.8 Where NE Marine Dr. curves left, continue straight onto NE Bridgeton Rd.

38.5 Left onto N. Gantenbein Ave., then right to continue on N. Marine Dr.

38.9 Right onto N. Anchor Way. Continue to end of street and go straight, then immediately right, onto path, which crosses under I-5 and continues alongside N. Marine Dr.

40.5 Path crosses N. Marine Dr. to parallel N. Portland Rd.

41.9 Path curves left to follow Columbia Slough. At first intersection, go right to cross slough.

42.5 At path's end, continue on N. Columbia Court. Go left onto N. Portsmouth Ave.

42.9 Right onto N. Fessenden St.

43.2 Left onto Peninsula Crossing Trail, just before bridge over tracks.

44.0 At path's end, continue on N. Carey Blvd., then left onto N. Willamette Blvd.

46.4 Right at N. Rosa Parks Way to stay on N. Willamette Blvd.

47.2 Right onto N. Greeley Ave.

48.8 Right onto N. Interstate Ave.

49.4 Stay right to exit N. Interstate Ave. and continue on N. Larabee Ave. Go right to cross Broadway Bridge and continue on NW Broadway.

50.5 Left onto NW Couch St.

50.8 Right onto NW Naito Pkwy.

51.5 Cross parkway at crosswalk to end at Salmon Street Springs fountain in Tom McCall Waterfront Park.

17 Forest Park

DIFFICULTY: Moderate
DISTANCE: 16.5-mile loop
ELEVATION GAIN: 1900 feet

Getting There: From I-405 north- or southbound, take exit 3 for US Hwy. 30, then take first exit—it comes soon—onto NW Vaughn St. Past stoplight, turn left onto NW 27th Ave., then immediately right onto NW Upshur St. Road dead-ends at Lower Macleay Park.

Transit: Take MAX Blue or Red Line to PGE Park Station and bicycle north on SW (then NW) 18th Ave. Go left onto NW Raleigh St., right onto NW 27th Ave., then left onto NW Upshur St. to parking area (approximately 2.1 miles; see map for Ride 4).

Forest Park is a favorite among local riders—especially the fitness types, who appreciate the hills, winding roads, and lack of stoplights. The experts test their mettle on long circumnavigations, linking US Highway 30 to NW Skyline Boulevard via steep and busy roads: Germantown, Newberry, McNamee, Cornelius Pass, Logie Trail.

These are all classic rides, but they don't actually get you into the park—just around its edges. If you're willing to endure a little dirt and gravel, though, you can ride right through the forest on unpaved but well-packed roads, suitable for all but the skinniest tires. This isn't mountain biking, but unless it's August, be prepared for a little mud.

The route follows a portion of Leif Erickson Drive closed to motorized traffic. The actual trailhead is at the end of NW Thurman Street, but Lower Macleay Park makes a more convenient starting point.

Here, where Balch Creek tumbles down an almost old-growth forest, Portland businessman Donald Macleay donated a 108-acre tract in 1897. He stipulated that the city provide a means for local hospital patients to visit it in summer. This act of generosity (or tax avoidance,

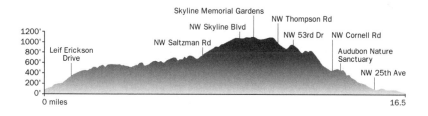

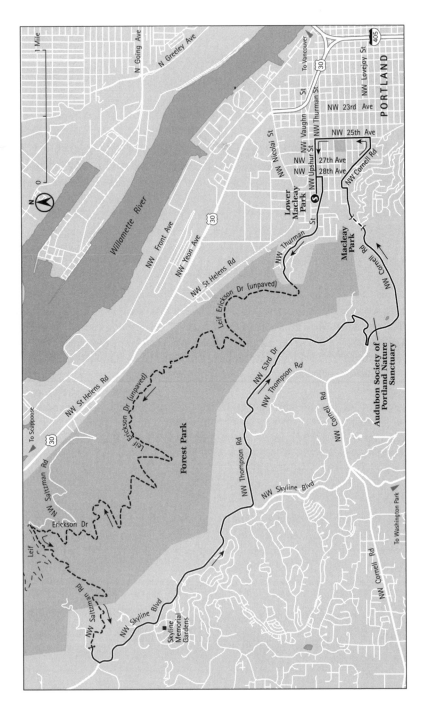

as Macleay's detractors claimed) kicked off a sporadic park-building effort that resulted, decades later, in what the city claims to be "the largest forested natural area within city limits in the United States."

From the Macleay parking area, strike west on NW Thurman Street. Soon you reach the end of the pavement and a gate. Beyond begins Leif Erickson Drive. The road climbs gradually, traversing ridges and ravines. It's almost impossible to keep track of where you are: the forest occasionally opens to admit a view to St. Johns, but just as rapidly closes in again. Even on the sunniest of days, twilight reigns for long stretches. As the miles click by, the park's quiet immensity starts to sink in.

HOW WE GOT FOREST PARK

Forest Park is Portland's crown jewel, a 5170-acre forest draping the Tualatin Hills north of downtown. Boosters call it the largest urban park in the nation. (The Trust for Public Land, which tracks city park facts nationwide, ranks it 19th—but never mind the facts.)

You might think Forest Park resulted from the foresight and planning for which Portland is known. Not so. Ignoring the Olmsted Brothers' 1903 recommendation to protect the area (see Ride 16), city fathers tried to jump-start real estate development by building a road through the forest. To pay for the road, which cost twice the projected amount, they assessed taxes to the neighboring property owners. Most refused to pay.

Then, in 1915, a major landslide blew out the road. More landslides followed. Dejected speculators gave up on their lots, which the city took in lieu of the delinquent property taxes. Forest thickened around the lonely road—now called Leif Erickson Drive.

Over the next decades, the park-in-waiting was logged, burned, and drilled for oil. Still the forest endured, and the voices in favor of preservation grew louder. In 1948, after a determined campaign by the City Club of Portland, the city officially declared it a park. To learn more, check out the Forest Park Conservancy (www.forestparkconservancy.org).

After about 6 miles, Leif Erickson intersects NW Saltzman Road, another mostly smooth, hard-packed gravel road. Saltzman provides a great route up and out of the forest to Skyline Drive. Though a bit steeper than Leif Erickson, it's surprisingly gentle. After 1.5 miles it delivers you back to the blacktop at NW Skyline Boulevard.

Leif Erickson Drive in Forest Park

Time to change gears now, both on the bike and in your head. You're mostly done climbing, but with no shoulder and plenty of traffic, Skyline demands vigilance. The steady stream of cyclists helps to keep the drivers in check, though.

Views across the Tualatin Valley soon open to the west at the Skyline Memorial Gardens. A path parallels the road here, allowing you a measure of calm to admire the vista. At NW Thompson Road, you plunge back into the forest on a screaming downhill, then up a short but stiff climb on NW 53rd Drive. It looks more like a Forest Service road than a neighborhood street, though, complete with some truly scary potholes. Watch out on the downhill!

NW 53rd Drive drops to NW Cornell Road, a busy thoroughfare following Balch Creek. You'll soon pass the Audubon Society of Portland's Nature Sanctuary, which shelters remnants of the great rain forest that once covered the Tualatin Hills. Stop to check out the wildlife care center, where Audubon volunteers nurse injured animals back to health.

Beyond the sanctuary, NW Cornell Road gets a bit white-knuckle, with fast drivers, nonexistent shoulders, and a tunnel thrown in for good measure. Soon enough, though, it releases you to the calm of Northwest Portland. Before returning the final blocks to Macleay Park, consider a detour down Thurman to NW 24th Avenue, where you can celebrate your ride with a pastry at the exquisite St. Honoré Bakery. You—and the other cyclists you'll no doubt encounter there—earned it.

MILEAGE LOG

0.0 Begin at Lower Macleay Park parking area. Exit on NW Upshur St. and go right onto NW 28th Ave., then right again onto NW Thurman St.

1.3 Enter Forest Park and continue on unpaved Leif Erickson Dr.

7.5 Very sharp left at four-way junction onto NW Saltzman Rd.

9.1 Continue past gate (cars here) on NW Saltzman Rd.

9.2 Left onto NW Skyline Blvd.

9.8 Skyline Memorial Gardens at right.

11.1 Left onto NW Thompson Rd.

11.7 Left onto NW 53rd Dr.

13.5 Left onto NW Cornell Rd.

14.0 Audubon Society of Portland Nature Sanctuary at left.

15.5 Left onto NW 25th Ave.

16.0 Left onto NW Upshur St.

16.5 End at Lower Macleay Park parking area.

18 Sauvie Island

DIFFICULTY: Easy to Moderate
DISTANCE: 12.1-mile loop
ELEVATION GAIN: 50 feet

Getting There: From I-405 northbound, take exit 3 for US Hwy. 30. Follow it 9.5 miles west and go right to cross Sauvie Island Bridge. At base of bridge, go left onto NW Gillihan Rd. and turn into parking area at TriMet bus stop.

Transit: Take TriMet bus No. 17 to Sauvie Island, end of the line.

This easy road loop around the southern end of Sauvie Island—the largest river island in the United States—is another classic Portland ride, loved by casual riders and weekend warriors alike. The roads lack shoulders, but traffic is low and people around here are used to cyclists. The only time likely to be busy—also the best time to visit—is autumn, when people flock to the island for hay rides, pumpkin patches, corn mazes, and Halloween fun.

Sauvie Island is a special place, a world apart despite its proximity to Portland. It's an extension of the Willamette's confluence with the Columbia, blurring the boundary between earth and water. The northern half is mostly a labyrinth of tidal sloughs, lakes, and wetlands that hardly qualify as land at all. The southern half is a board-flat mosaic of farms and fields kept mostly dry by levees. In summer it hums quietly with the din of agriculture. In winter, a dense fog often shrouds the island, furthering the sense of isolation.

The ride starts at the TriMet bus stop at the base of the Sauvie Island Bridge. From the parking area, head north along NW Sauvie Island Road, which parallels Multnomah Channel atop a dike. Houseboats line the channel. Across the water is Burlington Bottoms, a protected wetland rich in plants and animals that have become rare in the Willamette Valley: pond turtles, red-legged frogs, and coho salmon, to name a few.

After a mile, look for Howell Territorial Park at right. Make a short side trip here to visit the James Bybee House, built in 1856 by one of the island's first American settlers. It's now owned by Metro, the

Howell   Sauvie Island   NW Reeder Rd &
200' ┐ Territorial Park │ Church   NW Gillihan Loop Rd
  0' ┤
   0 miles   12.1

Hard charging on Sauvie Island, with Mount St. Helens behind

regional government. The restored house and farm grounds tell the story of the island, which was once the region's epicenter. Before Asa Lovejoy and William Overton staked their claim to the forest that would become Portland, before the Hudson's Bay Company set up shop in Fort Vancouver, before Lewis and Clark paddled down the Columbia en route to the ocean, this island was home to the Multnomah people, who numbered more than 2000 in at least 15 villages. That's almost twice the island's current population. At the time, it was probably the greatest concentration of people anywhere this side of Celilo Falls.

The Multnomahs lived from the river's abundant salmon runs and the island's wetlands, where they harvested the wapato plant in dugout canoes. When George Vancouver's ships—the first to explore up the Columbia River—approached the island, an armada of Multnomahs greeted them in canoes, armed but eager to trade. The Multnomahs kept the peace with the fur traders and settlers who followed. Their openness to newcomers proved their undoing, however, as trade

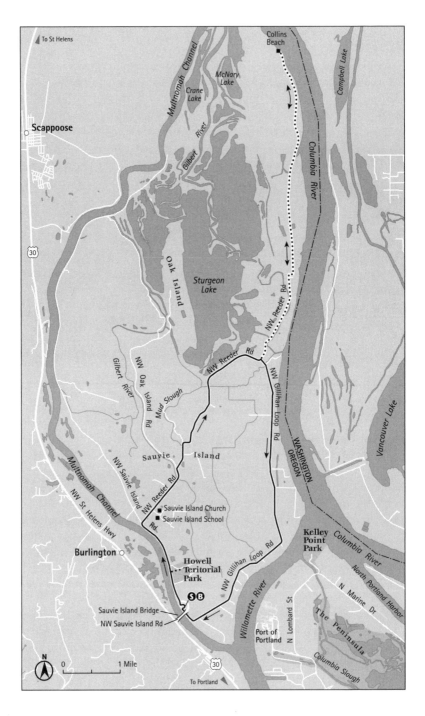

To St Helens

Collins
Beach

McNary
Lake

Campbell
Lake

Crane
Lake

Multnomah Channel

Gilbert River

Scappoose

Columbia River

30

Oak Island

Sturgeon
Lake

NW Reeder Rd

NW Reeder Rd

NW Oak Island Rd

Gilbert River

Mud Slough

NW Gillihan Loop Rd

WASHINGTON
OREGON

Vancouver
Lake

Sauvie   Island

NW Sauvie Island Rd

Multnomah Channel

NW St Helens Hwy

NW Reeder Rd.

■ Sauvie Island Church
■ Sauvie Island School

Burlington

Howell
Teritorial
Park

NW Gillihan Loop Rd

Kelley
Point
Park

Columbia River

North Portland Harbor

N Marine Dr

S B

Willamette River

The Peninsula

Sauvie Island Bridge

NW Sauvie Island Rd

Port of
Portland

N Lombard St

N

0   1 Mile

30

Columbia Slough

To Portland

exposed them to European diseases. An especially virulent epidemic, likely malaria, spread through the villages in the early 1830s, killing nearly everyone. The survivors fled the island, never to return.

Several years later, the Hudson's Bay Company set up a dairy farm on the now desolate island, managed by a French-Canadian named Laurent Sauvé. His name lives on, though he was not long for the island. James Bybee and a handful of other Americans soon followed, bringing dreams of a grand settlement. It never came. The flood of settlers opted instead for Portland, the Tualatin Valley, and points farther south in the Willamette Valley. Sauvie Island—almost exactly the same dimensions as Manhattan—settled into the quiet, rural character that has defined it since.

One sound often breaks the quiet, though: the singing, cackling, and honking of migrating birds. Continue north along NW Sauvie Island Road and NW Reeder Road, past the church and school, into the fields. Though you can't quite see it in this flat landscape, you're at the edge of Sturgeon Lake and the 12,000-acre Sauvie Island wildlife area, where in fall and spring thousands of migrating geese and sandhill cranes fill the skies and fields en route to and from Alaska.

At NW Gillihan Loop Road, turn right to head south along the Willamette River. (NW Reeder Road continues north; about 5 miles down the road, a series of very popular beaches—especially clothing-optional Collins Beach—make for a great side trip.) Gillihan is even quieter than Reeder Road, passing large farms and scattered homes. The Port of Portland's wharves, towers, and asphalt expanses lie only 0.5 mile across the water, a sharp contrast to the fields and oak groves on your right. Across the channel, dark firs cloak the Tualatin Mountains.

The final miles are uneventful, unless the aforementioned autumn sightseers are around. NW Gillihan Road loops westward back to Multnomah Channel and passes under the Sauvie Island Bridge. The bus stop and parking area are just beyond.

MILEAGE LOG

0.0 Begin at TriMet bus stop and parking area below bridge. Go right onto NW Gillihan Loop Rd., straight through stop sign, then left onto NW Sauvie Island Rd.

1.0 (**Side trip:** Howell Territorial Park at right.)

1.8 Right onto NW Reeder Rd.

6.1 Right onto NW Gillihan Loop Rd. (**Side trip:** Left to visit Collins Beach.)

12.1 End at TriMet bus stop.

19 St. Helens and Scappoose

DIFFICULTY: Moderate
DISTANCE: 35-mile loop; options: 22.5-mile St. Helens loop, 9.8-mile
   Scappoose loop
ELEVATION GAIN: 1100 feet

Getting There: Take US Hwy. 30 north from Portland to St. Helens and go right onto Bachelor Flat Rd.–Columbia Blvd. Go right onto S. 18th St., then right into McCormick Park.

Transit: Catch the Columbia County Rider on SW Salmon Street between SW 6th Avenue and SW Broadway. Get off at the St. Helens stop (Rite Aid Pharmacy), cross Highway 30, and continue on Gable Road to join the route at mile 34.8.

This ride can hardly be considered "in town," but it offers plenty of reasons to venture north of Forest Park on a bicycle, and it's not very far north of Sauvie Island. It links the old river towns of St. Helens and Scappoose on two loops, each with its own character. The St. Helens loop tours the old town center and riverfront before climbing to timberlands for views across the Columbia. The Scappoose loop is a flat lap through a low, lonely landscape of farms and gravel mines. Both loops are great, and both make good stand-alone rides. But if you're coming all the way from Portland, you might as well enjoy the whole thing.

   Begin in St. Helens at McCormick Park, named for the Michigan lumber family that once employed much of the town. Pick up Old Portland Road and follow it north into the old town center, where the imposing Columbia County Courthouse fronts a small plaza. Vacant storefronts and a derelict waterfront mill bear witness to effects of Oregon's shrinking timber industry.

   St. Helens was built to face the river, not the highway, which runs a mile to the west. Isolation has no doubt contributed to this downtown's hard times but also kept the blight of fast-food chains and big-box stores at bay. The elegant Columbia Theater on First Street dates from 1928. The Klondike Hotel at First and Cowlitz Streets, from 1910,

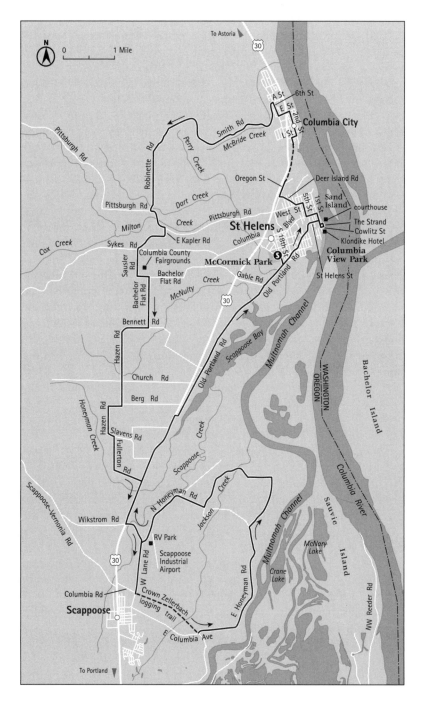

housed the town's many riverboat travelers. A restaurant still operates on the ground floor, but the hotel rooms above have been abandoned for decades. Paranormal buffs think they're haunted.

Hard to imagine now, but St. Helens once challenged Portland for preeminence. In the 1850s, conventional wisdom dictated that one of the many river villages—Portland, Linnton, St. Johns, Albina, Milwaukie, and others—would become the gateway to the Pacific Northwest. The rest would fade or be absorbed. Each town asserted its future greatness as a matter of geographic destiny, holding that *it* was the "natural" head of navigation on the river—and thus the logical seaport for Willamette Valley foodstuffs feeding the California Gold Rush.

Portland prevailed over most of the early challengers. But in 1853, St. Helens managed to convince the Pacific Mail Steamship Company, headquartered in San Francisco, to bring oceangoing steamships all the way up the Columbia—and make St. Helens its sole port. (Then as now, California money called the shots in Oregon.) So dire a threat was this to Portland's economic future that leading businessmen banded together to launch a competing steamship line, subsidizing trade voyages to San Francisco at a huge loss. The competitors eventually buckled; Portland emerged victorious, and its businessmen amassed great fortunes. St. Helens, its river ambitions dashed, settled into a humbler existence as a mill town.

Though never the port it once hoped to be, St. Helens attracts plenty of pleasure boats. From Columbia View Park, next to the courthouse off Strand Street, you can admire the yachts moored at the marina and across the channel at Sand Island Marine Park.

When you're done exploring downtown, head north on First Street and out of town via Deer Island Road. A bicycle path beginning at the animal shelter on Oregon Street leads a mile through woods to Columbia City, St. Helens's smaller and even quieter neighbor. Follow Second Street past City Hall and the school playground, where if the weather cooperates you can spot Mount Adams peeking through its foothills 70 miles east.

Now you leave the river to cross US Highway 30 and climb into the foothills. This begins with several miles of packed gravel on Smith Road, up a shady ravine along McBride Creek. Other than a bit of washboard and some mud if it's been raining, the road is doable on any bike. Beware the occasional logging truck.

The pavement resumes and the climbing ends at Robinette Road, where clear-cuts open huge views to the southeast. Robinette leads briskly down to Milton Creek, through an isolated valley ringed by

Fishing by bike, St. Helens

timberlands. After a short but busy stretch along Pittsburgh Road, peaceful riding resumes. Across Sykes Road, you'll pass the Columbia County Fairgrounds and a great Mount Hood view. The descent, now gradual, continues south along quiet roads with panoramic views across Scappoose Bay, Sauvie Island, and the Columbia.

Fullerton Road brings you back to the highway. Should you wish to shorten the loop, go left here to pick up Old Portland Road, 1.5 miles down US 30. To continue on the loop, go right instead. US 30 is busy but has a generous shoulder. The only stressful moment comes when you have to cross traffic to turn left onto W. Lane Road. Use extreme caution here.

Now begins the second part of this ride, a loop around Scappoose's floodplain. It's flat and rural, even a bit desolate. After 0.5 mile, W. Lane Road meets N. Honeyman Road. Continue south on W. Lane Road past a huge quarry.

At the Columbia Road intersection, go left to pick up a 1.5-mile stretch of the old Crown Zellerbach logging road. If a proposed expansion to the Urban Growth Boundary goes ahead, a road will someday push through here. As of this writing, though, it's still a car-free path, a bit overgrown but much loved by local walkers and cyclists.

At E. Columbia Avenue, go left. You're in lowland farm country now. Multnomah Channel is 100 yards or less to your right, but hidden from view behind a levee. Sauvie Island's treetops sway in the distance, above the levee. It's a remarkably empty place: nothing but fields and the occasional alder grove stretch to the distant levee, which forms a horizon. It's especially beautiful in autumn, when river mists spread inland, the foliage turns, and migrating birds fill the sky.

When Lewis and Clark passed through this area two centuries ago, it was a vast grassland roamed by elk herds. Birds gathered in flocks so large they darkened the sky—much to the astonishment and annoyance of the explorers, who struggled to sleep through the cacophony. These grasslands later attracted the Hudson's Bay Company traders at Fort Vancouver, in search of pastureland for the fort's growing horse herd. In 1828, Chief Factor John McLoughlin's stepson, Thomas McKay, established a ranch in the immediate vicinity. He was the area's first nonnative inhabitant. (For more on Fort Vancouver and John McLoughlin, see Rides 32 and 46.)

The wilderness of Lewis and Clark's day is a bit hard to recognize now, replaced by farm fields or removed altogether from the massive gravel quarries. N. Honeyman Road passes a few of these in its final miles. At the Scappoose Industrial Airport, a small county-run RV park (restrooms) offers a good place to park, should you want to ride just the Scappoose loop. Immediately beyond, a right turn on W. Lane Road leads back to US 30, where a few miles of highway riding lead to Old Portland Road and an uneventful but scenic return to McCormick Park.

MILEAGE LOG

0.0 Begin at McCormick Park in St. Helens. Go right to exit park onto S. 18th St., then left onto Old Portland Rd. at stoplight.

1.3 Old Portland Rd. curves right to become St. Helens St. Go right onto 1st St.

1.4 Left onto Cowlitz St., then left onto Strand St. Continue past Columbia View Park, courthouse, and Plaza Square. Return to 1st St. and go right.

1.9 1st St. curves left to become Columbia Blvd.

2.2 Right onto 5th St., left onto West St., then bear right onto Deer Island Rd.

2.8 Right onto Oregon St. Continue straight onto path (entrance is opposite the animal shelter).

4.4 Right onto L St., then left onto 2nd St. in "downtown" Columbia City.

4.9 Left onto E St. Cross US 30.

5.2 Right onto 6th St.

5.5 Left onto A St., which becomes Smith Rd. (hard-packed gravel).

7.9 Continue straight onto paved Robinette Rd. Great view.

10.0 Left onto Pittsburgh Rd.

10.5 Right onto E. Kapler Rd.

11.3 Cross Sykes Rd. to continue on Sausler Rd., which curves left at Columbia County Fairgrounds.

12.0 Right onto S. Bachelor Flat Rd.

13.0 Right onto Bennett Rd., which curves left to become Hazen Rd. (which curves several times).

15.8 Left onto Slavens Rd., then immediate right onto Fullerton Rd.

17.2 Right onto US 30. (**Option:** To skip Scappoose loop, go left onto US 30 for 0.9 mile and resume at mile 31.4 below.)

18.1 Left onto W. Lane Rd. Use extreme caution crossing US 30.

18.6 Straight at stop sign to continue on W. Lane Rd.

19.5 Left at Columbia Rd. onto Crown Zellerbach logging trail.

21.0 Left onto E. Columbia Ave., which becomes E. Honeyman Rd.

24.8 Road curves left to become N. Honeyman Rd.

28.2 Scappoose RV Park (restrooms) at left. (**Option:** Park here to do just the Scappoose loop.)

28.4 Right onto W. Lane Rd.

29.0 Right onto US 30.

31.4 Right onto Old Portland Rd. Cross tracks.

34.3 Right to stay on Old Portland Rd. Cross tracks.

34.8 Left onto S. 18th St.

35.0 Left to end at McCormick Park in St. Helens.

AROUND THE TUALATIN VALLEY

The Tualatin Mountains, or West Hills, separate downtown Portland from the broad Tualatin Valley. Spilling from Coast Range foothills at the region's western edge, the Tualatin River meanders generally southeastward to meet the Willamette River at West Linn. The Tualatin courses through a land of contrasts, home to Oregon's finest farm-land and fastest-growing suburbs. Rides in this chapter reflect these contrasts.

20 Rock Creek Greenway Trail

DIFFICULTY: Easy
DISTANCE: 7.6 miles; option: 9.7-mile loop
ELEVATION GAIN: 400 feet

Getting There: From US Hwy. 26 westbound, take exit 62B for Cornelius Pass Rd. Go right, then right again onto NW Rock Creek Blvd. Go about 0.5 mile to Rock Creek Powerline Park.

Transit: Take MAX Blue Line to Quatama station. Cross tracks onto pedestrian pathway, then go left onto NW 206th Ave. to exit housing development. Continue about 0.75 mile and go left onto NW Cornell Rd., then right onto Rock Creek Greenway Trail. Follow it under free-way and go left onto NW Rock Creek Blvd. to join the route near mile 8.9; continue west to start of route (adds about 4 miles round-trip).

This ride and the next explore lower suburban tributaries of the Tualatin River via greenway paths. Both rides offer car-free riding through parks and natural areas. In both cases, too, you have to deal with frustrating gaps in the greenways, the legacy of piecemeal and (until recently) uncoordinated growth. Even with gaps, these greenways are vital com-ponents of the region's alternative transportation infrastructure. (A lot

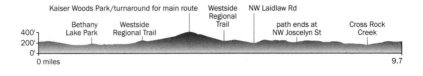

of people are working to close the gaps too; see "The Intertwine" side-bar in Ride 22.)

This ride tours the Rock Creek Greenway at the northern edge of Beaverton, in the fast-growing community of Bethany.

Begin at Rock Creek Powerline Park, just off NW Cornelius Pass Road. From the parking area, the path shoots straight east, past soccer fields and a golf course. Across NW Neahkahnie Avenue, it continues past Bethany Lake to end at NW 185th Avenue. Go left onto the sidewalk here and cross 185th at the stoplight. Continue a short distance in the bike lane on NW West Union Road, then cross West Union at the crosswalk to continue on the path.

The next mile has big views and mellow riding as the path climbs gradually to intersect with the Westside Regional Trail (see Ride 21). The path ends again at NW Kaiser Road, forcing you to make another detour on the sidewalk for 0.25 mile. The easy-to-miss entrance to Kaiser Woods Park is across NW Kaiser Road.

The path now climbs at a steeper grade, passing more homes at left. They're crowded even closer together here, separated by little more than a walkway. Then the homes—and the path—abruptly end at a large field near the base of wooded slopes rising to NW Skyline Boulevard and Forest Park.

Here at the edge of town, you can readily see a strange but not uncommon effect of the Urban Growth Boundary. It was designed to direct growth, not constrain it. In practice, though, planners have used it as a tool to create denser, and ostensibly more walkable and sustainable, communities. But since the older parts of the region are already built out—many areas in quarter-acre lots long associated with suburbia—planners have focused on the margins. As a result, the newest developments at the edge of town are often the densest—and in many cases farthest from the freeway, mass transit, and jobs.

Since you're out of park, it's time to turn around. The most straightforward route is back the way you came.

Alternatively, you can make a loop via a portion of the Westside Regional Trail and neighborhood streets. To do this, backtrack to the Westside Regional Trail junction and go left. The trail loops through

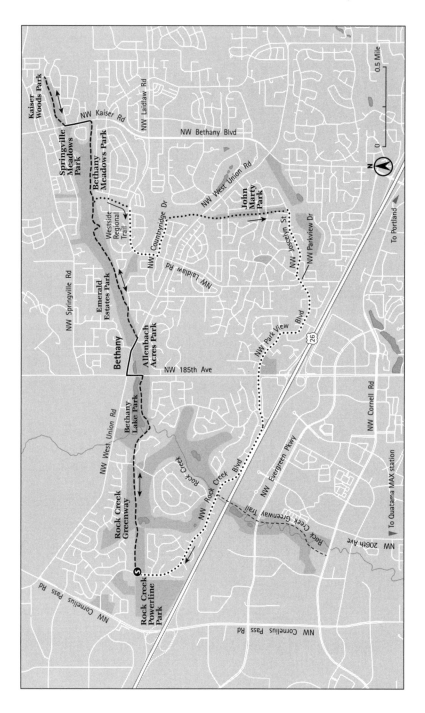

Big views on the Rock Creek Greenway

John Marty Park and eventually to NW Rock Creek Boulevard, where at mile 8.9 you cross Rock Creek and a lower segment of the Rock Creek Greenway Trail. (This is your return route if you began at the Quatama MAX station.) The road continues west, uphill now, another 0.75 mile to return to Rock Creek Powerline Park.

MILEAGE LOG

0.0 Begin at Rock Creek Powerline Park. Proceed east on Rock Creek Greenway Trail past soccer fields. Cross NW Neahkahnie Ave. and continue.

1.4 Path ends at Bethany Lake Park. Left onto sidewalk along NW 185th Ave. Cross 185th at stoplight and continue on NW West Union Rd. Cross West Union at crosswalk to resume path.

2.7 Westside Regional Trail at right; continue straight on Rock Creek Greenway.

3.3 Left at path's end onto sidewalk along NW Kaiser Rd.

3.6 Cross NW Kaiser Rd. and continue through gate into Kaiser Woods Park on Rock Creek Greenway Trail.

3.8 Path ends in Kaiser Woods Park. Retrace route to the start.

Optional loop return:

3.8 At end of path in Kaiser Woods Park, retrace route 1.1 miles.

4.9 Left onto Westside Regional Trail.

5.3 Path ends. Right onto NW Laidlaw Rd. (caution).

5.7 Left onto NW Countryridge Dr. At street's end, continue straight on path.

6.1 Cross NW West Union Rd. and continue south on path through John Marty Park.

6.8 Right at path's end onto NW Joscelyn St.

7.2 Left onto NW Parkview Dr. Cross NW 174th Ave. and continue on NW Park View Blvd.

8.1 Cross NW 185th Ave. onto NW Rock Creek Blvd.

9.7 End at Rock Creek Powerline Park.

21 Westside Regional Trail

DIFFICULTY: Easy
DISTANCE: 19 miles; option: 16.4-mile loop
ELEVATION GAIN: 1500 feet

Getting There: From US Hwy. 26 westbound, take exit 65 and go left onto NW Cornell Rd. Across freeway, go left again onto NW 158th Ave. Continue approximately 0.7 mile and go left at NW Schendel Ave. into Tualatin Hills Park and Recreation District's Howard M. Terpenning Recreation Complex.

Transit: Ride MAX Blue Line to Merlo Rd.–158th Ave. station in Beaverton and join route at mile 2.3.

The Westside Regional Trail runs north and south, following a powerline easement the length of Beaverton. As powerlines are wont to do, the path charges up and over hills with little regard for topography. The result is a roller-coaster ride with dramatic views and thigh-burning, but relatively short, climbs. The trail is a few notches tougher than the Fanno or Rock Creek Greenways, and like those paths it also suffers from some gaps. But even as a work in progress, it's a great ride.

Begin at the Howard M. Terpenning Recreation Complex, a sprawling temple to fitness. (Beaverton is a sporty town. Nike's world headquarters is around the corner, after all.) From the parking area, look behind the aquatic center for a path heading north, over a small

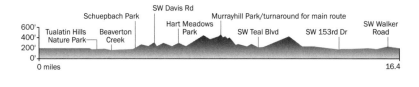

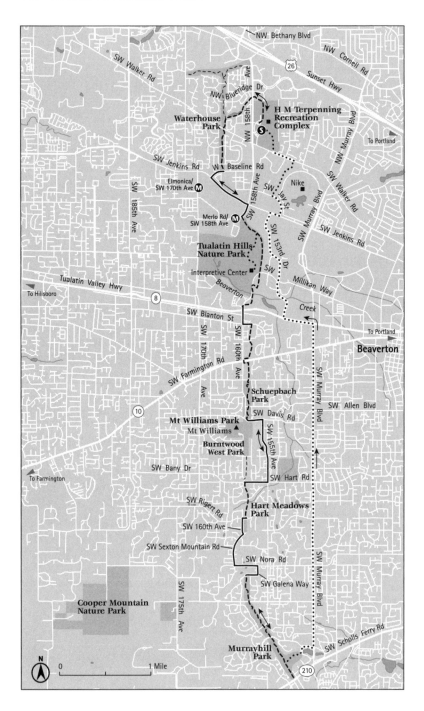

wetland and past baseball fields to a skate park. A left fork in the trail sends you out to NW 158th Avenue. Across 158th (cross at the nearby stoplight), the path continues into the woods of Waterhouse Park.

The path ends at W. Baseline Road—continue to SW Jenkins Road, a busy street with a good bike lane and the Merlo Road–158th Avenue MAX Station. This marks the entrance to the Oak Trail, which leads into a deep forest at the north end of Tualatin Hills Nature Park.

The park's trails aren't very well suited to bicycling—too many sharps turns, slippery boardwalks, and strolling families to frighten— so this route exits onto the Westside Regional Trail at the first junction. But if you've never been to this 222-acre patch of suburban wilderness at the confluence of Cedar Mill and Beaverton Creeks, you owe it to yourself to explore its many trails. The low, lush, and perpetually wet forest (there's not a hill anywhere around despite the park's name) feels ancient and vast. A good place to start is at the Interpretive Center; get there on the Oak Trail by staying right at the fork (near mile 2.6) where the main route heads left. Rejoin the main route at SW Millikan Way.

The Westside Regional Trail, meanwhile, skirts the park's eastern edge en route to the Tualatin Valley Highway (Oregon Route 8). This ugly and outsize thoroughfare was the valley's backbone until the Sunset Highway (OR 26) displaced it.

Two miles east of here, in 1847, a settler named Lawrence Hall claimed land at the "Beaver Dam," built a gristmill, and launched the valley's agricultural fame. Fertile soil meant nothing without access to markets, though, so the valley's farmers teamed up with fledgling Portland's business leaders to build a road. It ran from Hall's claim over the West Hills to Portland's waterfront. This rude highway—mostly cedar planks spanning an ocean of mud—played a decisive role in Portland's life-and-death struggle against competing river ports. The economic fates of Portland and Washington County have been inter-twined ever since.

Across the highway, the Westside Trail resumes. It's more of the same here: a meandering path under the powerlines, occasionally crossing a major road (SW Farmington) on a gradual uphill. Mount Williams looms above the path at Schuepbach Park, where the trail enters switchbacks.

With a mountain blocking further forward progress, go left onto Davis and then right onto SW 155th Avenue. Views open to the east as you traverse the side of Mount Williams. At SW Hart Road, head right to rejoin the path in Hart Meadows Park. It runs downhill, crosses Johnston Creek, and heads up the flank of Cooper Mountain to

Murrayhill Park

SW Rigert Road. Here, another gap necessitates a detour along neighborhood streets—pleasant enough, though it adds extra hill climbing.

The path resumes at SW Galena Way in Murrayhill Park. This stretch of trail is the most dramatic, with even bigger views east to Beaverton, Mount Sylvania, and the Southwest Hills of Portland. Straight ahead looms Bull Mountain, its broad summit and ravined flanks cloaked in monotonous tract homes—a rebuke to all who crow too loudly about our vaunted land use planning system.

The final descent to SW Scholls Ferry Road is truly a roller coaster, with short and steep ups and downs that will test your brakes and shifting skills. Use extra caution around pedestrians here, and keep an eye out for wet leaves and other trail hazards. Though the path is paved, the risk of a single-track-style wipeout is very real. It's one of the funnest stretches of greenway anywhere.

Sadly, it comes to a screeching halt at SW Scholls Ferry, another of those old rural routes now depressingly choked with suburban traffic. The powerline corridor continues across the road and sharply up Bull Mountain but, alas, there is no path. Nor are there any other connectors within easy reach. Your best bet, then, is to grab a bite at the strip mall next door and head back up the way you came.

Alternatively, if you want a more direct and less hilly loop return, follow SW Murray Boulevard. This charmless suburban express route is designed to speed drivers to their cul-de-sacs. Though it's no fun to ride, it gets you 3.2 miles back north to the Tualatin Valley Highway (OR 8) very quickly, via a good bike lane. The loop continues on SW 153rd Drive. Follow it over Beaverton Creek, across the MAX tracks, and past "Nike Woods," a chunk of Nike-owned forest whose eventual fate has been a source of conflict between Beaverton and its resident corporate behemoth for decades. The Terpenning Recreation Complex is just a few blocks farther.

MILEAGE LOG

0.0 Begin at Howard M. Terpenning Recreation Complex. Behind aquatic center, go left to follow path north to skate park. Go left here toward NW 158th Ave.

0.3 Cross NW 158th Ave. at NW Blueridge Dr. Backtrack on NW 158th 100 yards and go right onto path entering Waterhouse Park.

0.8 Left at trail junction. Cross SW Walker Rd. and continue on path.

1.4 Right onto W. Baseline Rd.

1.6 Left onto SW Jenkins Rd.

2.1 Right onto SW 158th Ave.

2.3 Cross MAX tracks and go left onto Oak Trail path in Tualatin Hills Nature Park. Caution on boardwalks. (**Side trip:** Follow side trail to Interpretive Center.)

2.6 Left onto unpaved path (walk bike). Pavement resumes shortly on Westside Regional Trail.

3.0 Cross SW Millikan Way and continue on path.

3.3 Left onto sidewalk along SW Millikan Way. Cross Beaverton Creek, then go left to continue on path.

3.6 Left at path's end onto SW Millikan Way. Cross Tualatin Valley Hwy. (OR 8) and continue on SW 160th Ave.

3.6 Left onto SW Blanton St. Continue 150 yards and go right onto Westside Regional Trail.

4.3 Right onto sidewalk at SW Farmington Rd. Cross Farmington at SW 160th Ave. and backtrack on Farmington to continue on path. Enter Schuepbach Park.

5.2 Left at path's end onto SW Davis Rd. (caution).

5.5 Right onto SW 155th Ave.

6.1 Right onto SW Hart Rd.

6.4 Left onto Westside Regional Trail at Hart Meadows Park.

7.0 Right onto SW Rigert Rd., then immediate left onto SW 160th Ave. Go right onto SW Sexton Mountain Rd. at T intersection.

7.6 Left onto SW Nora Rd. Steep downhill.

7.9 Right onto SW Galena Way.

8.2 Left onto path in Murrayhill Park. Caution on hills.

9.5 Path ends at SW Scholls Ferry Rd. Retrace route to return.

Optional loop return:

9.5 From SW Scholls Ferry Rd., backtrack on path 0.2 mile and go right on spur path. Follow it 0.3 mile, curving left at SW Murray Scholls Dr.

10.0 Right onto SW Teal Blvd.

10.2 Left onto SW Murray Blvd.

13.5 Left onto SW Tualatin Valley Hwy. (OR 8).

13.8 Right onto SW 153rd Dr.

14.3 Cross SW Millikan Way and continue north.

15.1 Right onto SW Jenkins Rd., then left onto SW Jay St. Nike World Headquarters at right.

15.4 Right onto path.

15.9 Left at path's end onto SW Walker Rd.

16.2 Right onto path running between baseball fields, then left at junction.

16.4 Path ends at parking lot in Howard M. Terpenning Recreation Complex.

22 Fanno Creek Greenway Trail

DIFFICULTY: Easy

DISTANCE: 15.8 miles; option: 11.5-mile loop

ELEVATION GAIN: 100 feet

Getting There: From I-5 southbound, take exit 294 for Oregon Rte. 99W. Cross OR 217 via overpass and go left onto SW Hall Blvd. Continue approximately 1 mile to Tigard Library.

Transit: Ride WES or TriMet bus to Tigard Transit Center station. Cross WES tracks west to transit center parking lot, go left, and bicycle south on path to SW Hall Blvd. Go right, through stoplight at SW Burnham St., and right past city hall to join Fanno Creek Greenway Trail at 0.2 mile on the mileage log.

Fanno Creek is the most urbanized tributary of the Tualatin River. Rising barely a mile west of the Willamette River in Southwest Portland, it flows west and then south, through Beaverton and Tigard, to meet the

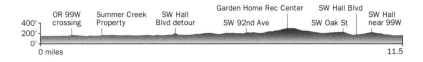

				Garden Home Rec Center		SW Hall Blvd		
	OR 99W	Summer Creek	SW Hall					SW Hall
400'	crossing	Property	Blvd detour		SW 92nd Ave		SW Oak St	near 99W
200'								
0'								
	0 miles							11.5

Tualatin at Cook Park (see Ride 23). This ride explores a stretch of the creek on the Fanno Creek Greenway Trail, a family-friendly but busy path connecting several large parks in Fanno's floodplain. It's a great counterpoint to the Rock Creek Greenway—an intimate, wooded ramble in contrast to Rock Creek's wide-open path and Tualatin Valley views.

Begin at the Tigard Public Library and go left onto the trail, which snakes behind the library and crosses Fanno Creek via a narrow wooden bridge—the first of several on this path—which can be treacherous when wet. Cross SW Hall Boulevard and continue on the path through forest, skirting city hall and the school district's bus barn. The path soon emerges at SW Main Street in downtown Tigard. Plans call for this section of the creek to be restored, complete with new meanders and a rerouted trail.

On the Fanno Creek Greenway Trail in Greenway Park (Tualatin Hills Park and Recreation District)

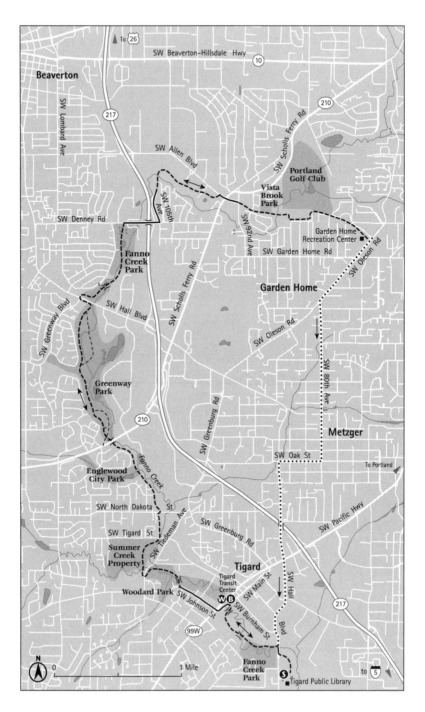

To 26

SW Beaverton–Hillsdale Hwy

10

Beaverton

217

SW Lombard Ave

SW Allen Blvd

SW Scholls Ferry Rd

210

Portland
Golf Club

Vista
Brook
Park

SW 105th Ave

SW Denney Rd

SW 92nd Ave

Garden Home
Recreation Center

SW Oleson Rd

Fanno
Creek
Park

SW Garden Home Rd

Garden Home

SW Hall Blvd

SW Greenway Blvd

SW Scholls Ferry Rd

SW Oleson Rd

SW 80th Ave

Greenway
Park

210

Metzger

SW Greenburg Rd

SW Oak St

To Portland

Englewood
City Park

Fanno Creek

SW North Dakota St

SW Tigard St

SW Tiedeman Ave

SW Greenburg Rd

SW Pacific Hwy

Summer
Creek
Property

Tigard

Woodard Park

Tigard
Transit
Center

W B

SW Johnson St

SW Main St

SW Burnham St

SW Hall Blvd

217

99W

N

0   1 Mile

Fanno
Creek
Park

S

Tigard Public Library

to 5

At Main Street, the route crosses Oregon Route 99W and follows neighborhood streets to Woodard Park where the path resumes. Continue across Fanno Creek and through the park's oak groves to SW Tiedeman Avenue. Across Tiedeman you enter the Summer Creek Property, a large natural area recently acquired by the City of Tigard.

THE INTERTWINE

On your bike map or a trail sign, at a park, or on the back of a bus, you might notice a little four-leaved icon above the word "Intertwine." This, as the promoters put it, is "our connected network of parks, trails, and natural areas in the Portland, Oregon, and Vancouver, Washington, region."

If that sounds a little vague, well, it is. Think of it this way: on any given ride, you might visit a natural area owned by Metro (the regional government), then follow a bike route maintained by the City of Portland. Then you might detour onto a walking trail in the City of Hillsboro, followed by a picnic lunch at a park in the Tualatin Hills Park and Recreation District (or in Clark County, at an Oregon State Park, or even a US Forest Service site—the list goes on). Then you head home via MAX, operated by TriMet, the regional transit agency.

All of these governments work (in theory!) toward the same thing: protecting the places we love and helping us experience them. But with so many cooks in the kitchen, the meal often lacks coherence. Hence the annoying gaps separating chunks of the Fanno Creek Greenway trail (which crosses four jurisdictions) or the difficult pedestrian access to the Tualatin River National Wildlife Refuge (a world-class urban wildlife sanctuary situated between two poorly connected suburban towns).

The Intertwine is dedicated to the idea that by bringing government agencies together—with nonprofits, businesses, and community leaders added to the mix—we can improve the system as a whole. Just as importantly, we can better connect the people of this region to their natural heritage, inspiring them to protect it by inviting them to *use* it.

By physically linking the region's parks, trails, and natural areas—and by linking those who care about it to one another—the Intertwine (www .theintertwine.org) exists to make one of the world's greatest places even better.

North of SW North Dakota Street, the path skirts extensive wetlands that in recent years have been home to some very industrious beavers. Trailside vegetation veils their feats of engineering, but if you look carefully at around mile 2.5 (as of this writing, that is—those critters are always on the move), you can make out some of the beaver dams.

It's pretty amazing, really. We're smack in the heart of suburbia, within earshot of OR 217, and miles from anything you'd properly call wilderness, yet here's a colony of beavers. They've received some help in recent years from extensive streamside restoration (see Ride 23). Now they're returning the favor, expanding wetlands that naturally clean Fanno's water and create fish habitat.

Continue through a narrow underpass under SW Scholls Ferry Road. Ride with caution here and respect pedestrians' right-of-way! North of Scholls Ferry you enter Beaverton—not that you can really tell the difference—and expansive Greenway Park. The main trail stays left; side trails fork right to visit wetland areas.

At the park's north end, SW Hall Boulevard presents another of the greenway's gaps—in this case a road crossing with no stoplight or crosswalk. You'll probably see riders dart straight across Hall to continue north on the path; this can be dangerous. The official route sends you 100 yards west up Hall on the sidewalk to SW Greenway Boulevard so you can cross at the stoplight and backtrack. This is annoying but probably a good idea.

Across Hall, the forest closes in again. The path soon forks; go right to cross the creek and continue past more wetlands. Homes crowd almost to the path's edge, but dense streamside vegetation mostly obscures them. The path ends at SW Denney Road; go right and follow Denney across OR 217 via an overpass, then go left (use caution crossing busy Denney) onto SW 105th Avenue. The path continues where 105th dead-ends, crossing more wetlands and following the creek in a narrow corridor between residences and commercial buildings.

The trail emerges to busy traffic again at SW Scholls Ferry Road (OR 210) then plunges back into woods beyond SW 92nd Avenue.

The path again enters a narrow wooded corridor, hemmed in by homes. It continues, an intimate forest path all the way to its end at the Garden Home Recreation Center on SW Oleson Road.

That's all for now. Someday, hopefully, you'll be able to continue car-free all the way to the Willamette. For now, retrace your route back to Tigard Library.

Alternatively, you can return via a faster loop; it includes some busy streets (with bike lanes) but should be suitable for anyone who knows the rules of the road. See the mileage log for details.

MILEAGE LOG

0.0 Begin at Tigard Public Library. Go left onto path at back end of parking lot.

0.2 Cross SW Hall Blvd. at crosswalk; continue on path in Tigard's Fanno Creek Park.

0.6 Left at junction to cross creek again, then right to continue north on greenway.

0.8 Left onto SW Main St. in Tigard.

1.0 Cross OR 99W at stoplight onto SW Johnson St.

1.3 Right onto Fanno Creek Greenway Trail to enter Woodard Park.

1.8 Left onto SW Tiedeman Ave., then right to resume path in Summer Creek Property.

2.1 Cross SW Tigard St. and continue on path.

2.3 Right onto SW North Dakota St., then immediate left to continue on path.

3.1 Path crosses under SW Scholls Ferry Rd. to enter Greenway Park. Main path stays left.

4.3 Path ends at SW Hall Blvd. Cross at crosswalk 150 yards west (at SW Greenway Blvd.) and backtrack to continue on path in Beaverton's Fanno Creek Park.

4.4 Right to cross bridge to continue north on path.

5.0 Right onto SW Denney Rd.; cross OR 217 and go left onto SW 105th Ave.

5.5 Continue on path at end of SW 105th Ave.

6.4 Left onto sidewalk at SW Scholls Ferry Blvd. Cross Scholls and SW Allen Blvd. at stoplight and continue east on sidewalk along Allen.

6.6 Cross SW 92nd Ave. at crosswalk to resume path.

7.9 End at Garden Home Recreation Center. Retrace route back to start.

Optional loop return:

7.9 Right onto SW Oleson Rd.

8.5 Left onto SW 80th Ave.

9.7 Right onto SW Oak St.

10.0 Left onto SW Hall Blvd.

11.5 Left to end at Tigard Public Library.

23 Tualatin River

DIFFICULTY: Challenging
DISTANCE: 23.5 miles
ELEVATION GAIN: 2000 feet

Getting There: From I-5 southbound, take exit 289 for Tualatin–Sherwood and go right onto SW Nyberg St., which curves left to become SW Tualatin–Sherwood Rd. Go right onto SW Boones Ferry Rd., then continue straight onto SW Tualatin Rd. Where road bends left, continue straight into Tualatin Community Park.

Transit: Ride WES or TriMet bus No. 96 to Tualatin. Station and bus stop are across street from Tualatin Community Park.

This ride loops a stretch of the lower Tualatin River, from suburbs to country and back. Along the way it visits the Tualatin River National Wildlife Refuge and climbs high above the river on Chehalem Ridge. It's a demanding ride rich with contrasts—one of my favorites.

Begin at the Tualatin Community Park in the town of Tualatin. In the 1850s, a town called Bridgeport sprang up across the river from here; it served as a river port for boats headed upstream to Scholls and Hillsboro and as a ferry point for overland travelers between Portland and Salem. In 1886, the Portland and Willamette Railway Company routed its new Portland-Salem line across the river from Bridgeport, effectively dooming the town to obsolescence. As elsewhere in the Willamette Valley, the shift from river to rail shifted fortunes as well. In this case, Tualatin was the winner.

Not that it boomed, exactly. Nearly a century after its triumph, it still barely topped 1000 souls. Then came Interstate 5, which again reordered the fate of communities up and down the Willamette Valley. Between 1970 and 2010, Tualatin's population grew 35 times over. Much of the "old" town disappeared. (Tualatin's new downtown, the Commons, was previously home to a famously "aromatic" pet food factory that finally closed its doors in 1987. Is that a whiff of kibble wafting

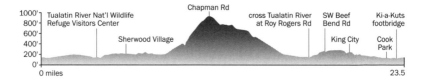

Low water on the Tualatin River, Cook Park

through the plaza?) A generation ago, the broad floodplain west of town was farmland; now it's a sprawling district of warehouses, light industry, and gravel mines. Beyond, though, lies another recent invention: the Tualatin River National Wildlife Refuge.

That's where you're headed. From Tualatin Community Park, go right onto SW Tualatin Road; follow it across railroad tracks and past subdivisions and office parks to SW 124th Avenue. A right turn here leads you to Oregon Route 99W. Follow this very busy but ample-shouldered highway out of town.

A mile and half down the highway, a driveway at right leads up to the refuge's Visitor Center. It's a beautiful building, full of wood and light. Windows look out over an expanse of wetlands, which flood and contract with the changing seasons. Dioramas, plaques, and exhibits relate the refuge's natural and human history—including how this refuge came to exist at all. There aren't many refuges like this one, established on degraded farmland in the midst of a growing urban

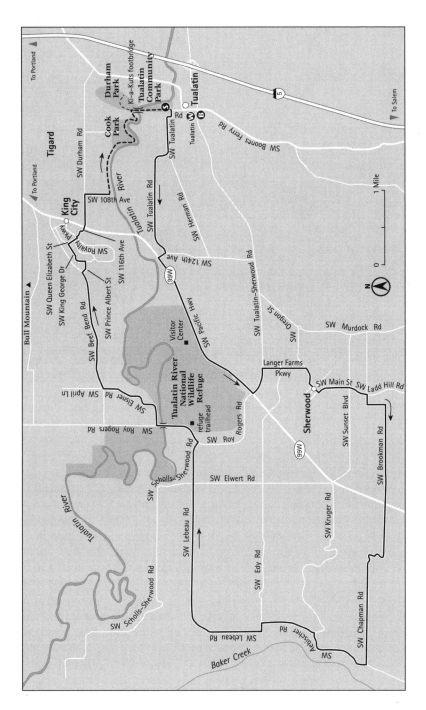

region. It owes its existence largely to local citizens, whose tireless advocacy prompted the federal government to accept a 12-acre donation. From this humble beginning 20 years ago, the refuge has grown to several thousand acres, gradually reclaiming the river and its floodplain for wildlife.

A RIVER'S REBIRTH

Though it drains a vast watershed, the Tualatin can be an elusive river. Cloaked for much of its length in dense vegetation, it flows through some of the region's most densely populated areas almost unnoticed. A lucky few own homes fronting the lazy river, but the rest of us can hardly even *see* the Tualatin, let alone access it.

For decades this low profile suited the river, since it was a place you'd rather not see—or smell or taste, for that matter. A century ago it was a tourist destination, drawing swimmers and anglers to its clear, gentle waters at spots like Avalon Park, just upstream from today's Oregon Route 99W bridge. Then the Tualatin Valley filled with farms, towns, industry, roads, and ever more people. The forests and wetlands that once cooled and cleaned the river gave way to parking lots and lawns. Farmers and city builders "tidied up" the river, clearing much of the bushes and trees along its banks. Fertilizer, industrial pollution, and even raw sewage flowed unchecked into the Tualatin.

Stripped bare and loaded with a chemical soup of runoff, the river warmed up. The laws of chemistry dictate that warmer water holds less oxygen—too little for native fish like cutthroat trout and chinook salmon. Conditions got dicey for the fish but better for algae, which thrived in the bouillabaisse of warm water and chemicals. The slimy green algae bloomed, consumed even more oxygen, killed off even more fish, and warmed things up further. By the 1970s, the now stinking and nearly lifeless river was Oregon's dirtiest, an embarrassment that finally prompted the federal government to crack down in the 1980s.

A sensible way to clean up a polluted river is to stop putting pollutants into it. This tends to put people out of business, though. Another approach is to build massive plants to clean water before it goes into the river (and, in this case, before it comes back out, since the river we foul is the same river we drink from). It's really expensive and often not up to the job. Fortunately, the leaders charged with cleaning the Tualatin listened to the engineers proposing a fancy new solution: let nature do the work.

Over the last two decades, this approach has been tried out in the Tualatin on a large scale. The feds have agreed to let the local authorities clean the Tualatin by restoring it. The valley's residents and businesses now pay—through their sewer and water bills—to plant more than 2 million trees along the river to shade and cool the water. Meanwhile, the clean water cops target specific sources of pollution for elimination.

Engineers still build plants to clean runoff, but the main technology in these "plants" is, well, plants. The local water authority, now called Clean Water Services, has restored vast tracts of degraded riverside wetlands and routed its stormwater collection pipes into these wetlands, where plants, bugs, and bacteria cooperate to turn nasty water into relatively clean water.

While the engineers work, citizens are organizing to advocate for and connect people to the river. The Tualatin Riverkeepers lead paddle trips and educational outings, advocate for smart growth, and call polluters to account. Metro and other local governments work to protect the river as well, acquiring sensitive properties and nursing them back to ecological health. Most significantly, the Tualatin River National Wildlife Refuge plants a flag for wildlife here at the growing edge of the region.

The stink is gone, birds are back, and even the fish are (gradually) returning. We'll never return the Tualatin River to anything like the condition we found it in. But signs are good that we'll at least have a living river—and, hence, living people—as we move forward.

~~~~~~

Beyond the refuge, follow the highway to the outskirts of Sherwood, another Tualatin Valley village mushrooming into suburbia. Pass strip malls and gas stations to reach Sherwood's charming old town center. Continue across the tracks up Main Street, south and out of town. Where the subdivisions suddenly stop, follow quiet SW Brookman Road back to OR 99W.

Across the highway, get ready for a stiff climb up the east flank of Chehalem Ridge on idyllic SW Chapman Road. A tough but beautiful 1.5 miles later, it curves north and begins a gradual descent back down to the river, which cuts a green, serpentine strip far below. Back at the river, carefully cross SW Roy Rogers Road. When you're safely across, look for a small country lane leading right—it ends a short distance at a trailhead for the refuge, where several miles of seasonal walking trails (no bikes allowed) invite another detour.

Continue north on Roy Rogers across the Tualatin River, then go right onto SW Elsner Road. Follow it past a few final farms to SW Beef Bend Road, which returns you to suburbia. This is another busy, narrow road that demands vigilance and a cool head. It rewards your efforts with an easy climb over the shoulder of Bull Mountain and views across the river.

At SW Prince Albert Street—an easy turn to miss—go right into King City. This golf course development has streets named for the English royal family. It looks like something dropped from Palm Springs. At the downhill end, sneak around a strip mall to cross OR 99W and continue on SW Durham Road.

A right turn at SW 108th Avenue sends you on another antiseptic suburban street, at the end of which an unobtrusive sign indicates the Tualatin River Greenway Trail. Follow this path east through woods and fields into Tigard's Cook Park, where at the boat launch you finally get a good close-up of the elusive river. Just beyond, follow a short stretch of dirt trail to a butterfly garden and bird-watching pavilion. The trail, paved once again, continues along the river to meet another path paralleling the Westside Express tracks. Go right here and cross the river on the recently built Ki-a-Kuts footbridge, which affords a long, lovely view downstream. You'd never know the interstate is around the bend! Tualatin Community Park is just beyond.

MILEAGE LOG

0.0   Begin at Tualatin Community Park. Go right onto SW Tualatin Rd. Cross railroad tracks and go right at next intersection to stay on Tualatin.

0.7   Right at intersection with SW Herman Rd. to stay on SW Tualatin Rd.

2.2   Right onto SW 124th Ave., then left onto SW Pacific Hwy. (OR 99W) at stoplight.

3.6   Tualatin River National Wildlife Refuge Visitor Center driveway at right.

4.6   Left onto SW Tualatin–Sherwood Rd.

5.0   Right onto Langer Farms Pkwy.

5.6   Right onto SW Oregon St. Continue onto SW 1st St. through Sherwood Village.

6.1   Left onto SW Main St. Cross tracks and continue on SW Main St., which becomes SW Ladd Hill Rd. after intersection with SW Sunset Blvd.

6.8   Right onto SW Brookman Rd.

8.5   Cross SW Pacific Hwy. (OR 99W) and continue west on SW Chapman Rd. Long hill.

10.9   SW Chapman curves right to continue downhill.

11.9   Left onto SW Aebischer Rd.

12.6   Left onto SW Edy Rd., which becomes SW Lebeau Rd.

15.6   Continue straight onto SW Scholls–Sherwood Rd.

16.2 Left onto SW Roy Rogers Rd. (caution). (**Option:** Detour to refuge trailhead at right.) Cross Tualatin River.

16.9 Right onto SW Elsner Rd.

18.0 Right onto SW Beef Bend Rd. Caution on this narrow road.

19.6 Right onto SW Prince Albert St.

19.8 Left onto SW King George Dr.

20.2 Right onto SW Queen Elizabeth St.

20.3 Left onto SW Royalty Pkwy., then immediate right (dogleg), to stay on SW Queen Elizabeth St.

20.4 Right onto SW 116th Ave.

20.5 Cross OR 99W and continue east on SW Durham Rd.

20.7 Right onto SW 108th Ave.

21.3 At street's end, continue straight onto Tualatin River Greenway, which curves left. Stay right at all junctions on path.

22.4 Paved path ends at boat ramp in Cook Park. Continue through parking area onto dirt path.

22.6 Go right onto paved path. (**Option:** detour to butterfly garden at left.)

23.0 Cross under rail tracks and go right onto Ki-a-Kuts footbridge across Tualatin River.

23.5 End at Tualatin Community Park.

THE UGB

Way back in 1970, Oregon passed some aggressive laws to limit sprawl and protect farmland. Every city was required to draw a line—an Urban Growth Boundary—around itself on the map. Outside the line, urban development is restricted; inside the line, government planners encourage dense, walkable, and public transit–friendly development. The goal isn't to stop growth but to direct it, in the hope of creating more livable communities that cost tax-payers less to service. As land develops, the boundary gradually expands.

The UGB is, and always has been, controversial. Some say it drives up housing prices and works against the "free" market. It has unquestionably succeeded in limiting sprawl, though—just look across the Columbia to see how things might have turned out. (We won't go into the question of whether or not Portland's UGB is to blame for Vancouver's sprawl.)

All this wonkiness aside, the UGB is what allows us to get off MAX and bicycle right into the countryside. The UGB is invisible, of course, but in places you can practically see the line written on the landscape, places where condominiums face farm fields across the road. It's a defining feature of our region.

24 Hillsboro to Helvetia

DIFFICULTY: Moderate to Challenging
DISTANCE: 28-mile loop
ELEVATION GAIN: 700 feet

Getting There: From US Hwy. 26, take exit 62A for NW Cornelius Pass Rd. and go left. Go right after 1 mile onto NW Cornell Rd. and follow it about 4 miles into Hillsboro. Go right onto E. Main St. Continue through downtown and go left onto S. First Ave., cross SE Washington St., and go right into a parking garage.

Transit: Ride MAX Blue Line to its last stop, Hatfield Government Center in Hillsboro.

The Tualatin Mountains drop steeply eastward to the Willamette River, creased with ravines. Forest Park and the timberlands beyond cloak these hills in forest. Over the ridge, the mountains slope more

A New Year's visit to the Helvetia Community Church

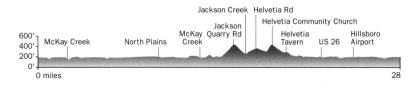

gradually to the Tualatin Valley, blanketed by farms and vineyards. This is Helvetia.

Farther south, US Highway 26 cuts arrow-straight across the valley, dividing Helvetia from Hillsboro and Beaverton. More than the freeway separates urban from rural, though. The real dividing line is invisible: the Urban Growth Boundary, or UGB—a line on the map beyond which it is decreed no city shall grow (see "The UGB" sidebar after Ride 23).

This ride visits both sides of the magic line, looping from fast-growing Hillsboro to Helvetia's rural byways and back. While the ride isn't meant to be a land-use planning lesson—we're here for the idyllic countryside and dramatic views—it does offer a particularly potent example of the UGB line's influence. More on that below.

The ride begins in downtown Hillsboro, a little farm town that several decades ago grew some high-tech appendages. Now it's home to Oregon's "Silicon Forest," anchored by Intel. While the downtown remains a bit sleepy, Hillsboro's margins are booming. But the UGB limits the town's westward march at McKay Creek. Beyond lies farmland as far as you can see.

The route crosses McKay Creek on NW Hornecker Road, then makes a long arc to the west and north on mostly quiet rural roads. At NW Gordon Road, cross US 26 to the little burg of North Plains. Its main drag, NW Commercial Street, is so quiet you can almost hear the tumbleweeds rolling. It's a world away from Hillsboro's office parks and shopping malls, just over the freeway.

At the end of Commercial Street, head left onto NW Shadybrook Road and follow it north into the Tualatin Mountain foothills. The next few miles traverse the hills, following the boundary between farm and forest. Views to the south take in Helvetia's farms and estates, behind them the freeway and then suburbs beyond suburbs.

A sharp drop to the old Jackson Quarry interrupts your generally upward progress. The climb back up is tough but enjoyable, on a very quiet and narrow lane deep in forest. Back out of the ravine, the route continues through open country along NW Helvetia Road. You soon reach the intersection with NW Logie Trail, where ambitious riders can detour up to NW Skyline Boulevard on a very scenic climb. (From

Skyline, the detour returns via Rock Creek, adding a total of 12.6 miles and 1150 feet of elevation gain.)

The main route saves Logie Trail for another day, though, and instead continues straight ahead on NW Helvetia Road. Swiss immigrants settled this area in the 1870s (they were the "Germans" at the end of Germantown Road), and their heritage endures. Swiss names dot century-old farms, some with farmhouses built in the traditional Swiss style. Around mile 17.8 you pass the historic Helvetia Community Church, which until the Second World War conducted services primarily in German.

Helvetia's Swiss descendents have long valued the area's bucolic quality and have watched Hillsboro's relentless expansion with unease.

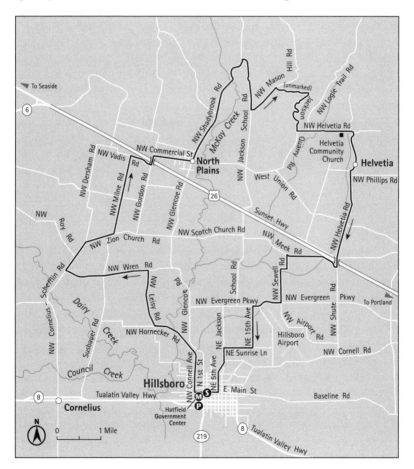

The issue came to a head in 2009 when Metro, the regional government, convened the mother of all planning processes, intended to coordinate and map regional growth for the next 50 years. No urban region in the United States had ever attempted to plan this far into the future; the process held potentially huge implications for communities across the region.

Helvetia was one such community. As part of this ambitious planning process, Hillsboro produced maps showing much of Helvetia hopefully annexed to the city and zoned for high-density industrial and residential development. For many residents, this proposal meant the destruction of all they loved about Helvetia.

Hearings on the proposals drew hot tempers to packed houses. During a particularly contentious meeting, one resident determined to preserve Helvetia's rural character and heritage yodeled her testimony. This may have clinched the deal: the politicos ultimately decided to leave Helvetia off-limits to the developers. The controversy illustrated just how difficult it is to plan for growth; as the region's population grows and pressure to expand the Urban Growth Boundary mounts, more such battles are to be expected.

The old community church, set in a fold of the Tualatin Mountains' rolling foothills, is a great place to ponder Helvetia's past and future. Continuing on Helvetia Road, though, it's a good idea to focus on the present moment. As the road drops back to the valley floor, traffic picks up noticeably. Watch for congestion (and grab refreshment if you're so inclined) at the Helvetia Tavern, the community's unofficial town hall.

Continue underneath a trestle and past the intersection with NW Phillips Road. Traffic ratchets up another notch here. Helvetia Road now shoots over the freeway. Just beyond, NW Meek Road returns you to quiet farmland. (Its days are numbered, though; this area was added to the Urban Growth Boundary in 2011 as future industrial land.) NW Sewell Road leads you to NW Evergreen Parkway, Hillsboro's northern thoroughfare. Follow it past the airport to NE 15th Avenue, where a left turn leads you past one of Intel's massive "campuses." Several suburban miles later, you reach Main Street, where a valedictory cruise through downtown Hillsboro ends at the MAX station.

MILEAGE LOG

0.0 Begin at Hatfield Government Center MAX station in Hillsboro. Go left onto W. Main St. and then right onto NW Connell Ave., which becomes NW Hornecker Rd. Soon cross McKay Creek.

2.2 Right onto NW Leisy Rd.

3.6 Left onto NW Wren Rd.

5.6 Right onto NW Cornelius–Schefflin Rd.

7.0 Left onto NW Milne Rd.

8.8 Right onto NW Vadis Rd.

9.4 Left onto NW Gordon Rd. Cross US 26 and go right onto NW Commercial St. in North Plains.

10.3 Left onto NW Shadybrook Rd. Eventually cross McKay Creek.

13.0 Right onto NW Jackson School Rd.

14.2 Left onto NW Mason Hill Rd.

15.0 Right onto (unmarked) Jackson Quarry Rd.

17.0 Left onto Helvetia Rd. (for an extended loop to NW Skyline Blvd., go left at mile 17.2 onto NW Logie Trail Rd.). Helvetia Community Church at right in about 1 mile.

21.6 After US 26 overpass, first right onto NW Meek Rd..

22.9 Left onto NW Sewell Rd.

24.1 Right onto NW Evergreen Pkwy., past airport.

24.9 Left onto NE 15th Ave.

25.8 Right onto NE Sunrise Lane.

26.5 Left onto NE Jackson School Rd. Continue straight onto NE 5th Ave.

27.6 Right onto E. Main St.

28.0 End at Hatfield Government Center MAX station on W. Main St.

25 Forest Grove

DIFFICULTY: Moderate
DISTANCE: 19.2-mile loop
ELEVATION GAIN: 600 feet

Getting There: From US Hwy. 26 westbound, take exit 57 for Glencoe Rd. Go left over freeway, then right at stoplight onto NW Zion Church Rd., which becomes NW Cornelius–Schefflin Rd. Follow signs for Forest Grove through two traffic circles: right onto NW Verboort Rd., then left onto NW Martin Rd. Go left onto Oregon Rte. 47–Quince St., then right

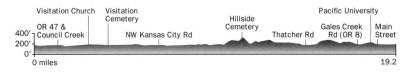

Back roads beyond Forest Grove

onto Pacific Ave. in Forest Grove. Go left onto Elm St., then right onto 17th Ave. to Rogers Park.

Transit: Take MAX Blue Line to Hillsboro Central/SE Third Transit Center, then catch bus No. 57 to Forest Grove or bicycle west along Baseline Rd. (OR 8) through Cornelius to OR 47 and follow directions above (approximately 12 miles round-trip).

Tucked against the Coast Range foothills and bounded by Gales Creek and the Tualatin River, Forest Grove has a compact, friendly atmosphere. It's an all-American kind of place that's maintained its identity and charm despite a gradual transformation from farm town to Portland suburb. Its hinterland—the far western edge of the Tualatin Valley—is close by. This ride explores a bit of that country on a short and very scenic loop.

Begin at Rogers Park, in the shade of towering Douglas firs. The route leads from here through neighborhoods, across Oregon Route 47 and out of town. As you cross Council Creek on Porter Road, the scenery abruptly shifts from homes to fields. This is incredibly fertile land, some of the most productive anywhere in Oregon. It's intensely cultivated, too, so devoid of natural features as to seem almost industrial. Yet it's indisputably beautiful as well.

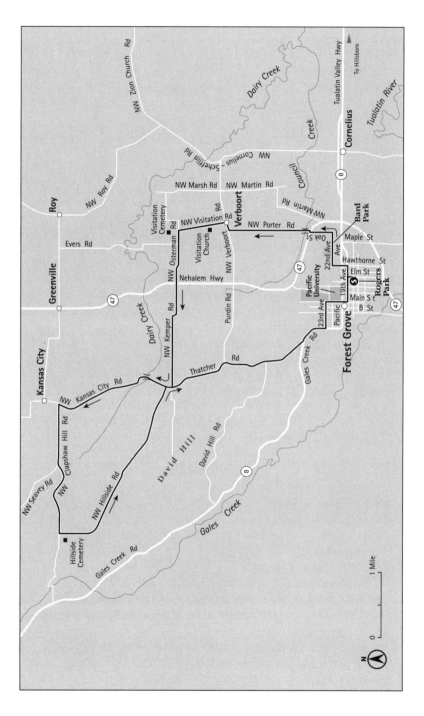

There aren't too many distractions from the scenery on this loop, though you might stop to admire the fine Visitation Catholic Church in the village of Verboort. The present building is only about 60 years old, but the parish dates to 1875, when six Dutch families settled in the area. The massive sequoias shading the church are reputedly from seeds collected during the California Gold Rush. If you plan your ride for the first Saturday in November, you can catch Verboort's Sausage and Kraut dinner, an annual tradition dating back to 1934.

Farther down Visitation Road is the Visitation Cemetery, full of pioneer graves meticulously tended by the church. The ride now heads west on NW Osterman Road toward the Coast Range. The country empties out a little more as you again cross OR 47 and then turn north at Thatcher Road. The land rolls and the farms grow wider apart.

At NW Clapshaw Hill Road, the route continues west and climbs gradually, affording views eastward across the western Tualatin Valley—still entirely rural out here beyond the microchip factories and shoe companies. The Hillside Cemetery stands at another lonesome crossroad. Turn left here and start downhill. David Hill, cloaked in timber, rises steeply at right.

Back at Thatcher Road, continue south into Forest Grove's northwestern margin, where stalled-out subdivisions wait, forlornly, for the housing market to recover. At 23rd Avenue, go left to reach Pacific University—home of the town's namesake grove—and the historic downtown. Main Street offers plenty of opportunities to stop and linger over coffee or a glass of wine from one of the many local wineries. From here, it's a short trip back to Rogers Park.

MILEAGE LOG

0.0 Begin at Rogers Park. Go left onto Elm St., then right onto 19th Ave.

0.4 Left onto Hawthorne St.

0.6 Right onto 22nd Ave.

1.2 Left onto Oak St. Cross rail tracks, OR 47, and Council Creek to continue on NW Porter Rd.

3.0 Right onto NW Verboort Rd., then immediate left onto NW Visitation Rd. Visitation Church at left.

4.0 NW Visitation Rd. curves left to become NW Osterman Rd. (Visitation Cemetery at right), then crosses OR 47 to become NW Kemper Rd.

6.6 Right onto NW Kansas City Rd.

8.8 Left onto NW Clapshaw Hill Rd.

9.8 Stay left to stay on Clapshaw Hill Rd.

11.1 Left onto NW Hillside Rd. Hillside Cemetery at right.

14.5 Right onto Thatcher Rd.; base of David Hill at right.

17.2 Left onto Gales Creek Rd. (OR 8).

17.7 Left onto 23rd Ave.

18.2 Right onto Main St. Pacific University campus at left.

18.5 Left onto 19th Ave.

19.0 Right onto Elm St.

19.2 Right to end at Rogers Park.

26 Hagg Lake

DIFFICULTY: Moderate
DISTANCE: 31.8-mile loop; option: 10.4-mile lake loop
ELEVATION GAIN: 1450 feet

Getting There: See Ride 25's directions to Rogers Park in Forest Grove.

Alternatively, to ride only around the lake, drive to Oregon Rte. 47 in Forest Grove (see Ride 25) and continue south to SW Scoggins Valley Rd., following signs for Hagg Lake. Parking area on W. Shore Dr., on far side of dam, makes best starting place; parking fee.

Hagg Lake is another classic road loop, one of the best beginner rides around. A lightly traveled road circles a reservoir tucked against the Coast Range at the edge of the metro area. Trailheads, boat launches, and parks ring the lake. On summer weekends it's overrun with humanity—but plenty of those humans are on bikes.

The shorter lake loop, at 10.4 miles and approximately 800 feet of climbing, is doable by just about any rider. If you have the time and energy, though, I highly recommend adding it to the longer loop described here. For the full loop, start at Rogers Park in Forest Grove and head west on 17th Avenue. A left onto A Street leads you to the B Street trail and out of town, where the broad Tualatin River wetlands stretch low to your left and the Coast Range foothills rise to your right.

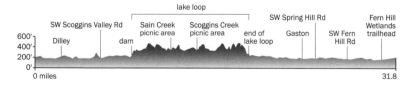

At trail's end, continue on Old Oregon Route 47 to the tiny crossroads of Dilley, where Montinore Estate winery stands ready to fortify you for the ride.

After a very short stretch on OR 47, go right to return to Old OR 47. Go right onto SW Scoggins Valley Road, where a wide shoulder keeps the boat-hauling pickup trucks at bay. You pass the Stimson Lumber Company's mill, home to one of Oregon's oldest timber giants. Immediately beyond is the Hagg Lake entrance booth, sometimes backed up with vehicles waiting to buy a parking pass. (One more reason to bike!)

At the intersection of W. Shore Drive and Scoggins Valley Road, you can choose to loop clockwise or counterclockwise. I prefer clockwise, which makes it easier to stop at the various lake access points along the way. A left on W. Shore Drive takes you across the dam—beware occasionally fierce winds here—and past the large parking area (an alternate starting point).

The loop now climbs to lake views at around mile 11. This is the

Peace and quiet at Hagg Lake

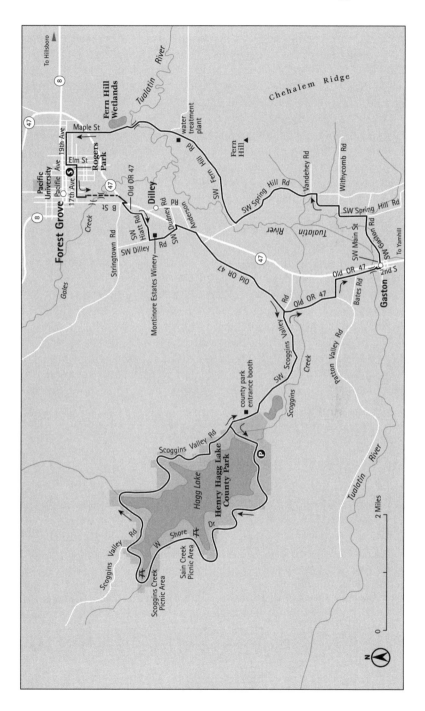

only real climb on the ride, and it amounts to only a few hundred feet. (The remainder of the lake loop has plenty of smaller ups and downs, though.) Tucked away in narrow, wooded arms of the lake are picnic areas (Sain Creek around mile 12 and, even better, Scoggins Creek around mile 14), ideal for a lunch stop and leg-stretching lakeshore hike.

While you're pedaling around the lake's quiet back side, imagine it suddenly bigger, with all those boat launches and picnic sites drowned. It may well happen in the coming years. Hagg Lake provides most of Washington County's water—for drinking, irrigation, and industry—and the county's booming growth is stretching the lake to its limits. What's more, the dam holding back Hagg Lake is not up to snuff for resisting a major earthquake. So local leaders are lobbying furiously for some federal money to raise the dam by as much as 40 feet and make seismic upgrades.

Continuing around the lake, you reach another high point near the loop's end and then drop quickly down to the junction with W. Shore Drive, where you began the loop. Now it's back out to Old OR 47 and south to Gaston, where you return to Forest Grove via Spring Hill Road in the shadow of Chehalem Ridge.

Around mile 29 you pass the facility that treats all that water from Hagg Lake before sending it to hundreds of thousands of homes and businesses. Some of the wastewater coming back from those homes, and from the basin's highly productive farms, filters through the Fernhill wetlands. You pass these around mile 30, where a parking area and trailhead offer access and good birding, especially in winter. A short pedal across OR 47 and through Forest Grove returns you to Rogers Park.

MILEAGE LOG

0.0 Begin at Rogers Park. Proceed west on 17th Ave.

0.5 Left onto A St., then left onto 16th Ave. Immediate right onto B St. trail. Path crosses Gales Creek, then parallels Hwy. 47.

1.5 At trail's end, cross B St. and continue on Old OR 47.

1.8 Right onto SW Hiatt Rd.

2.3 Left onto SW Dilley Rd.

3.0 Right onto OR 47.

3.3 Right onto Old OR 47.

5.6 Right onto SW Scoggins Valley Rd.

7.9 Entrance booth to Henry Hagg Lake County Park.

8.2 Left onto W. Shore Dr. (**Option:** Start lake loop here.)

11.0 Climb for lake views.

12.0 Sain Creek picnic area at right.

14.0 Scoggins Creek picnic area at right.

14.2 W. Shore Dr. becomes SW Scoggins Valley Rd.

18.6 At W. Shore Dr. (**option:** end of lake loop), continue straight on SW Scoggins Valley Rd.

21.3 Right onto Old OR 47.

22.2 Curve left to stay on Old OR 47.

22.5 Right to stay on Old OR 47.

23.3 Cross Tualatin River, right onto OR 47 in Gaston, then immediate left onto SW Main St.–SW Gaston Rd.

24.3 Just after bridge over creek, left at stop sign onto SW Spring Hill Rd.

27.2 Right onto SW Fern Hill Rd. just before Tualatin River.

29.0 Water treatment plant at left.

30.6 Fern Hill Wetlands trailhead at right.

30.8 Cross OR 47 and continue north on Maple St. in Forest Grove.

31.1 Left onto 19th Ave.

31.7 Left onto Elm St., then right onto 17th Ave.

31.8 End at Rogers Park.

27 Banks–Vernonia State Trail

DIFFICULTY: Easy (Loop: Challenging)
DISTANCE: 44.6 miles; option: 57-mile loop
ELEVATION GAIN: 1300 feet; option 1900 feet

Getting There: Follow US Hwy. 26 westbound approximately 21.3 miles from Portland and go left onto Banks Rd. (0.5 mile beyond Oregon Rte. 6 intersection). Continue 1.7 miles and go right onto Sellers Rd. (OR 47). Trailhead immediately at left.

Transit: At Union Station in Portland or at Sunset Transit Center in Beaverton, catch "The Wave," aka Tillamook County Bus (Route 5), to Banks. Get off at Sunset and Main and ride north on Main Street (OR 47) 0.3 mile to NW Banks Road. Go right across rail tracks, then

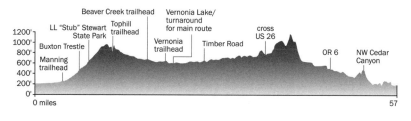

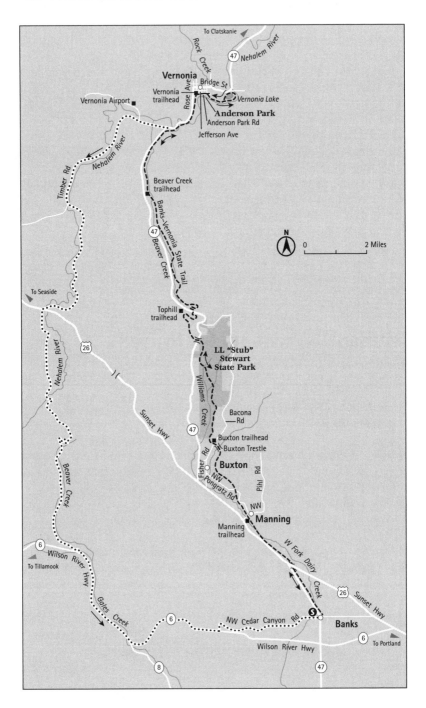

immediately left onto trail. Alternately, from the Hatfield Government Center MAX (Blue Line) in Hillsboro, follow Ride 24 to mile 6, then go left onto NW Roy Road, left onto NW Wilkesboro Road, right onto NW Aerts Road, left onto NW Banks Road, and right onto NW Sellers Road to trailhead (12.2 miles one way).

The Banks–Vernonia State Trail is popular, but not as popular as it should be. It's simply one of the best rails-to-trails in the United States, a 21-mile ride deep into the Coast Range foothills. It climbs gently from Tualatin Valley farmland into timber country, crossing a dozen bridges en route to the logging village of Vernonia. If it were a little closer to Portland, it would probably be mobbed. Instead, odds are good you'll have plenty of the trail to yourself.

The quiet era may soon come to end, though. In 2010, Oregon State Parks (the trail's owner) paved its last gravel stretch, opening the floodgates to casual road riders. Now is the time to visit!

The trail begins in the little town of Banks, a far suburban outpost situated where the two main coast routes, the Sunset Highway (US Highway 26) and Wilson River Highway (Oregon Route 6), split. It heads northwest up a fork of Dairy Creek, through a narrow valley. Farms crowd the bottomland; timber lots cover the hills. US 26 runs parallel to the trail, but a screen of trees blocks out most noise.

At mile 4 the trail crosses NW Pihl Road in the hamlet of Manning. There's a trailhead here, the first of four between Banks and Vernonia. The trail now crosses the valley, away from the highway, toward the base of timbered hills. After crossing NW Pongratz Road, it curves north to follow Mendenhall Creek opposite the village of Buxton. Here, where the Nehalem Highway (OR 47) strikes north from the coastbound Sunset Highway, farmland gives way to timber country. The valley narrows and forest closes in. The trail's steady grade gets noticeably steeper.

Near mile 6.5, the trail crosses Mendenhall Creek and Bacona Road over the Buxton Trestle, a 700-foot long, 80-foot-high wooden viaduct. Slow down here: the trail across the trestle can be slippery when wet—as is the case with the many other wooden bridges on this ride. It'd be a shame to hurry past this spot, anyway. Views down Mendenhall Creek from the trestle are great. Just beyond the trestle, a spur trail leads right, down to the Buxton trailhead.

Just past mile 7 beyond the trestle you enter L. L. "Stub" Stewart State Park. "Stub" was a lumberman and long-standing member of the Oregon Parks Commission; his namesake park, which opened in 2007,

Rest stop on the Buxton Trestle, Banks–Vernonia State Trail (Ray Hennings)

is one of Oregon's newest. It fills most of the valley of Williams Creek, a high tributary of Dairy Creek. A lot of the park still looks like the industrial timberland it used to be: young, dense, monotonous. With time and management, it will transform into that rarest of Oregon landscapes: a mature Coast Range forest.

Past mile 10 you cross the park's entrance road. A half mile later the trail exits the park, crossing over OR 47. The trail now climbs steadily over a low divide to drop steeply (beware: 11 percent grade!) to the Tophill trailhead. Congratulations: you've now officially left the Tualatin Valley. Beaver Creek—which you cross just past the trailhead and OR 47, before climbing back *up* an 11 percent grade!—flows into the Nehalem River and thence to the Pacific.

After the short but steep climb from Beaver Creek, the trail begins a long downhill cruise, high above OR 47, to Vernonia. Near mile 16.5, a short spur leads left across the creek to the Beaver Creek trailhead. A mile beyond, the trail crosses the creek to parallel the highway. The hills recede and farm fields return as you enter the flatlands surrounding Beaver Creek's confluence with the Nehalem River past mile 19. Timber Road (an optional return loop) meets the highway at left.

The final miles follow the Nehalem River to Vernonia. At Anderson Park, detour three blocks north to visit "downtown." Established in the 1880s, Vernonia was a remote, hardscrabble farm town until 1924, when the Oregon-American Lumber Company opened what it claimed to be the largest sawmill in the world. It built a rail line (you just rode it) to the Tualatin Valley. Vernonia boomed. But in a mere 30 years, the timber was mostly all cut, the mill obsolete, and the lumber company absorbed by ever-larger timber conglomerates. The mill closed in 1957, a few days before Christmas.

Like most Oregon timber towns, Vernonia has never fully recovered from this loss and the timber industry's subsequent decline. To make things worse, floods devastated the town in 1996 and again in 2007. The town has repeatedly bounced back, though, rebuilding despite the terrible economic times. It has an understated charm and even a hint of bohemianism.

From Anderson Park, the trail crosses Rock Creek and continues through the old mill site, now overgrown. It loops Vernonia Lake, the old millpond. A ruined mill building overlooks the pond, its roof long gone. Maples grow up through it. This is the end of the line. Follow the trail back to Anderson Park, explore the town a bit, and then take the trail all the way back to your starting point.

Alternatively, if you'd prefer to loop back via a significantly more challenging road, backtrack on the trail a few miles to the Timber Road intersection. Leave the trail here and follow Timber Road west, past the airport and up narrow Nehalem River valley. This is hard-core timber country, cut over and gloomy, but also very quiet. Timber Road crosses the Sunset Highway and immediately returns to the forest, passing the tiny hamlet of Timber before climbing steeply out of the valley to Coast Range views.

After topping 1100 feet in elevation, Timber Road dives down to Beaver Creek (a different Beaver Creek—this one flows into Gales Creek and the Tualatin River) through switchbacks. Five lonely forest miles later, it returns to some semblance of civilization at the Wilson River Highway (OR 6). Go left and follow this highway through a couple of frankly stressful miles until a wide shoulder appears.

The highway crosses several low hills en route to Banks. Go left onto Cedar Canyon Road for a final few miles of quiet and scenic riding above the highway. Cross OR 47 to enter Banks. The trailhead—your starting point—is immediately at left.

MILEAGE LOG

0.0   Begin at Banks trailhead. Proceed north on Banks–Vernonia State Trail.

4.0   Manning trailhead at left. Cross NW Pihl Rd. and continue.

5.1   Cross NW Pongratz Rd.

6.8   Cross Mendenhall Creek and Bacona Rd. on Buxton Trestle.

7.3   Enter L. L. "Stub" Stewart State Park.

10.6   Exit park; cross over OR 47 on trestle.

12.2   Tophill trailhead at left. Cross OR 47 and Beaver Creek and continue.

16.5   Spur trail to Beaver Creek trailhead at left.

18.9   Timber Rd. leads off left (optional loop return).

20.8   Vernonia trailhead at Anderson Park. Trail continues along road.

21.2   Veer right onto trail for Vernonia Lake.

21.8   Vernonia Lake. Continue on loop around lake.

22.8   End of loop. Retrace route to return.

Optional loop return:

22.8   From Vernonia Lake, retrace route 2.9 miles.

25.7   At Timber Rd., leave Banks–Vernonia Trail and cross OR 47 (caution!). Continue on Timber Rd.

36.1   Cross US 26 and continue on Timber Rd.

46.1   Left onto OR 6.

53.1   Left onto NW Cedar Canyon Rd.

57.0   Cross OR 47 and rail tracks, then left onto Sellers Rd. to end at Banks trailhead.

28 Cape Lookout

DIFFICULTY: Moderate
DISTANCE: 30.8-mile loop
ELEVATION GAIN: 1600 feet

Getting There: Follow US Hwy. 26 westbound to Banks, then Oregon Rte. 6 (Wilson River Hwy.) west to Tillamook. In Tillamook, turn left onto Laurel Ave. and park near county courthouse at Second St. The 74-mile drive from Portland takes about 1½ hours.

Transit: At Union Station in Portland or Sunset Transit Center in Beaverton, catch "the Wave," aka Tillamook County Bus (Route 5), to Tillamook; buses stop along US 26 en route to the coast.

Bike vacation, Cape Lookout State Park (Okay, so maybe they didn't ride all the way here!) (Oregon State Parks)

I'm tucking this Oregon Coast ride into a book about Portland bicycling for two reasons: (1) it's just too good to miss, and (2) with a little advance planning, you can do it without a car. Catch a bus at Union Station in Portland on a weekday or a Saturday morning, spend a night or two at Cape Lookout State Park, then return on Sunday evening. It's a great first overnight tour.

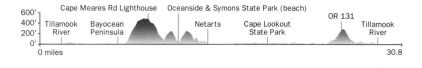

The ride loops around Cape Meares and Netarts Bay to Cape Lookout, then back to Tillamook. It's scenic from the very first mile, and the traffic is manageable. Best of all, Cape Lookout State Park welcomes you with 40 first-come, first-served hiker-biker campsites—a rarity on the car-oriented coast. (Yurts and cabins are available by reservation; plan well in advance if you want one, or visit in the off-season).

If you decide to take the bus, call to confirm schedules and let them know you're bringing a bike. The driver will make every effort to accommodate you if the bus's two bike racks are full (be prepared to disassemble your ride if necessary).

The bus drops you off in front of the county courthouse in downtown Tillamook. If you have time, visit the Tillamook County Pioneer Museum across the street. It's one of the coast's hidden treasures, with more extensive, and much better, exhibits than you might expect from a small-town museum. The best reason to visit may be the second-floor collection of taxidermy, dioramas, shells, and rocks, preserved in more or less the same display for the last half century. It's a museum of museum making, a poignant reminder of how we once saw the natural world.

From Tillamook, strike westward through the dairy farms ringing Tillamook Bay. This was once a vast wetland, where five rivers met to form an estuary. Dikes and drainage tiles have turned it into world-class dairy land. This has produced some yummy cheese but has also badly degraded the water quality of Tillamook Bay and created major flood hazards. Recent years have seen efforts by the Tillamook Estuaries Partnership (www.tbnep.org) to restore the bay and strike a new balance between economy and ecology.

Across the pungent fields, the route crosses the Tillamook River and hugs the bay toward Bayocean Peninsula—former home of Bayocean, the most spectacular real estate failure Oregon has ever known.

Envisioning a West Coast version of Atlantic City here, resort developers started selling lots in 1906 when the peninsula was nothing but sand and beach grass. By the 1920s, Bayocean had elegant hotels, a school, a dance hall, a bowling alley, tennis courts, and an enormous natatorium, or indoor swimming pool. Built right on the ocean and fed with heated seawater, it boasted electric lights, a wave generator, a bandstand, and viewing galleries to seat 1000 people.

Most visitors to Bayocean came via ferry across Tillamook Bay's frequently rough waters. This inconvenience prompted the resort's owners to lobby the federal government to build jetties at the bay's outlet in hopes of making a smoother ride. But jetties aren't cheap, and the

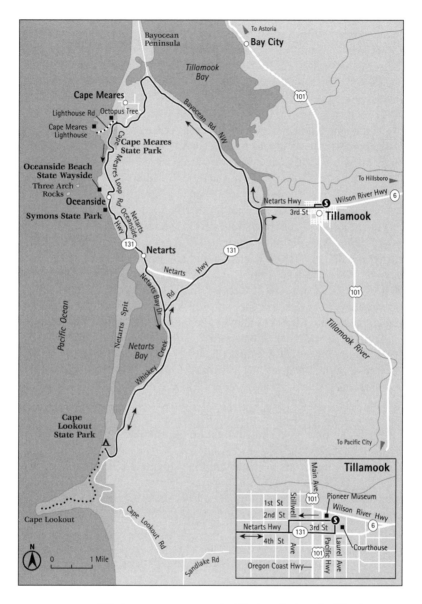

resort owners didn't want to pay much. Their solution: build a jetty on only one side of the bay.

Alas, this cost-saving measure altered the movements of surf and tide, rapidly and dramatically increasing erosion at Bayocean. The town literally fell into the sea: first the natatorium, then the hotel, then just about everything else. A few lingering ruins were removed in the 1960s, among them the Bayocean schoolhouse, now serving as nearby Cape Meares's community center. (For more on this remarkable story, see Bert and Margie Webber's *Bayocean: The Oregon Town That Fell into the Sea.*)

From Bayocean, the route heads south and up (and up!) to Cape Meares State Park. Check out the famed "octopus tree," a fantastically weathered spruce, and the historic lighthouse. A long descent down Cape Meares's south side ends at the quiet resort of Oceanside, where Three Arch Rocks rise from the ocean just offshore.

These sea stacks have history to match their beauty. In the early 1900s, plumage hunters feeding the millinery industry started slaughtering the rocks' birds en mass. Fearing the total destruction of these populations, Portland photographer and ornithologist William L. Finley raised the alarm. His photographs and advocacy convinced President Theodore Roosevelt to designate Three Arch Rocks a bird refuge—the first of its kind on the West Coast. From a handful of such sites developed what would become the nation's system of national wildlife refuges. The William L. Finley Refuge near Corvallis honors his legacy.

From Oceanside it's a quick cruise south to Netarts, where you leave the ocean to follow quiet Netarts Bay to Cape Lookout State Park. The masses descend on this park in summer, turning the 200-plus car and RV sites into a miniature city. Mercifully, the hiker-biker campsites are screened by a small patch of woods, affording a surprising degree of seclusion.

From the park you can hike for miles along the beach at Netarts Spit or tackle the stiff hike up to Cape Lookout, a narrow finger of land reaching 1.5 miles out to sea. Climbing through old-growth spruce forests, the trail ends atop cliffs at the cape's very tip. It's hands-down one of the most dramatic views in Oregon. In spring and fall, you'll likely spot migrating whales. (You can shortcut the hike by riding from the park approximately 3 steep miles to the upper trailhead, where it's only 4 miles by foot out and back.)

From the park, the route now returns to Tillamook via the Netarts Highway. This is a pretty fast ride—nice if you're rushing to catch the bus—but also busy, so beware.

There's plenty more to explore if you have more time and ambition: continue southward through Sand Lake dunes to Clay Meyers State Natural Area at Whalen Island, a nearly pristine coastal estuary (a great out-and-back day trip from Cape Lookout). Better still, extend your tour to Pacific City via Sandlake Road and Cape Kiwanda; from Pacific City you can catch the bus back to Tillamook and transfer to a Portland-bound bus. Or you can boldly return to Portland via the Nestucca River Road, a two- to three-day odyssey across the Coast Range.

MILEAGE LOG

0.0 Begin at Tillamook County courthouse. Proceed west on 2nd St.

0.2 Left onto Stillwell Ave., then immediate right onto 3rd St., which becomes Netarts Hwy. (OR 131).

1.9 Right onto Bayocean Rd. NW across Tillamook River.

6.9 Entrance to Bayocean Peninsula.

7.2 Left onto Cape Meares Loop Rd., which becomes Bayshore Dr.

9.2 Junction with Cape Meares Lighthouse Dr. (**Side trip:** Go right to visit lighthouse.)

11.7 Slight left to join Netarts Oceanside Hwy. W (OR 131) in Oceanside. Symons State Park (beach access) is just beyond.

14.2 Right in Netarts onto Netarts Bay Dr., which becomes Whiskey Creek Rd.

19.5 Right to enter Cape Lookout State Park.

20.0 Beach and campground. Turn around.

20.6 Left onto Whiskey Creek Rd. to exit park and return to Tillamook. (**Side trip:** Go right for Cape Lookout upper trailhead, Sand Lake, and points beyond.)

24.5 Right to stay on Whiskey Creek Rd.

25.7 Merge with Netarts Hwy. (OR 131; caution).

29.2 Cross Tillamook River.

30.8 Left onto Laurel Ave. to end at courthouse.

29 Chehalem Ridge

DIFFICULTY: Very challenging
DISTANCE: 48.2-mile loop
ELEVATION GAIN: 2000 feet

Getting There: From I-5 southbound, take exit 294 for Oregon Rte. 99W. Continue southwest approximately 16 miles to Newberg, continue through downtown, and go right onto N. Main St. Continue another 0.5 mile to Jaquith Park at right.

Transit: Ride MAX Blue Line to Hatfield Government Center station in Hillsboro. Go right onto W. Main St., right again onto S. First Ave.,

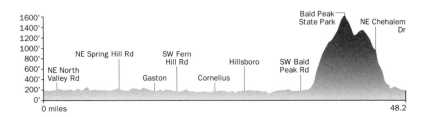

and left onto SW Walnut St. to join the route near mile 26.7. Or take TriMet bus or WES to Tigard Transit Center; transfer to Yamhill County Transit Area bus to Newberg. Get off at the Thriftway on E 1st St. and ride north on N. Main Street 0.7 mile to Jaquith Park.

This rigorous tour laps Chehalem Ridge, the broad mountain rising southwest of Hillsboro. It's another test piece for local cyclists, with sustained climbing, white-knuckle downhills, and views from the Coast Range to the Cascades. This version begins in Newberg and loops the broad ridge clockwise, following the Tualatin River through Gaston, Cornelius, and Hillsboro before attacking the ridge itself. I prefer this route, but you could just as easily begin in Hillsboro—convenient if you're riding MAX.

Begin at Jaquith Park in Newberg, where new subdivisions give way to vineyards and orchards. At NE North Valley Road, the loop truly begins; go left to head up the broad Chehalem Valley via a quiet and scenic route. (The main drag, Oregon Route 240, runs parallel about a mile south.) These are easy miles, passing Chehalem Ridge at right and the Red Hills of Dundee at left.

Past the intersection with NE Ribbon Ridge Road, the valley narrows considerably. North Valley Road curves north, hugging the hillside above the increasingly wet valley bottom. Wooded slopes edging the valley floor draw to within 0.25 mile of one another, momentarily closing out the vistas. Then, almost imperceptibly, you cross the watershed boundary from Chehelam Creek—which meets the Willamette River in Newberg—to the Tualatin River, passing tiny Ayers Creek en route to the Wapato Lakebed.

The wet fields on your left may not seem to qualify as a "lake." A century ago, however, this was indeed a lake ringed by wetlands. In winter the lake would spread, swollen with the Tualatin's floodwaters, to 1500 acres or more. The Atfalati people lived in permanent villages ringing the lake, subsisting on its vast fields of wapato. In 1855, though, after a decade of encroachment by settlers, the dwindling Atfalati

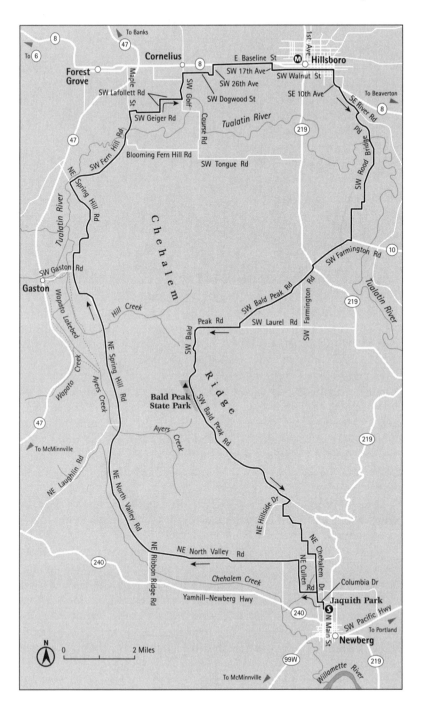

To Banks
To 6
8
47
To 6
Cornelius
8
E Baseline St
Hillsboro
1st Ave
SW 17th Ave
Forest
Grove
Maple St
SW 26th Ave
SW Walnut St
To Beaverton
SW Lafollett Rd
SW Golf Course Rd
SW Dogwood St
SE 10th Ave
SE River Rd
8
SW Geiger Rd
Tualatin River
SW Rood Bridge Rd
47
SW Fern Hill Rd
Blooming Fern Hill Rd
219
SW Tongue Rd
NE Spring Hill Rd
Tualatin River
C h e h a l e m
SW Gaston Rd
SW Farmington Rd
10
Gaston
Wapato Lakebed
Hill Creek
SW Bald Peak Rd
Farmington Rd
Tualatin River
Peak Rd
SW MS Bald
SW Laurel Rd
219
MS
NE Spring Hill Rd
Ayers Creek
Wapato Creek
R i d g e
Bald Peak
State Park
SW Bald Peak Rd
47
Ayers Creek
219
To McMinnville
NE Laughlin Rd
NE North Valley Rd
NE Hillside Dr
NE Chehalem Dr
240
NE North Valley Rd
NE Ribbon Ridge Rd
Chehalem Creek
NE Cullen Rd
Columbia Dr
Jaquith Park
Yamhill–Newberg Hwy
240
SW Pacific Hwy
To Portland
N Main St
Newberg
N
0   2 Miles
99W
219
To McMinnville
Willamette River

Clouds blanket the Chehalem Valley, clear to the Coast Range, in this view from Bald Peak.

"agreed" to join other Kalapuyan peoples at Grand Ronde, the newly created reservation in the Coast Range foothills.

Farmers moved in. In the 1930s, they diked and drained the lake to expand their fields. The peaty soil has never managed to produce as many onions as farmers had hoped, though. So over the last decade, government agencies have started buying up the lakebed in the hopes of one day restoring wetlands. This effort got a big boost in 2007, when the US Fish and Wildlife Service added a large part of the Wapato Lakebed to the Tualatin River National Wildlife Refuge. In the future, perhaps soon, the lake may return.

Cruising along the lakebed, notice the long, high ridge at right. In a few miles you'll be way up there, about 1500 hundred feet above the valley bottom.

This side of Chehalem Ridge is heavily forested and only sparsely populated. It's going to remain that way thanks to the Metro Regional Government, which in partnership with the Trust for Public Land recently acquired more than 1100 acres of the ridge from the Stimson Lumber Company. It's cutover timberland right now but in the coming years will be restored to native vegetation—a mix of oak woodlands, savannas, and conifers—and someday blossom into a superb regional park.

The route continues between ridge and river for several more miles, turning northeastward at SW Fern Hill Road. The meandering Tualatin River gradually makes its way around the ridge to flow east and south— and so do you, passing through the sleepy streets of Cornelius to strike eastward for several busy (but bike-laned) miles on OR 8 to Hillsboro. (MAX users join the route here.) At the far end of downtown, SE River Road and SE Rood Bridge Road lead back across the meandering river and into the countryside again. Old farmhouses and spreading oaks dot the land; Chehalem Ridge looms at the horizon.

The hill is closer than it looks, though. After a few more flat, bucolic miles, you cross the valley's main north-south road, OR 219, and finally begin the epic climb up SW Bald Peak Road. Things start out gently enough, but soon the road shoots uphill, gaining almost 800 feet in 2 relentless miles. Views back to the east are stunning—assuming you're not too stunned to notice. The grade eases again near the ridgetop, where SW Bald Peak Road curves south to reveal equally magnificent views over the Wapato Lakebed.

Don't rest yet, though: the next 2 miles climb another 500 feet, demanding full effort all the way to Bald Peak State Park. The park is not much more than a viewpoint, but the view is worth the work. Leave the bike and hike out a few hundred yards to fully appreciate it. The land drops sharply away, revealing the Chehalem Valley, the North Yamhill Valley beyond, and the Coast Range silhouetting the horizon. It's almost mythic—a vision of pastoral grandeur lifted from the canvas of some 19th-century landscape painter celebrating Manifest Destiny. That is, if the clouds don't get in the way.

The long descent back to Newberg is a joy. SW Bald Peak Road follows the forested ridge as it gradually falls, then turns to drop more sharply down NE Chehalem Drive. Make sure your brakes are in good working order. The grade finally mellows again as you cross NE North Valley Road and return to Newberg. Your starting point, Jaquith Park, is 1.5 miles farther.

MILEAGE LOG

0.0 Begin at Jaquith Park in Newberg. Go right onto N. Main St.

0.2 Left onto Columbia Dr.

0.5 Right onto N. Chehalem Dr.

0.8 Left onto NE Cullen Rd.

1.9 Left onto NE North Valley Rd.

6.2 Slight right to stay on NE North Valley Rd.

10.1 Cross NE Laughlin Rd. and continue straight, now on NE Spring Hill Rd.

14.6 Gaston a short distance at left, across OR 47.

17.6 Right onto SW Fern Hill Rd.

20.3 Right onto SW Geiger Rd.

21.4 Left onto SW Lafollett Rd.

22.2 Left onto SW Golf Course Rd.

22.8 Right onto S. Dogwood St. in Cornelius.

23.8 Left onto SW 26th Ave.

24.1 Right onto E. Baseline St. (OR 8).

25.7 Right onto SW 17th Ave., which becomes SW Walnut St. in Hillsboro.

27.6 Right onto SE 10th Ave.

28.1 Right onto SE River Rd.

29.3 Right onto SE Rood Bridge Rd.

33.0 Right onto SW Farmington Rd.

34.2 Left onto SW Hillsboro Hwy. (OR 219) and immediate right onto SW Bald Peak Rd.

37.0 Bear right to stay on SW Bald Peak Rd.

40.1 Bald Peak State Park at right.

44.3 Right onto NE Chehalem Dr.

46.6 At NE North Valley Rd., continue straight on NE Chehalem Dr.

47.8 Left onto Columbia Dr.

48.0 Right onto N. Main St.

48.2 Left to end at Jaquith Park.

30 Parrett Mountain

DIFFICULTY: Challenging
DISTANCE: 16.2-mile loop
ELEVATION GAIN: 1650 feet

Getting There: From I-5 southbound, take exit 283, Wilsonville, and go right onto SW Wilsonville Rd. Graham Oaks Park is approximately 1.5 miles on the right.

Transit: Ride WES to Wilsonville station. Go right onto SW Barber St., left onto SW Kinsman Rd., then right onto SW Wilsonville Rd. to Graham Oaks Park (1.8 miles total).

Parrett Mountain is well traveled by serious cyclists, the types who ride a "century" every Saturday. This is Tour de France stuff: lung-busting

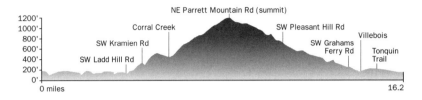

hills, huge views, narrow country roads. I've selected a short but rigorous route to give you a taste for the area, with no spandex necessary (unless you're into it, of course).

Begin at Graham Oaks Park. Here, the Metro Regional Government is turning back the clock, restoring old fields and orchards to their native grasses and oak trees. In 30 years or so, with careful tending, Metro will be the proud owner of an oak savanna. These once blanketed the Willamette Valley but have been ploughed under and built upon for a century and a half. Ecologists estimate that less than 3 percent of the valley's oak savannas remain.

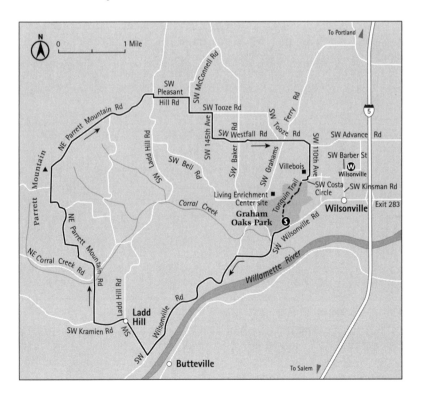

A right turn out of the parking area puts you on SW Wilsonville Road. To be honest, this is white-knuckle riding. On some country rides, it's the occasional snarling dog or swaying log truck that adds a touch of excitement. Not here. Many of these rural folk are actually executives, and these executives tend to own very nice cars, which they tend to enjoy driving very quickly on the winding, leafy roads. It's a scene straight out of a luxury-car commercial, except that in the commercial there's never a bicyclist sucking exhaust fumes after barely escaping that Ford Escape. Bottom line: with no shoulders or bike lanes, this road demands of bicyclists a certain Zen-like calm. The BMW or Porsche that will inevitably charge up behind you can no doubt afford to be late to wherever it's going. Just make sure you're visible and take the whole lane if you need it.

Wilsonville Road leads southwest along the Willamette River past monumental horse farms and riverfront mansions tucked just out of view. It's a manicured landscape to be sure, but pleasingly immaculate. At SW Ladd Hill Road, near the site of the old ferry to Butteville (see Ride 33), turn right to begin climbing in earnest.

Ladd Hill Road climbs to the tiny crossroads of Ladd Hill. The terrain rolls gently up, then down into the wooded Corral Creek drainage, then decisively up on NE Parrett Mountain Road. Climbing ever higher on this road, you start to get a sense of Parrett Mountain's prominence, which barely tops 1200 feet but really *feels* like a mountain. It soars straight up from the Willamette, forcing the great river to detour eastward around it. And it stands alone, separated from the larger massif of Chehalem Ridge by a low pass through which Oregon Route 99W runs.

Around mile 8, sloping meadows foreground a panorama of farms, cities, timbered foothills, and the Cascades, crowned by Mount Hood 60 miles distant. It's a vantage that more or less sums up this corner of the world, where a generation of Oregonians have thought about, fought about, and compromised over how to balance urban growth with protecting farmland and natural places. On balance, the result is inspiring.

The views east just keep coming as you head back downhill toward Wilsonville, past the estate homes, the picturesque farms (holdouts from a bygone, truly agricultural era), the exurban development slowly creeping uphill, and into the 21st-century ersatz community of "Villebois," a master-planned development attempting to replicate a small town. For now, limping half-built through the real estate bust, the place looks more like a stage set than an actual community, but hopefully time will change that.

Running on empty near the top of Parrett Mountain

A side note: Villebois stands on the site of the Dammasch State Hospital, an old-school state-run insane asylum. At Dammasch, as at its famous counterpart in Salem (where Ken Kesey's *One Flew Over the Cuckoo's Nest* is set), doctors carried out electroshock therapy and forced sterilization on "defectives"—epileptic, developmentally disabled, and psychotic patients, as well as convicted rapists. An official Eugenics Board, established by state law, oversaw the sterilizations, which, incredibly, took place as recently as the 1970s. The eugenics law was on the books until 1983—long after its "scientific" basis was thoroughly discredited.

Dammasch was unceremoniously razed in 2005—only a few years after an unidentified state employee "accidentally" shredded most of the hospital's eugenics records. Still standing nearby, however, is the former Callahan Center, a rehabilitation facility built in the 1970s for injured state workers. A hulking, bunkerlike mass of concrete, the Callahan Center was connected to Dammasch by a subterranean passageway more than a mile long. Apparently—though I haven't been able to confirm this—the buildings were intended to serve as a radiation treatment center in the event of nuclear war.

In 1992, a new-age church bought the facility to create a megachurch and retreat center. The saga of the Living Enrichment Center, as it was called, is too long to relate here. Suffice it to say, it began with spiritual idealism and ended a mere dozen years later with financial misdeeds, a shattered congregation, and a gigantic abandoned building. It still stands, windows broken and "No Trespassing" signs posted, right next to Villebois and Graham Oaks Park. (To actually see the building, venture south on SW Grahams Ferry Road from Villebois.)

Your ride ends with a tour through Graham Oaks Park on a section of the new Tonquin Trail, which will one day link Wilsonville with Sherwood and Tualatin to the north. For now, enjoy the car-free asphalt covering a final mile back to the parking area.

MILEAGE LOG

0.0   Begin at Graham Oaks Park; go right onto SW Wilsonville Rd.

3.9   Right onto SW Ladd Hill Rd.

4.6   Left onto SW Kramien Rd.

5.2   Right onto NE Parrett Mountain Rd., which turns to packed gravel at mile 5.5.

5.9   Left onto NE Corral Creek Rd., then immediate right onto NE Parrett Mountain Rd. (dogleg; pavement resumes).

8.5   Summit of NE Parrett Mountain Rd.

10.8   Right onto SW Ladd Hill Rd., then immediate left onto SW Pleasant Hill Rd. (dogleg).

11.5   Curve right onto SW McConnell Rd.

11.7   Curve left onto SW Tooze Rd.

12.1   Right onto SW 145th Ave., which curves left to become SW Westfall Rd.

13.8   Cross SW Grahams Ferry Rd. to continue on SW Tooze Rd.

14.3   Right onto SW 110th Ave. Continue straight through roundabout at Villebois development onto SW Costa Circle. (**Side trip:** Go right at roundabout to see "town center" area.)

15.1   Left onto path (Tonquin Trail) into Graham Oaks Park.

16.1   Right at four-way intersection to return to parking area.

16.2   End at Graham Oaks Park.

31 Stafford

DIFFICULTY: Very challenging
DISTANCE: 25.6-mile loop
ELEVATION GAIN: 2200 feet

Getting There: From I-5 southbound, take exit 299A for Oregon Rte. 43 south, toward Lake Oswego. Follow OR 43 approximately 6.6 miles through downtown Lake Oswego and go left onto Ladd St., then right onto Furnace St. into George Rogers Park.

Transit: Take TriMet bus No. 35 to S. State St. and Middle Crest Rd. Bicycle east on Wilbur St. 2 blocks to Furnace St.; go right into George Rogers Park.

This ride has a little bit of everything: suburban exploration, a stretch of Willamette riverfront, hills to climb, and great views. It's a ride for when you want both a workout and a few good reasons to stop along the way. Be warned: it's got four long hills and a few stretches of road with a nonexistent shoulder and swift traffic. Residents are used to bicyclists around here, though, so if you stay visible and polite, everything should be fine.

Begin at George Rogers Park, a gem of a park that's home to Lake Oswego's original river landing—now an inviting beach—and the remains of its iron furnace. (Yes, before the lakeside mansions and upscale boutiques, Lake Oswego was one of the West's original industrial towns.)

Cross Oregon Route 43 and continue up McVey Avenue, where the climbing starts gently enough. There's a bike lane of sorts here, but its twists, turns, and interruptions will probably persuade you to ride in the roadway. A proper path begins past the Oswego Pioneer Cemetery. At left is historic Luscher Farm, owned by the City of Lake Oswego. Visitors come to learn organic farming and gardening, work a community garden plot, or just poke around the farm's restored turn-of-the-20th-century buildings.

At the traffic circle, you cross Rosemont Road and begin the long descent into the lower Tualatin Valley (also known as the Stafford Basin). If you're wondering how it is that you so abruptly moved from suburbia to countryside, remember those three magic letters: UGB (see "The UGB" sidebar before Ride 24).

Stafford has recently become a land-use planning battleground. With great views and good access to freeways, it tempts developers with dreams of the millions to be made replicating the high-end housing just over the hill in Lake Oswego and West Linn. Not everyone

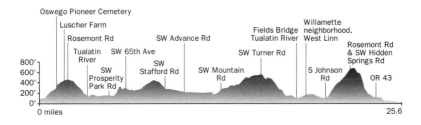

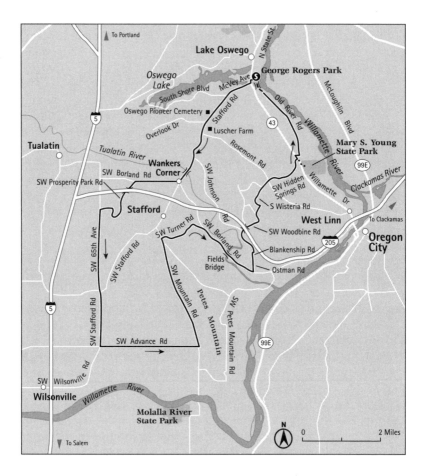

shares these dreams, though, and some of them, already proud owners of their 10 acres of Stafford heaven, are dug in against further growth.

The issue came to a head in 2009, when Metro, the regional government, launched a far-sighted effort to plan for long-term growth. The final product was a map designating which areas will urbanize and which will remain rural for the next 50 years. Stafford proved to be one of the most contentious areas. After protracted debate, the developers won out. So enjoy this countryside while you still can.

But for now, focus on the road! Stafford Road in this stretch has a soft dirt shoulder, maybe a foot wide, next to a bike-eating ditch. Don't even try to let cars pass. Take the whole lane—you probably won't have trouble reaching the 40-mile-per-hour speed limit anyway. You soon cross the Tualatin River and reach the traffic circle at Wankers Corner (that

Lake Oswego's heritage: the old iron furnace in George Rogers Park

really is the name—though locals insist it's pronounced "Wonkers") and strike westward on SW Borland Road.

Soon you head left onto SW Prosperity Park Road, under Interstate 205 and into deep woods. A mile and half later, you emerge into open country sloping gently toward the Willamette River. Go left onto SW 65th Avenue, turn right onto on SW Stafford Road and cross Boeckman Creek. Though it looks a little more convincingly rural out here, chances are still good that the roaring engine about to pass you powers a Hummer, not a tractor. At SW Advance Road the route skirts Wilsonville's Urban Growth Boundary and then strikes eastward.

The country empties out as you cross Newland Creek. Petes Mountain looms ahead. Now comes a highlight: the long, gradual climb up aptly named SW Mountain Road, with views west toward Parrett Mountain (Ride 30) and Chehalem Ridge (Ride 29). After nearly 3 miles of climbing, you gain the ridgetop—then immediately plunge down the other side on a steep descent down SW Turner Road to the Tualatin River. Go right at SW Borland Road to cross the river, into West Linn's Willamette neighborhood. A few neighborhood streets later, a left turn on SW Johnson Road leads right back out of town.

At SW Woodbine Road, you begin the last and biggest climb. Narrow and winding, lined with horse farms, gated mansion drives, and the occasional old farmhouse, Woodbine Road just about sums up Stafford's charms. Chances are good, though, that the next housing boom will transform this area. What might development look like? A likely answer awaits you at the top of the hill, across Rosemont Road in the ultrasuburban Hidden Springs neighborhood.

That said, the 16 percent grade on SW Hidden Springs Road focuses your attention on the road, not the houses. It leads very quickly down to OR 43 (a quick side trip to the right leads to Mary S. Young State Park; see Ride 2) and then to Old River Road, a quiet, wooded lane following the Willamette. Where Old River Road curves away from the river to become Glenmorrie Drive, look for a narrow path at right. It leads a final 0.5 mile to a bridge over Sucker Creek (Oswego Lake's outlet stream) and back to George Rogers Park.

MILEAGE LOG

0.0 Begin at George Rogers Park. Exit on Green St. and cross Willamette Dr. (OR 43) to continue uphill on McVey Ave., which becomes Stafford Rd. after intersection with S. Shore Blvd.

1.3 Oswego Pioneer Cemetery at right.

1.7 At Overlook Dr., path to Luscher Farm Park is at left.

2.1 At traffic circle at Rosemont Rd., go straight to continue downhill on Stafford Rd. and cross Tualatin River.

3.5 Right at traffic circle (Wankers Corner) onto SW Borland Rd.

4.7 Left onto SW Prosperity Park Rd.; pass under I-205.

6.4 Left onto SW 65th Ave.

8.7 Right onto SW Stafford Rd.

9.9 Left onto SW Advance Rd.

12.6 Left onto SW Mountain Rd.

15.6 Right onto SW Turner Rd.

16.9 Right onto SW Borland Rd. Cross Tualatin River on Fields Bridge.

18.3 Left onto Ostman Rd.

19.0 Right onto Blankenship Rd.

19.7 Left onto S. Johnson Rd.

20.4 Right onto SW Woodbine Rd., pass underneath I-205, and continue uphill. Woodbine becomes S. Wisteria Rd.

22.1 Cross Rosemont Rd. and continue downhill on SW Hidden Springs Rd.

23.3 Lest onto OR 43, then right at stoplight onto Cedar Oak Rd., then left onto Old River Rd. (**Side trip:** Go right onto OR 43 to visit Mary S. Young State Park.)

25.2 Right onto path (just before road curves sharply left) to continue along river.

25.6 Path crosses bridge to end at George Rogers Park.

UP THE WILLAMETTE VALLEY

The Willamette Valley stretches 100 miles upstream from Wilsonville, the metro region's southern boundary. The valley is a cycling paradise that could fill a guidebook of its own; here, I offer a sample of the country roads, quaint towns, and rural vistas to be found just beyond the Portland city limits.

32 Willamette Falls

DIFFICULTY: Challenging
DISTANCE: 26.8-mile loop
ELEVATION GAIN: 2000 feet

Getting There: From I-205 southbound, take exit 9 for Oregon Rte. 99E and go right onto McLoughlin Blvd. (OR 99E). Go left at first stoplight onto Dunes Dr., then left onto Clackamette Dr. John Storm Park is at right, under freeway bridge.

Transit: Ride MAX Green Line to Clackamas Town Center (see map for Ride 8); bicycle south on I-205 bike path. Across Clackamas River and past Clackamette Cove, path ends at Main St. in Oregon City. Go right and follow Main St. to Clackamette Dr. and John Storm Park (approximately 12.4 miles round-trip). Or catch TriMet bus No. 33 to Oregon City Transit Center; bicycle right onto Main St. to join the route near mile 0.5.

This ride visits some historic sites in Oregon City, followed by a scenic loop of rural riding, topped off with a ferry ride. If you're not up for the loop, you should nevertheless spend a few hours in Oregon City sightseeing by bike. On the other hand, if you're just here to ride, feel free to skip the historic sites and head straight out of town.

Since Oregon City is essentially a suburb of Portland, it's easy to overlook the place's significance. Established in 1829, it was the first

permanent American settlement west of the Mississippi, thousands of uncharted miles from the nearest town. Fort Vancouver was its only neighbor, and not a particularly friendly one. Present-day Portland was nothing but a riverside campsite hacked from the forest. (Isolation is relative, of course. Since time immemorial, Willamette Falls has been a mecca for Native people, a fishing site rivaling Celilo Falls on the Columbia.) Though a bit worn and faded today, and ringed by sprawl, Oregon City wears its heritage proudly. It's hard to pedal a block without encountering a historic site.

Begin your ride at John Storm Park along the Willamette River, where a path leads up to a promenade along McLoughlin Boulevard. Across McLoughlin, continue south on Main Street through downtown, which looks to be still partially stuck in the 1950s—in a good way. At the south end of downtown, take the elevator up to Seventh Street.

The elevator?

Yes. Oregon City happens to own and operate the only outdoor municipal elevator in the United States, whisking pedestrians and bicyclists 130 vertical feet up to the top of the bluff.

Why an elevator? Soon after its founding, Oregon City outgrew its narrow riverside bench and sprawled up the bluff, sprouting a second downtown on Singer Hill. To get from the lower town to the upper, residents had to climb 722 steps. By the early 20th century they were pretty tired of this arrangement, so they taxed themselves to build the "vertical street."

Up on Seventh Street, you'll immediately find yet another reason to stop: the John McLoughlin House, former home to the "Father of Oregon." It's on Center Street between Seventh and Eighth Streets—a stone's throw from the elevator. McLoughlin's home was moved here from the lower town and now, brilliantly restored, is a part of the Fort Vancouver National Historic Park. Tours are free (www.mcloughlin house.org). For more on McLoughlin, see the "Fort Vancouver" sidebar after Ride 46.

A few blocks down Seventh, turn right onto John Adams Street. It leads past the Francis Ermatinger House, where, according to lore,

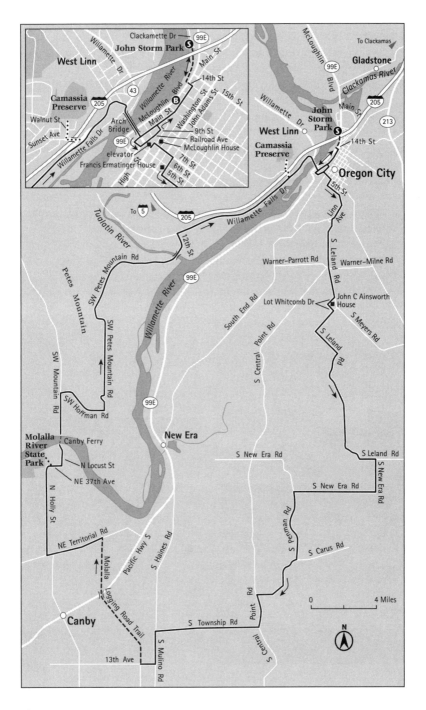

West Linn

Clackamette Dr — 99E
John Storm Park S

Willamette Dr

14th St

Camassia Preserve 205

Main St

43

McLoughlin Blvd

Washington St

John Adams St

15th St

Walnut St

Sunset Ave

Arch Bridge

Willamette Falls Dr

9th St
Railroad Ave
McLoughlin House

elevator
Francis Ermatinger House

7th St
6th St
5th St

High

99E B

To Clackamas

McLoughlin Blvd

99E **Gladstone**

Clackamas River

Willamette Dr

John Storm Park S

Main St

205

213

West Linn

14th St

Camassia Preserve

5th St

Oregon City

Linn Ave

Tualatin River

To 5

205

Willamette Falls Dr

12th St

Warner–Parrott Rd

S Leland Rd

Warner–Milne Rd

99E

Petes Mountain

SW Petes Mountain Rd

Willamette River

South End Rd

S Central Point Rd

John C Ainsworth House

Lot Whitcomb Dr

S Meyers Rd

S Leland Rd

SW Petes Mountain Rd

SW Mountain Rd

SW Hoffman Rd

99E

Molalla River State Park

Canby Ferry

N Locust St

NE 37th Ave

N Holly St

New Era

S New Era Rd

S New Era Rd

S Leland Rd

S New Era Rd

S Penman Rd

S Carus Rd

NE Territorial Rd

Pacific Hwy S

S Haines Rd

Molalla Logging Road Trail

Point Rd

S Central Rd

Canby

S Township Rd

13th Ave

S Mulino Rd

0   4 Miles

N

Francis Pettygrove and Asa Lovejoy held their famous coin toss. The two men were clearing a new settlement downstream; each wanted to name it after his hometown. The winner? Hint: Pettygrove was from Portland, Maine. Ermatinger's house is the oldest building in Clackamas County and one of the very first houses in Oregon.

There are dozens more historic sites around, but by now you're probably itching to ride. So go left onto Fifth Street and start cranking uphill, past newer neighborhoods to the edge of town. A quick detour off Leland Road goes past the John C. Ainsworth House, another of Oregon's earliest homes.

Now you speed downhill and out of town. The next few miles traverse some especially scenic country, past horse farms and humble ranches. The land slopes gradually toward the Willamette, flattening out at the outskirts of Canby.

At 13th Avenue you'll pick up the Molalla Logging Road Trail, a rail-to-trail path. It carries you into Canby and—mercifully—over Oregon Route 99E. (Canby's downtown is a few blocks to the west.) Soon you

Hot times on the Canby Ferry (Jonathan Maus/*Bike Portland*)

return to the countryside and reach the Willamette River. If you've got time for more detours, visit Molalla River State Park, where a trail leads along the Willamette to the Molalla's mouth.

Now that you've ridden an elevator, you might as well take a ferry. It runs year-round save for a few holidays (but double-check!) and is free for bicycles. You might have to wait a little while, but be glad for the rest: immediately off the ferry you start climbing.

Things look a little different on this side of the river: more mansions, fewer farms, fancier cars, lots of horses. This is country-squire country. From the ferry, climb SW Mountain Road to SW Hoffman Road, which turns into SW Petes Mountain Road and *really* climbs. The grade eases near the top. The view up here is fantastic, taking in the river, Oregon City, Mount Hood, and just about all of Clackamas County.

Now the road plunges down the north side of Petes Mountain as steeply as it climbed. Make sure your brakes are in good working order! At the bottom, it crosses the Tualatin River to enter West Linn. A quick climb from the river through the Willamette neighborhood brings you to Willamette Falls Drive, lined with boutiques and restaurants. Continue on Willamette Falls Drive past 10th Street, where most of the traffic disappears. Now the road draws nearer to the Willamette River, with periodic views across the water.

Just past a wastewater treatment plant, a spur road veers left to meet Sunset Avenue. If you're up for a 0.5-mile side trip, follow Sunset to Walnut Street, where at street's end an unobtrusive signs marks the entrance to Camassia, a 26-acre nature preserve owned by the Nature Conservancy. In April and May, Camassia's namesake camas flowers blossom a brilliant purple among restored oak groves. Views across the falls from Camassia's unique basalt outcroppings, scoured millennia ago by the Missoula Floods (see "The Floods" sidebar in Ride 43), make it worth a visit any time of year.

Back on Willamette Falls Drive, you soon reach what was once downtown West Linn, before I-205 ran it over. Not much remains. (Why *West* Linn, you ask? The original version, Linn City, was swept away in 1861's cataclysmic Willamette River flood. Residents prudently rebuilt higher up the hill.) A right turn onto OR 43 brings you to the historic Arch Bridge, built in 1923. As of this writing it's closed for renovation, scheduled to reopen in early 2013 (www.archrehab.com). In the meantime a shuttle carries bicyclists and pedestrians over the nearby I-205 bridge.

Back in Oregon City, loop back on Main Street and Railroad Avenue to retrace your route to John Storm Park.

MILEAGE LOG

0.0 Begin at John Storm Park. Go right onto Clackamette Dr., continue under I-205, then continue on path across Clackamette Dr. Path parallels McLoughlin Blvd. along a promenade.

0.4 Cross McLoughlin Blvd. at crosswalk on 14th St. Continue 1 block and go right onto Main St.

0.9 Left onto 6th St., left onto Railroad Ave., then immediate right into tunnel under railroad tracks to elevator. Elevate!

1.0 Exit elevator and follow path left. Cross at crosswalk and go right onto 7th Ave. McLoughlin House immediately at left.

1.2 Right onto John Adams St. Francis Ermatinger House at right.

1.3 Left onto 5th St., which curves right to become Linn Ave.

2.7 At Warner–Milne Rd., Linn Ave. becomes S. Leland Rd.

3.1 Right onto Lot Whitcomb Dr., just before S. Meyers Rd. John C. Ainsworth House at left (19130 Lot Whitcomb Dr.).

3.4 Right onto S. Leland Rd.

6.4 Right onto S. New Era Rd., which curves right.

8.2 Left onto S. Penman Rd.

9.2 Right onto S. Carus Rd.

10.2 Left at T intersection onto S. Central Point Rd.

10.7 Right onto S. Township Rd.

12.3 Left onto S. Mulino Rd.

12.8 Right onto 13th Ave.

13.1 Right onto Molalla Logging Road Trail through Canby.

15.2 Left onto NE Territorial Rd.

16.1 Right onto N. Holly St., which curves right to become NE 37th Ave.

17.4 Riverpark Dr. at left. (**Side trip:** Go left here to visit Molalla River State Park.) Continue on NE 37th Ave., which curves left to become N. Locust St.

17.8 Cross Willamette River on Canby Ferry; continue on SW Mountain Rd. Steep uphill!

18.7 Right onto SW Hoffman Rd., which curves left to become SW Petes Mountain Rd. Another steep uphill.

21.6 Begin descent of Petes Mountain.

22.8 Cross Tualatin River; road becomes Tualatin Ave., then curves left to become 12th St. in West Linn's Willamette neighborhood.

23.2 Right onto Willamette Falls Dr.

25.2 Chestnut St. at left. (**Side trip:** Go left to Sunset Ave., then immediately right onto Walnut St., which ends at Camassia Preserve.) Continue on Willamette Falls Dr.

25.7 Right onto OR 43 (Willamette Dr.). Cross Willamette River on Arch Bridge.

25.9 Right at bottom of bridge onto Main St., then left onto 6th St. and left onto Railroad Ave., which curves left to become 9th St.

26.2 Right onto Main St.

26.4 Left onto 14th St. Cross McLoughlin Blvd. (OR 99E) and go right onto promenade.

26.8 End at John Storm Park.

33 Champoeg

DIFFICULTY: Easy
DISTANCE: 8.5-mile Butteville Loop, 16.3-mile French Prairie Loop
ELEVATION GAIN: Butteville Loop 650 feet; French Prairie Loop 225 feet

Getting There: From I-5 southbound, take exit 278 toward Donald and Aurora. Go right onto Ehlen Rd. NE. After approximately 2.5 miles, go right onto Case Rd. NE, which curves left to become Champoeg Rd. NE. Park entrance is at right, approximately 6 miles from I-5. At entrance booth, go left and continue 1 mile to Riverside Day-use Area.

Transit: Take TriMet bus or WES to Tigard Transit Center; transfer to Yamhill County Transit Area bus to Newberg. Get off at the Safeway on SW 99E and N. Springbrook Rd. Ride south on Springbook; go left on S. St. Paul Hwy. (OR 219), cross river, and go left onto Champoeg Rd. NE to park entrance (12.4 miles round trip).

This ride tours Oregon's "birthplace," Champoeg State Park, where a 4-mile paved path visits historic farm fields, oak groves, and a wild

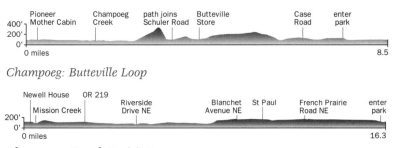

Champoeg: Butteville Loop

Champoeg: French Prairie Loop

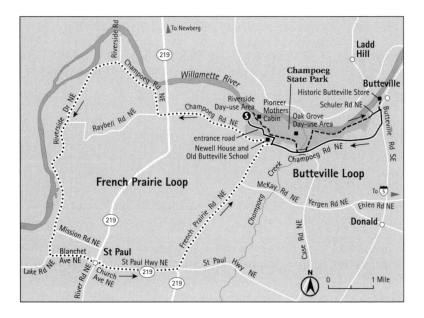

stretch of Willamette riverfront to end at the historic town of Butteville. It's one of the most scenic family rides anywhere in the state. For good measure, I've thrown in an easy road loop around French Prairie.

For the Butteville Loop, begin at the Riverside Day-use Area. The bike path leads east into woods, past a field, and to the Pioneer Mothers Cabin. The cabin dates only to 1931—a replica, built and maintained by the Daughters of the American Revolution—but is filled with artifacts donated by descendants of actual pioneers. It's open seasonally for tours.

The path continues southeast through more fields and woods to the Oak Grove Day-use Area, where the valley's iconic oaks spread high and wide. This place is beautiful in every season. In spring, the buds glow green; in summer, the dense foliage casts welcome shade; in autumn, golden leaves blanket the path; in winter, river winds make the naked oak limbs dance. Here you can understand why so many generations of newcomers regarded Oregon as a promised land.

The path briefly joins the park's entrance road to cross Champoeg Creek and then veers left. For the next mile or so it parallels the Willamette River, then climbs several hundred feet into the forest. This short but surprisingly steep hill is the only stretch likely to challenge beginners. The path drops again to meet Schuler Road NE, a narrow lane leading to Champoeg Road NE. The path resumes here and follows the road's shoulder (against traffic) for a few hundred yards to end in Butteville.

Like Champoeg, Butteville is an old river town, a place to which nearby farmers hauled their harvest of wheat, packed in hand-stitched sacks, for shipment to Portland and beyond. Butteville survived the catastrophic 1861 flood that drowned so many river towns (including Champoeg), but it was nevertheless doomed as rail lines and, later, automobiles stole trade from the riverboats. Its lifeblood gone, Butteville withered.

A few buildings remain from the heyday, most notably the Historic Butteville Store. In business since 1863, it's now owned by Oregon State Parks and operated seasonally by the nonprofit Friends of Champoeg. Stop in for a sandwich and check out the Heritage Room. It claims to be the oldest continually operating business in Oregon.

To return, you can simply retrace your route (8 miles round-trip), but to see a little more of the surrounding country, instead loop back on a highly scenic stretch of Champoeg Road NE. Back at Champoeg State Park, follow the entrance road left at the ranger station to ride park roads back to the Riverside Day-use Area.

~~~~~~

THE CHAMPOEG STORY

How did the village of Champoeg (pronounced "sham-POO-ee"), never more than a few souls, earn the title of "Oregon's Birthplace"? Here's a quick version of the story.

In the early 1800s, fur traders employed by the Hudson's Bay Company ventured up the Willamette Valley to trade with the native Kalapuya people. They built trading posts, including one at Champoeg in 1813. Most of the traders were French Canadians, recruited from poverty-stricken, frigid Quebec villages. Enchanted by the valley's fertile soil and benign climate, many chose to quit the grueling fur trade and take up farming.

When the Oregon Trail opened in the 1840s, Americans poured into the valley. By that time, so many Hudson's Bay men had settled around Champoeg that the Americans called the area French Prairie. More settlers meant more conflicts. Since Britain and the United States both claimed the Oregon Territory, there was no government to which the settlers could turn for redress. Left to take care of their own affairs, they began meeting to hash out common concerns—first and foremost, the threat posed by wolves. (Yes, wolves!) These meetings helped establish some basic rules for coexistence.

Nevertheless, settlers struggled over the issue of government. The Americans considered Oregon to be American territory. Most of the French

Canadians, though no lovers of the British, feared drowning in a sea of Americans and thus supported Britain's territorial claim. The issue came to a head in May 1843, when American settlers proposed to establish a provisional government. A contingent of French Canadians and Americans met to vote on the idea. Since this provisional government was patterned after American territorial governments, a "yes" vote was essentially a vote for American sovereignty.

Lore has it—the actual historical record is conflicted—that the final vote was 52 to 50 in favor, with all Americans voting yes and all but two French Canadians voting no. This vote, ostensibly, marked the "beginning" of Oregon as we know it.

That was the official story for the next 100 years or so, promoted by red-blooded Oregon boosters as Oregon's Plymouth Rock and Constitutional Convention rolled into one, whereby scruffy farmers arguing about wolves spontaneously created a virtuous democracy in the wilderness. In its most inflated form, the story of Champoeg's vote credits the heroic pioneers—and especially those two French guys who voted with us!—with securing the Pacific Northwest for the United States and thus fulfilling the promise of Manifest Destiny. (It probably goes without saying that this story omits plenty. The Kalapuya, for one, didn't get to vote with the settlers usurping their land.)

What became of Champoeg? Months after the vote, the provisional government moved to Oregon City. Within a few years, the United States secured Oregon and replaced the provisional government with a territorial one. Champoeg resumed its humble existence as a riverfront farm town. In 1861, already fading as railroads drew trade away from the river, Champoeg drowned under the cataclysmic Willamette River flood of 1861. It was never rebuilt. Today it's the site of a state park.

~~~~~~

The second loop is a straightforward road tour through the fertile farmland of French Prairie, Oregon's original breadbasket. It begins at the park entrance and heads west on Champoeg Road NE, which has a good shoulder here and fairly light traffic. Immediately at right is the Newell House Museum, a reconstructed 1852 home also owned by the Daughters of the American Revolution. It's a worthwhile side trip to tour the house, grounds, and the old Butteville School, a pre–Civil War era one-room schoolhouse. This is quiet rural country, right across the river from suburban Wilsonville and Newberg, but a world apart. Views stretch north to Parrett Mountain and south across French Prairie.

After it crosses Oregon Route 219, Champoeg Road NE loses its

Among the oaks at Champoeg State Park (Oregon State Parks)

shoulder but also its traffic, becoming Riverside Drive NE, a lonely back road connecting a handful of farms along the Willamette. Chances are good you'll have the place to yourself, aside from a few farmers and sightseers.

Looping back east along Blanchet Avenue NE, you pass through the bustling metropolis of St. Paul—bustling, that is, if you happen to visit on the Fourth of July, when this tiny burg mounts one of the nation's most elite rodeos. (This is a serious affair: nearly 1000 cowboys and cowgirls, including the top pros, flock here from across the nation to compete for cash prizes running into six figures.) From St. Paul, continue east on OR 219 to French Prairie Road NE, another quiet byway that returns you to Champoeg.

There are a lot more cycling possibilities in this scenic area, such as the excellent tour along the Willamette Valley Scenic Bikeway to Willamette Mission State Park. Make a night of it: both Champoeg and Willamette Mission have hiker-biker campsites, which are nearly always available. You could ride here straight from Portland via Stafford, the Canby Ferry, and Aurora.

MILEAGE LOG

Butteville Loop:

0.0 Begin at Riverside Day-use Area in Champoeg State Park.

0.2 Pioneer Mothers Cabin parking area. Path continues at far end of parking lot.

1.0 Intersection (at crosswalk) with trail back to visitor center. Continue on path toward Oak Grove Day-use Area and campground.

1.6 Path briefly follows road on left shoulder (opposite traffic) to cross Champoeg Creek, then immediately heads left toward Willamette River.

3.4 Path joins Schuler Rd. NE.

3.8 Left to stay on path as it follows Butteville Rd. NE on left shoulder (opposite traffic).

4.0 Left onto Butte St. NE at path's end. Historic Butteville Store at right. (**Option:** Retrace route to return, 8 miles round-trip.) From Butteville Store, retrace route to Schuler Rd. NE and continue straight on Butteville Rd. NE.

4.5 Right onto Champoeg Rd. NE.

6.5 At stop sign at Case Rd. NE, continue straight on Champoeg Rd. NE.

7.4 Right to enter park.

7.5 Left at entrance booth to follow park road to Riverside Day-use Area.

8.5 End at Riverside Day-use Area.

French Prairie Loop:

0.0 From park entrance, right onto Champoeg Rd. NE.

0.2 Right at stop sign to stay on Champoeg Rd. NE. Newell House at right.

2.8 Cross OR 219 and take first right to continue on Champoeg Rd. NE.

4.5 Road curves left to become Riverside Dr. NE.

9.6 Left onto Blanchet Ave. NE.

10.7 Left onto River Rd. NE in St. Paul, then right onto Church Ave. NE, which becomes St. Paul Hwy. NE (OR 219).

12.7 Left onto French Prairie Rd. NE.

16.1 Right onto Champoeg Rd. NE.

16.3 Left into Champoeg State Park to end at park entrance.

34 Yamhill Wine Country

~~~~~~

DIFFICULTY: Moderate to Challenging
DISTANCE: 29.5-mile loop
ELEVATION GAIN: 1100 feet

Getting There: From I-5 southbound, take exit 294 and follow Oregon Rte. 99W southwest to Newberg, then continue west on OR 240 to Yamhill. On summer weekends, when OR 99W gets terribly backed up,

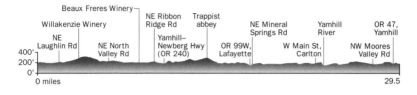

you're better off going to Forest Grove and continuing south on OR 47 approximately 15.5 miles to Yamhill. At stoplight in Yamhill, proceed south on OR 47, then left onto E. Third St. to Beulah Park at right.

Transit: Take MAX (Blue Line) to Hillsboro Central station and transfer to Yamhill County Area Transit bus 33 to Yamhill. Weekdays only.

Yamhill County is Oregon's wine heartland, home to the pinot noirs that have won worldwide acclaim. It's a territory of grape-clad, rolling hills and unpretentious towns, single-stoplight places where tractors and logging trucks still roll down Main Street. This ride visits several of those towns on a loop linking the Chehalem Creek and Yamhill River valleys. Along the way, it passes a few of Oregon's elite wineries, plus a Trappist abbey set in the forest.

Though Yamhill is a very scenic place to ride, some roads are busy and few have a shoulder. Most of this ride sticks to back roads, but even these require a certain amount of vigilance, especially if you choose to sample the local goods. No doubt some of the drivers have too.

Begin at Beulah Park in Yamhill, a little town whose low-key atmosphere belies the world-class grapes growing all around. The first mile or two out of town can be busy. You leave most of the traffic behind at NE Laughlin Road, which climbs past the massive Willakenzie Winery (at left) to a low divide. On the back side, Laughlin drops into the upper reaches of Chehalem Creek and then briefly, imperceptibly dips into the Tualatin basin along Ayers Creek. A right turn at NE North Valley Road returns you to Chehalem Creek. Seven miles into the ride, you've already visited three watersheds!

Beaux Freres winery is about 2 miles down NE North Valley Road on the left. A few miles farther, the hills recede and the valley widens. Go right onto NE Ribbon Ridge Road and right again onto the Yamhill–Newberg Highway (Oregon Route 240). Be cautious on this busy road, especially so at the intersection with NE Kuehne Road 0.5 mile farther.

NE Kuehne Road leads past some giant vineyards and across another low divide, back into the Yamhill basin. After NE Hendricks Road splits off to the right, things quiet down as you follow NE Abbey Road. The road skirts Our Lady of Guadalupe Trappist Abbey, tucked at the base of a broad, forested ridge. Monks pursue the contemplative traditions of their thousand-year-old order, supporting themselves by binding books, storing wine for nearby wineries, and managing their 1300-acre forest. They welcome visitors.

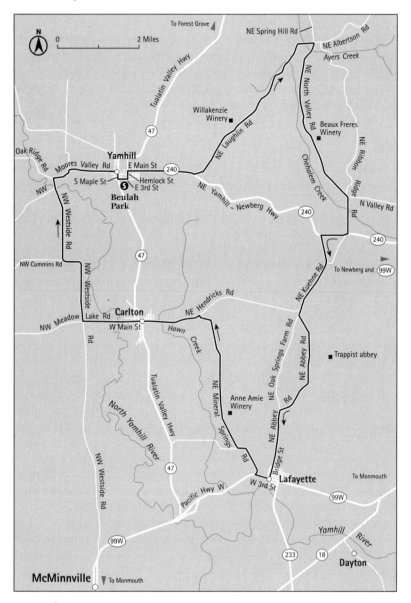

~~~~~~

THE WINE BOOM

Yamhill is a relative newcomer among wine regions. Though the Willamette Valley has produced wine since the earliest pioneer days, for a century that wine was mediocre at best and strictly for local consumption. In the 1960s a new generation of winemakers arrived, many of them Napa Valley exiles in search of cheaper land and a more down-to-earth atmosphere. In Yamhill County they found a climate slightly drier than the rest of the valley—sheltered by the Coast Range—and volcanic soils similar to that of certain wine regions in France.

Winemakers elsewhere were skeptical. So were local farmers, accustomed to growing fruit, nuts, and timber. But after some trial and error, Yamhill's wine pioneers homed in on the pinot noir grape. Four decades later, Yamhill pinots are among the world's elite. This has brought fame and a measure of fortune to what was long a hardscrabble county. It's also attracted newer wine entrepreneurs, ranging from wealthy hobby-farming retirees to European wine scions in search of fresh opportunities. Vineyards have spread, gourmet restaurants have opened, and mansions have sprouted on the hills like weeds, many in the faux-Tuscan style.

Wine success has made Yamhill more chic and a lot more expensive, but it hasn't fundamentally changed the rural feel. Most wineries are still small-scale affairs, family-owned and operated. The older economy—grazing, timber, fruits, nuts—persists. Towns like Carlton, Yamhill, and Dundee remain the kind of places where plenty of the wine drinkers still have mud on their boots.

~~~~~~

Abbey Road continues down a tranquil valley to the town of Lafayette and OR 99W. Almost as soon you've reached the highway, you leave it again, heading right onto NE Mineral Springs Road and up to more wine country in the beautiful, broad valley of Hawn Creek. Anne Amie winery, near mile 19, sits atop a hill at the end of a long driveway to the right.

Mineral Springs Road climbs gradually among heavily cultivated fields. The scenery could be Tuscan, minus hilltop castles. It's an exquisitely picturesque, though thoroughly humanized, landscape. (The oak grasslands that once predominated here are nearly all gone, ploughed under the vineyards. In fact this habitat type, once common across the Willamette Valley, is now rarer than the old-growth conifer forests that have occasioned so many battles over logging and endangered species.)

Clearing storm, Spring Hill Road

When you turn onto NE Hendricks Road, the traffic returns. It slows again at the edge of Carlton, a town where wine-tasting rooms far exceed stoplights. Now that you're on the home stretch, this is a good spot to sample the local fare. Then continue west, across the North Yamhill River on NW Meadow Lake Road, and go right onto NW Westside Road. Follow it north through a plain at the edge of the Coast Range. You'll cross the river a second time before NW Moores Valley Road, which carries you up and out of this shallow valley, back to Yamhill and Beulah Park.

MILEAGE LOG

0.0 Begin at Beulah Park. Go left (north) onto Hemlock St., then right onto E. Main St. (OR 240).

1.7 Left onto NE Laughlin Rd.

3.2 Willakenzie Winery on left.

6.0 Right onto NE North Valley Rd.

8.5 Beaux Freres Winery at left.

9.7 Slight right onto NE Ribbon Ridge Rd.

10.6 Right onto Yamhill–Newberg Hwy. (OR 240).

11.3 Left onto NE Kuehne Rd. (also called NE Carlton–Chehalem Creek Rd.).

13.1 When NE Hendricks Rd. veers off to right, continue straight.

13.2 Bear left onto NE Abbey Rd.

14.2 Trappist abbey entrance at left.
16.5 NE Abbey Rd. becomes Bridge St. in Lafayette.
17.2 Right onto W. 3rd St. (OR 99W) in Lafayette.
17.5 Right onto NE Mineral Springs Rd.
19.0 Anne Amie Winery at right.
21.5 Left onto NE Hendricks Rd.
22.9 At stoplights in Carlton, continue straight on W. Main St., which crosses Yamhill River west of town and becomes NW Meadow Lake Rd.
24.2 Right onto NW Westside Rd.
27.7 NW Westside Rd. curves right to join NW Moores Valley Rd.
29.2 Right at stoplight onto S. Maple St. (OR 47) in Yamhill, then left onto E. 3rd St.
29.5 End at Beulah Park.

35 Eola Hills

DIFFICULTY: Challenging
DISTANCE: 53.5-mile loop
ELEVATION GAIN: 2250 feet

Getting There: From I-5 southbound, take exit 260A, Salem Pkwy., and continue approximately 4.8 miles south into downtown Salem. Turn right onto Union St. NE and follow it south under bridges to Riverfront Park.

Transit: You can get to Salem on Amtrak (www.amtrakcascades .com), but the schedule will likely necessitate an overnight. Alternately (and weekdays only), take WES to Wilsonville and transfer to South Metro Area Regional Transit (SMART) bus to Salem Transit Center. Join the route on Chemeketa Street NE around mile 0.4.

The good people of Salem might understandably balk at being annexed to Portland, even if only for the purposes of a bicycling guidebook. Clearly, we're not in the Portland metro area anymore. But the countryside around Salem is so pleasant, and so easy to reach, that it'd be a shame to skip it in the name of geographical precision. Besides, you have a civic duty to visit our state capitol at least once.

Begin at Riverfront Park. For most of the 20th century, this site was a paper mill, powering Salem's economy and fouling its air. Citizens had long dreamed of a park here, so when the plant closed in the 1980s,

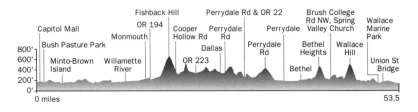

the city bought the land; the park finally opened in 1996. A token of the site's past remains in the form of a massive concrete ball. It stored acid for pulping wood; now it's been covered in about 86,000 decorative tiles and rechristened *Eco-Earth.*

From the park, ride east through downtown on Chemeketa Street NE to reach the Capitol Mall. At the mall's far end looms the capitol building, a massive cylinder capped by the *Golden Pioneer,* a gilded, 22-foot-tall statue of an idealized Oregonian, ax in hand. The building is Oregon's third capitol, built in 1938 after the first two burned. Its vast rotunda is worth a look, as are the sumptuously wood-paneled legislative chambers.

Continue south past the capitol and through Wilson Park on Winter Street SE. It leads you past Willamette University. This, the oldest university west of the Mississippi River, dates back to Salem's beginnings as a Methodist mission to the native Kalapuya people. When the Kalapuya inexplicably declined to trade their ancient ways for lives of servitude at the Methodists' Indian Labor School, the school foundered, as did the entire missionary venture. Fortunately for the missionaries (though not for the Kalapuya), rapid settlement created plenty of American children in need of learning. So the Indian Labor School reinvented itself as the Oregon Institute—later renamed Willamette University—to educate the state's future leaders.

Winter Street ends at Bush Pasture Park, the former estate of Asahel Bush, founder of Salem's newspaper. A paved path loops through the stately park to end at Bush's old mansion, now a museum. The barn next door houses contemporary art.

Now you're ready to head south out of town on River Road S. After a mile, go right onto Minto Island Road SW to loop through 898-acre Minto-Brown City Park, a patchwork of farm fields, orchards, and natural areas filling the Willamette's floodplain. From the road, go left onto a path leading along a slough. The Salem Hills rise abruptly to the southeast. City gives way to country quickly and gracefully.

The path ends at Homestead Road. Go left to return to River Road S. and turn right. After 10 miles of quiet country riding, you cross a

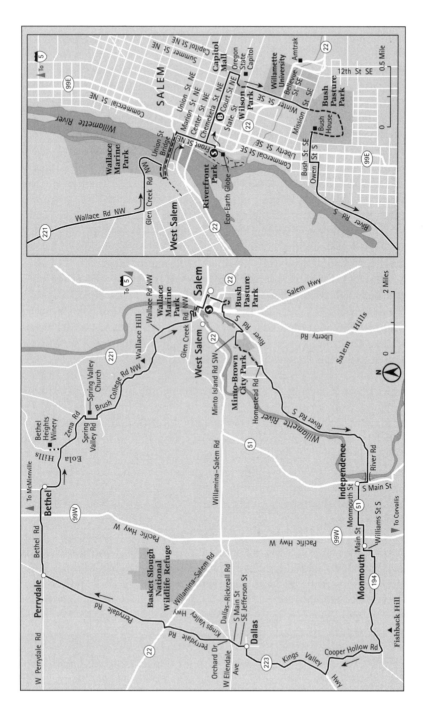

lonesome reach of the Willamette River to arrive at Independence. Founded in the 1840s by emigrants from that more famous Independence (in Missouri), the town was once a bustling river port. That changed when roads and rail displaced the river as the major means of travel. Life then got very quiet. Unlike the many other Willamette River towns that simply disappeared, Independence turned its isolation into a virtue, preserving and restoring its quaint downtown.

The route now heads west on Oregon Route 51, crossing OR 99W to reach the only slightly busier town of Monmouth and then continuing west to the Coast Range foothills. Go right onto Cooper Hollow Road and right again onto the Kings Valley Highway (OR 223). You're now heading north, following a stretch of the old Applegate Trail, which brought early settlers up from Southern Oregon and California. It's classic Willamette Valley country: tidy farms, tumbledown homesteads, and polished estates housing California retirees.

The highway swings through the town of Dallas. Several miles later, it crosses OR 22 and into gently rolling terrain below the Eola Hills. Vineyards climb knolls above the wetlands of Basket Slough National Wildlife Refuge. Lone oaks and crumbling barns mark the old farmsteads. On summer afternoons, crisp ocean breezes sneak through a gap in the Coast Range while the sun tints hills gold.

At the crossroad of Perrydale, head right. You recross OR 99W in the flats near Bethel and then begin a long climb up and over the Eola Hills via Zena Road. Wineries abound. A convenient one for a side trip is Bethel Heights, just up Bethel Heights Road from Zena Road's summit. The wine and views are superb—and the ride from here is mostly downhill! Back on Zena Road, go right onto Spring Valley Road, which brings you to the Spring Valley Presbyterian Church, built in 1858. The church presides over a landscape scarcely changed since then. Orderly fields stretch down to the Willamette; firs and maples clad the highest Eola Hills above.

With a little luck, this pastoral scene will endure. Salem's Urban Growth Boundary keeps the capital's sprawl from encroaching this farmland. Far-sighted landowners have also taken steps to protect the Eola hilltops, working with the Trust for Public Land to put conservation easements over thousands of acres of forest, ensuring they'll continue to provide wood and wildlife habitat in perpetuity. (The alternative, sooner or later, is McMansions.)

Spring Valley Church, desolate in midwinter

210 UP THE WILLAMETTE VALLEY

The final cruise down Brush College Road abruptly transports you from the 19th century into the 21st, with pioneer farms giving way to subdivisions. Go right onto Wallace Road NW and cruise a few miles through West Salem to reach Wallace Marine Park. From here, a recently built pedestrian path crosses the Willamette via the old Union Street rail bridge. Riverfront Park is just a few hundreds yards south down the road to your right.

MILEAGE LOG

0.0 Begin in Riverfront Park. Go left onto Front St. NE, then right onto Chemeketa St. NE.

0.7 Right onto pedestrian path (just before underpass) into Capitol Mall. Cross Court St. NE, proceed right around capitol, and continue through Wilson Park. Cross State St. at crosswalk and continue south on Winter St. SE.

1.4 Cross Mission St. SE into Bush Pasture Park and continue on path circling Willamette University sports fields. Past baseball field, follow path's right fork to loop back through park to Bush House.

2.1 Left onto Bush St. SE to exit park.

2.4 Left onto Commercial St. SE, then right onto Owens St. S., which becomes River Rd. S.

3.6 Right onto Minto Island Rd. SW, then left onto path past parking area. Stay left at all intersections (slough and orchards at right).

5.9 Path ends at Homestead Rd. Left to continue under rail trestle, then right onto River Rd. S.

13.5 Cross Willamette River on Independence Bridge (caution), then go right onto S. Main St. (OR 51) in Independence.

13.9 Left onto Monmouth St., which soon becomes Monmouth–Independence Hwy. (OR 51).

16.8 Left onto Whitman St. S. in Monmouth, which becomes Monmouth Hwy. (OR 194) upon leaving town.

20.4 Crest of Fishback Hill.

21.4 Right onto Cooper Hollow Rd.

24.3 Right onto Kings Valley Hwy. (OR 223).

28.3 Left onto SE Jefferson St. in downtown Dallas; merges with S. Main St.

29.0 Cross W. Ellendale Ave. and go left onto Orchard Dr., which becomes Perrydale Rd.

31.9 Cross OR 22 to continue on Perrydale.

37.6 Right onto Bethel Rd. in Perrydale.

41.2 Past OR 99W intersection, Bethel Rd. becomes Zena Road NW in Bethel.
43.3 Side trip: Go left off Zena Rd. to visit Bethel Heights Winery.
45.1 Right onto Spring Valley Rd. NW, then immediate right onto Brush College Rd. NW. Spring Valley Church at left.
48.2 Crest of Wallace Hill.
50.5 Right onto Wallace Rd. NW.
52.2 Left onto Glen Creek Rd. to enter Wallace Marine Park.
52.9 Bear right onto ramp, then left onto Union St. Bridge.
53.2 Right onto Water St. NE.
53.5 End in Riverfront Park.

36 Mount Angel and Silverton

DIFFICULTY: Moderate
DISTANCE: 36.6-mile loop; option: 22.1-mile loop
ELEVATION GAIN: 1600 feet; option 425 feet

Getting There: From I-5 southbound, take exit 282A for Canby-Hubbard. Follow Portland-Hubbard Hwy., then Oregon Rte. 99E, south through Hubbard and Woodburn. In Woodburn, go left onto Young St. at a stoplight and follow OR 214 east and south to Mount Angel.

This tour visits Mount Angel and Silverton, a pair of charming Willamette Valley towns surrounded by nurseries, grass-seed and flower farms, and Christmas trees. The isolated volcanic butte named Mount Angel, crowned by a Benedictine abbey, rises above the Pudding River's broad plain like an island and Mount Hood dominates the far horizon. There may be no other place in Oregon where human and natural landscapes complement one another so perfectly.

The full tour climbs high into the Silverton hills to magnificent valley views. If you're short on time or energy, follow the shorter and mostly flat 22.1-mile alternate route. Both are well worth the hour's drive from Portland.

Begin at College and Main Streets in Mount Angel, a tidy farm town that wears its German Catholic heritage prominently on its sleeve. If the half-timbered building facades don't clue you in, the recently built glockenspiel—reputedly the largest in the United States—will. The majestic spire of St. Marys Church, set against the forests and

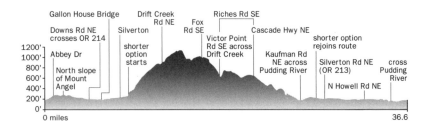

vineyards climbing Mount Angel's flank, gives the town a plausibly European look. What really defines Mount Angel, though, is its annual Oktoberfest, when visitors descend on this burg by the thousands to drink beer, eat pretzels, and listen to oompah bands.

Looming over town is Mount Angel itself. To the Kalapuya people it is Tapalamaho, a place of spiritual significance. Since 1883 it's also been home to a Benedictine abbey. The abbey's monks came here from a village high in the Swiss Alps called Engelberg, German for—you guessed it—"Mount Angel." Fearing persecution in their homeland, they followed a wave of German Catholic settlers to the Willamette Valley. They've been worshiping, teaching, and offering visitors a place for rest and spiritual contemplation ever since.

College Street leads southeast right past the abbey's entrance. A 1.5-mile, 200-foot out-and-back detour on Abbey Drive, lined with stations of the cross, climbs through a deep forest to the abbey's hilltop campus. There's a lot to explore up here, but don't miss the library. Designed by the famed Finnish architect Alvar Aalto, it's a masterpiece of light and quiet, framing broad valley views. On the other end of the aesthetic spectrum, check out the museum, home to Civil War artifacts, a two-headed sheep, and what it claims is the world's largest pig hairball.

Back on the main route, skirt Mount Angel's flank on E. College Street, then loop around to the west on Downs Road NE. Country lanes lead you across Oregon Route 214 south to Gallon House Bridge. Built in 1916 and recently renovated, it's Oregon's oldest covered bridge.

A few miles farther south you arrive in Silverton, a strong contender for the title of quaintest town in Oregon. Restaurants, cafes, and antique shops fill lovingly restored buildings in the immaculate town center, while massive Douglas firs shade Coolidge-McClaine Park (restrooms) on Silver Creek. Every block seems to have a church of some sort. Somehow, the small-town perfection feels genuine. This is an actual community, not a movie set. (That said, it *has* been used as a movie set. Remember *Bandits*?)

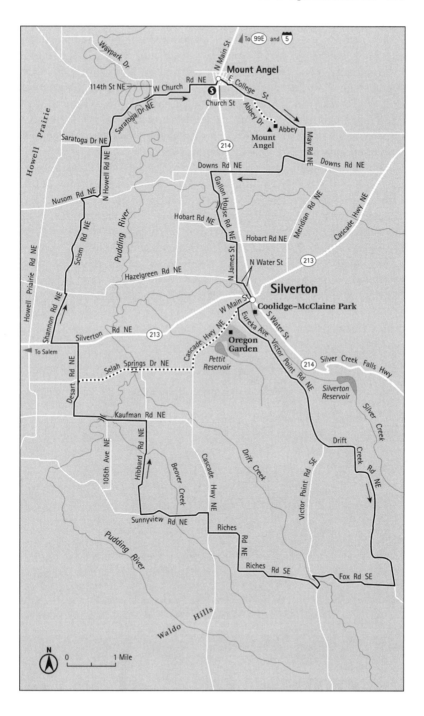

You could while away an afternoon in Silverton, but the bike beckons! So pedal up W. Main Street and head left, up Eureka Avenue. (Alternatively, you can continue straight on W. Main to the Cascade Highway for a shorter loop, which rejoins the main route at about mile 27.2. If you take the shorter option, you'll have plenty of time to visit the Oregon Garden, an elaborately landscaped showcase for Oregon's nursery industry. There's also a relocated Frank Lloyd Wright designed home here, restored and open to the public.)

On the main route, get ready for a climb. Eureka Avenue carries you up and out of town, becoming Victor Point Road NE. You now climb high above Silverton's reservoir and the surprisingly grand "canyon" of Silver Creek. The climbing continues on Drift Creek Road NE, with views opening in nearly every direction: southeast toward Silver Falls State Park, east to the High Cascades, west and south across the valley.

Fox Road SE turns you west, climbing to yet another sweeping view before a long, rolling descent down to the valley floor at Howell Prairie. Big views continue most of the way, especially on the Cascade

Gallon House Bridge, oldest covered bridge in the state

Highway (but watch for trucks here) and Sunnyview Road SE. Lone oaks and bunched stands of Douglas fir dot the rolling fields, accompanied by old farmsteads and the occasional McMansion.

The final miles follow forks of the meandering Pudding River through woods and fields on very quiet back roads. A short climb up from the river brings you back to Mount Angel. Time for the celebratory pretzel and beer!

A final note: you could easily extend the main route in any direction. Head east to Scotts Mills in the Cascade foothills, north along Meridian Road to Monitor and Aurora, west to French Prairie and Champoeg (see Ride 33), or—best of all—farther south along Drift Creek Road NE to Silver Falls State Park. This last suggestion makes for a great overnight tour.

MILEAGE LOG

0.0 Begin at N. Main St. (OR 214) and E. College St. Go left (east) on E. College St.

0.2 Left to stay on E. College St.

0.8 Abbey Dr. at right. (**Side trip:** Go right to visit abbey.) Continue on E. College St.

2.1 Right onto May Rd. NE.

2.8 Right onto Downs Rd. NE.

4.6 Cross OR 214 and continue.

5.1 Left onto Gallon House Rd. NE.

5.8 Cross Gallon House Bridge.

6.2 Left onto Hobart Rd. NE.

6.7 Right onto N. James St.

7.5 Left onto N. Water St. Cross W. C St. into downtown Silverton.

8.1 Right onto W. Main St.

8.5 Veer left onto Eureka Ave., which becomes Victor Point Rd. NE. (**Option:** Continue straight on W. Main St. for shorter 22.1-mile loop; street becomes Cascade Hwy. NE past Oregon Garden. Go right onto Selah Springs Dr. NE, then right at Desart Rd. NE to rejoin route near mile 27.)

11.9 Victor Point Rd. becomes Drift Creek Rd. NE.

16.0 Right onto Fox Rd. SE.

17.8 Left onto Victor Point Rd. SE to cross Drift Creek, then right onto Riches Rd. SE.

21.2 Right onto Cascade Hwy. NE.

21.6 Left onto Sunnyview Rd. NE.

23.1 Right onto Hibbard Rd. NE.

25.0 Left onto Kaufman Rd. NE. Cross Pudding River in about 1 mile.

26.5 Right onto Desart Rd. NE. (**Option:** Shorter loop rejoins main route in about 0.7 mile.)

28.0 Left onto Silverton Rd. NE (OR 213).

28.6 Right onto Shannon Rd. NE.

29.7 Left onto Hazelgreen Rd. NE, then immediate right onto Scism Rd. NE.

31.7 Right onto Nusom Rd. NE.

32.1 Left onto N. Howell Rd. NE.

33.1 Right onto Saratoga Dr. NE.

34.9 Just after crossing Pudding River, left onto 114th St. NE, then immediate right onto W. Church Rd. NE.

36.6 Left onto N. Main St. (OR 214) to end in Mount Angel.

37 Molalla River

DIFFICULTY: Challenging
DISTANCE: 28.4 miles; option: 33.9-mile loop
ELEVATION GAIN: 1100 feet; option 2500 feet

Getting There: From I-205 southbound, take exit 10 for Oregon Rte. 213 toward Molalla. Follow OR 213 approximately 16.5 miles, then go left onto OR 211 (W. Main St.) in Molalla. At far end of town, go right onto S. Mathias Rd., then veer left onto S. Feyrer Park Rd. Go about 1.6 miles to Feyrer County Park at left.

Transit: Take TriMet bus No. 99 (weekdays only) or No. 33 to Clackamas Community College in Oregon City; transfer to South Clackamas Transportation District bus to Molalla. Bicycle south along N. Molalla Ave.; cross Main St. (OR 211) and continue on S. Molalla Ave. Go left onto E. Fifth St., turn right onto S. Mathias Rd., and bear left onto S. Feyrer Park Rd.; follow it to Feyrer County Park (6.2 miles round-trip).

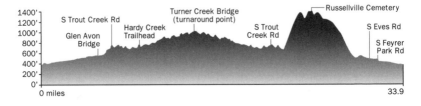

A mercifully dry January day on the Molalla Forest Road

This ride tours the Molalla River, a major tributary of the Willamette. In its lower reaches, the Molalla is lazy and meandering, lined with gravel bars and swimming holes. Upstream of the town of Molalla, it's a completely different river. Rugged and wild, it flows through a dramatic basalt canyon, slackening in crystalline pools at narrow spots and surging over rock ledges in clouds of whitewater. It's a paddler's and angler's dream—and a great place for biking.

Molalla Forest Road parallels the river deep into the mountains before turning to gravel near Table Rock Wilderness. While ambitious riders might want to go all the way to pavement's end, you can experience the canyon's grandeur on a shorter ride. It's an out-and-back, so you choose how far to go. (Alternatively, you can ride an optional return loop, which climbs out of the Molalla's canyon to expansive Willamette Valley views.)

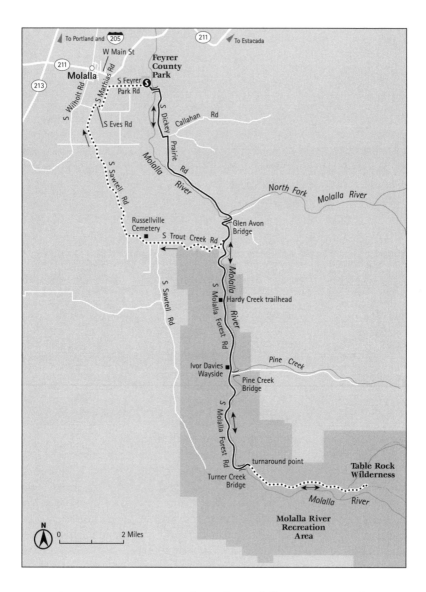

Begin at Feyrer County Park on the Molalla River. Cross the river and go right onto S. Dickey Prairie Road. Follow it south past farms and riverside homes to Glen Avon Bridge, where you turn right to recross the river and pick up S. Molalla Forest Road. The narrowing canyon now pins the road against the river, forcing it high above the water in places.

Near mile 6.8, S. Trout Creek Road shoots uphill to your right (this is the turn for the optional return loop on your way back). Continue south to venture upriver as far as your time and energy will carry you.

In another 0.5 mile you reach the boundary of the Molalla River Recreation Area, owned by the federal government—in other words, you and me—and overseen by the Bureau of Land Management. At mile 9.2 is Hardy Creek trailhead (restrooms), a good alternate starting point for a shorter trip that still gets you up the canyon.

Evidence of the canyon's volcanic origins is everywhere, notably in hexagonal basalt columns formed by ancient lava and exposed by the river's relentless carving. An especially striking formation lies across the river near mile 10.5, where perfectly formed columns of rock curve and swirl up from the water's surface to form a sheer cliff.

At mile 11 is the Ivor Davies Wayside, which overlooks Baby Bear Rapids, the lowest in a 4-mile stretch of whitewater beloved by paddlers. Turner Creek Bridge, at mile 13.7, makes a logical turnaround. The riding past here is excellent, but it gains a lot of elevation over the final 4.5 paved miles to the trailhead for Table Rock Wilderness. (Table Rock, by the way, is the lowest-elevation wilderness area in the Cascades and a classic hike. Here's an idea: Talk some friends into doing the hike, and bring your bike along. You can ride back out the Molalla River Road—downhill—while they hoof it up Table Rock. Reunite at Feyrer County Park.)

However high you ride, at some point turn around and retrace your route to return as you came.

Alternatively, at the S. Trout Creek Road intersection, go left for the optional loop return, climbing a punishing hill up to S. Sawtell Road. After a little less than 2 miles you'll reach a high point, emerging from deep forest. Mount St. Helens marks the horizon at right.

After a steep descent and a second, shorter climb, you'll reach S. Sawtell Rd.; Russellville Cemetery is just beyond. Views open across the entire northern Willamette Valley, clear to Portland and the Coast Range. Now begins a long descent through classic Clackamas countryside: timber lots, isolated hideaways, hayfields, nurseries. Near the outskirts of Molalla, S. Feyrer Park Road leads back down to the river at—you guessed it—Feyrer County Park.

A final note: the Molalla River, long loved but overlooked, is finally getting the respect it's due. Once notorious for vandalism, car prowlers, and littering partiers, the recreation corridor is now cleaner and more peaceful, thanks to a citizen-led stewardship campaign. The river is also benefiting from conservation and protection efforts, most notably a proposal inching through Congress to designate a long stretch of it as Wild and Scenic. The future for one of Oregon's wildest rivers is bright.

MILEAGE LOG

  0.0 Begin at Feyrer County Park. Go left onto S. Feyrer Park Rd., cross Molalla River, and go right onto S. Dickey Prairie Rd.

  5.6 Right onto Glen Avon Bridge to cross Molalla River, then left at fork onto S. Molalla Forest Rd.

  6.2 S. Trout Creek Rd. at right; continue straight. (**Option:** Go left here on the return for loop.)

  9.2 Hardy Creek trailhead at right.

11.0 Ivor Davies Wayside at right.

11.3 At Pine Creek Bridge, continue straight.

14.2 Turner Creek Bridge; turnaround point. Retrace route to return.

Optional loop return:

22.2 Left onto S. Trout Creek Rd. Steep uphill.

25.4 Continue straight onto S. Sawtell Rd. Russellville Cemetery at right.

31.1 Continue straight onto S. Eves Rd., which curves right.

31.5 Left onto S. Mathias Rd.

32.2 Right onto S. Feyrer Park Rd.

33.9 Left to end at Feyrer County Park.

EAST TO THE FOOTHILLS

Portland's eastern neighborhoods merge seamlessly into suburbs such as Gresham, Fairview, and Troutdale. Then the city suddenly ends, giving way to farmland and the timbered foothills of Mount Hood. These rides explore the region's eastern edge, visiting wild rivers, deep forests, and expansive parks.

38 Clackamas Countryside

DIFFICULTY: Very challenging
DISTANCE: 43.8-mile loop; option: 21.8-mile loop
ELEVATION GAIN: 2500 feet

Getting There: From I-205 southbound, take exit 10 for Oregon Rte. 213. Go right at first light onto Washington St. After about 1 mile, cross Abernethy Rd. and go left into small parking area for Abernethy Creek Park.

Transit: Ride MAX Green Line to its terminus at Clackamas Town Center (see map for Ride 8); bicycle south on I-205 bike path past Clackamette Cove in Oregon City. Go left from path onto Main St., continue under I-205, and go left onto 17th St. Cross Abernethy Rd. to Aberbethy Creek Park (adds 13 miles round-trip). Or catch TriMet bus No. 33 to Oregon City Transit Center, bicycle two blocks east on 12th St. to Washington St., turn left, and go 4 blocks to Abernethy Creek Park at right.

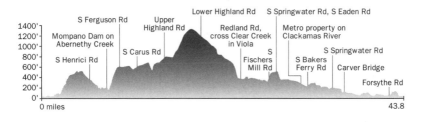

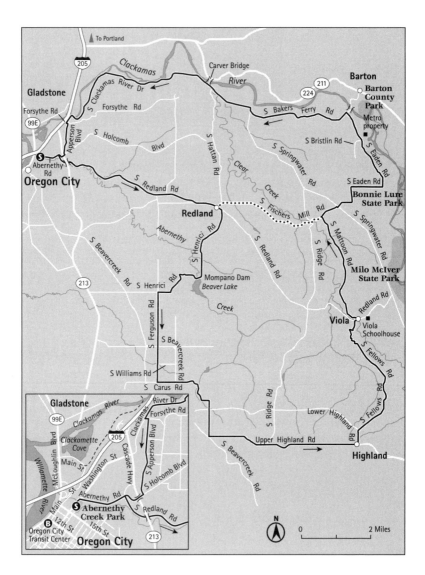

If Oregon has a heartland, it's Clackamas County—home to wealthy suburbs, downtrodden logging towns, bygone villages, iconic scenery, and relentless growth. It was the end of the Oregon Trail, a beacon to those who trekked the continent in search of good farmland, a second chance, or simple escape from whatever Midwestern village trapped them. Now it offers would-be country squires their five acres of heaven at a reasonable price. As a result, rural sprawl blankets much of the

Mount Hood and the middle of nowhere, Clackamas countryside

county, especially around Oregon City. Some of it is regrettable, but much of it makes for great bicycling.

This tour takes in the Clackamas countryside via back roads. It has a few long hills and several stretches of busy traffic, but for the most part it's mellow and manageable for intermediate riders.

Begin at Abernethy Creek Park in Oregon City, just north of the old downtown. Follow Abernethy Road to S. Redland Road, which crosses under Oregon Route 213 and speeds you into the countryside. Follow this busy rural highway—with a good bike lane—5 miles to the tiny crossroad of Redland, where you turn right onto S. Henrici Road. (Alternatively, go left onto S. Fischers Mill Road just before Henrici to shorten the ride to a 21.8-mile loop, rejoining the main route at mile 27.6.)

Henrici drops down into the Abernethy Creek drainage, an attractive little valley poised between its rural past and its suburban future. The latter is on display at Beaver Lake Estates, an upscale gated community seemingly parachuted into these backwoods from Dunthorpe or Lake Oswego. Henrici passes the imposing spillway on Mompano Dam—which creates the Beaver Lake surrounded by said estates—then begins a stiff climb back to the highlands. Use caution on this steep and twisty road.

Mellow riding resumes on S. Ferguson Road, which leads past some actual farms and deeper into the countryside. Cross S. Beavercreek Road; beyond, Ferguson turns into a narrow country lane, then diminishes further to a potholed driveway at S. Williams Road. Pavement resumes a short distance later near S. Carus Road, where big views over the Molalla River drainage open to your right. Go left here.

Carus Road briefly dips into a ravine before climbing to Lower, and then Upper, Highland Road. As the name suggests, you're in higher country now, with views spreading in every direction. By the time you reach the high point around mile 18, you'll have climbed more than 1300 feet from Oregon City.

S. Fellows Road carries you down again, through a tunnel of trees with sweeping curves and periodic views north. It drops all the way to Redland Road, where an old one-room schoolhouse marks the hamlet of Viola. Cross Clear Creek on Redland and go left onto S. Mattoon Road, through a pastoral valley nestled between high, forested ridges.

Where Mattoon ends, go right onto busy S. Fischers Mill Road. It climbs up to Springwater Road, which follows the divide between Clear Creek and the Clackamas River, closely following the old Oregon Trail. Cross Springwater and continue on S. Eaden Road, which leads downhill through a residential area, almost to the Clackamas River.

By this point you're itching—I hope—to actually *see* the county's eponymous river. Aside from a couple of great parks like Milo McIver, Barton, and Bonnie Lure, most of its banks are privately owned or otherwise hard to access. But from Eaden Road you can make a short side trip to the river at a spot that, if not quite secret, is hardly being advertised by its owner, Metro Regional Government.

Around mile 31, start looking for S. Bristlin Road leading left. Just past it, at right, look for a small pullout and a narrow, unsigned driveway. It leads 100 yards to a gate marked by a small Metro sign. Continue past the gate, now on gravel (it's a good idea to walk your bike), another several hundred yards downhill. You'll soon reach the river at a dramatic, sweeping bend. In fact, the river is currently eating your road, so you can't easily go much farther. This is a great spot to stop for a picnic or just to admire the powerful, wild river doing its work. Right around the downstream bend, the crowds at Barton County Park are loading their inner tubes with beer for the party float down to Carver— but here you'll likely be alone.

Back at Eaden Road, continue a short distance to S. Bakers Ferry Road and go left. The next several miles, on Bakers Ferry and then S. Springwater Road, are more trafficked than what you've been on recently. Be especially careful around the Carver Bridge, where many drivers haven't yet noticed they're not on Interstate 205 anymore. Beyond the bridge, continue on Clackamas River Drive for 5 very scenic and slightly quieter miles. If this road only had a shoulder, it would be one of the region's great routes. Hugging the river's flood-plain, through forest and fields, it's an especially nice ride in the fall, when the riverside maples turn bright yellow and orange.

Just before you reach OR 213, go left onto Forsythe Road and then right onto S. Apperson Boulevard, which leads along a bluff to Holcomb Boulevard. Go right, cross OR 213 via an overpass, and continue through the stoplight onto Abernethy Road. Abernethy Creek Park is another 0.5 mile down the road at left.

MILEAGE LOG

0.0 Begin at Abernethy Creek Park. Go right onto Washington St., then immediately right onto Abernethy Rd.

0.6 Right onto S. Redland Rd. Continue under OR 213.

5.8 Right onto S. Henrici Rd. (**Option:** Go left here to shorten loop to 21.8 miles; rejoin route at mile 27.6.)

8.1 Mompano Dam on Abernethy Creek at Beaver Lake.

9.6 Left onto S. Ferguson Rd.

11.0 Cross S. Beavercreek Rd.

11.5 Continue straight at S. Williams Rd. onto packed gravel road. (Pavement resumes after 0.4 mile.)

12.0 Left onto S. Carus Rd. Caution: visibility limited here. Cross S. Beavercreek Rd. and continue.

14.9 Left onto S. Upper Highland Rd. Caution: cars come quickly at right from S. Beavercreek Rd.

19.3 Left onto S. Lower Highland Rd.

20.1 Right onto S. Fellows Rd. Long downhill.

24.2 Right onto Redland Rd. to cross Clear Creek in Viola.

24.3 Left onto S. Mattoon Rd.

27.6 Right onto S. Fischers Mill Rd. (**Option:** Shortcut rejoins route here.)

28.1 Right onto S. Springwater Rd., then left onto S. Eaden Rd.

31.5 Metro property entrance at right, just beyond intersection with S. Bristlin Rd.

32.3 Left onto S. Bakers Ferry Rd.

35.3 Right onto S. Springwater Rd.

36.9 Carver Bridge at right. Continue straight on S. Clackamas River Dr.

42.1 Left onto Forsythe Rd., then immediate right onto S. Apperson Blvd.

43.0 Right onto S. Holcomb Blvd. Cross OR 213 on overpass.

43.3 Straight at stoplight onto Abernethy Rd.

43.8 Left onto Washington St., then immediate left to end in Abernethy Creek Park.

39 Faraday Road

DIFFICULTY: Easy
DISTANCE: 8.8 miles
ELEVATION GAIN: 275 feet

Getting There: From I-205 southbound, take exit 12A, Oregon Rte. 212–OR 224, toward Clackamas. After 3.5 miles, go right onto OR 224 and continue to Estacada. Approximately 1 mile beyond, go right onto E. Faraday Rd. Continue 0.3 mile to parking area on right side of road.

Transit: Ride TriMet bus 30 to Estacada and continue east on OR 224 approximately 1 mile to E. Faraday Rd.

Below Estacada, the Clackamas River winds through a widening plain past great parks like Milo McIver and Barton. Above Estacada, it's a steep mountain river pinned between basalt walls. At the point where it changes character, humanity has interrupted the river to harness its current for electricity. Dams have diminished the river's otherwise abundantly wild character. They've also diminished fish runs on this, the largest of rivers draining the Cascades' wet west side.

There's a silver lining to this development, though. The dams—three of them—require an access road; the road's owner, Portland General Electric (PGE), has opened it to bicyclists. While traffic rumbles along Oregon Route 224 far above the river, lonely E. Faraday Road winds through the canyon, out of sight and sound.

Begin about 0.5 mile down Faraday Road from OR 224, at the Faraday Lake parking area. A pedestrian bridge leads from the parking lot across the river to Faraday Lake, a reservoir created adjacent to the river's natural channel by a diversion dam 2 miles upstream. This design allows the Faraday Powerhouse (at the far end of the lake) to generate electricity with minimal effect on migrating salmon. The lake is stocked with fish and attracts plenty of anglers. It's worth a quick detour on foot.

Now ride east on Faraday Road, away from the river and up a slight hill. This part of the road is open to cars, but traffic is very light,

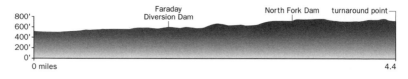

generally limited to PGE workers. After about 0.75 mile the road returns to the river, now more than 100 feet below you in a narrow canyon.

Around mile 1.6 you reach the diversion dam. When the original structure, called the Cazadero Dam, was built in 1907, this area was truly a wilderness. The current dam is from 1965. It doesn't produce power, it only diverts water into Faraday Lake. To help fish around the diversion dam, and the North Fork Dam farther upstream, PGE has built a nearly *2-mile-long* fish ladder, which it claims is the longest operating fish ladder in the world. It parallels Faraday Road.

Above the dam, the Clackamas River's rapids and riffles disappear under a narrow, curving lake. This stretch of road, closed to all non-PGE vehicles, is especially nice. From the green, still water, forested slopes rise steeply to the sky, shutting out everything else.

Around a bend, the road leads to the North Fork Dam. Here the long journey for those ladder-climbing fish ends at the North Fork Reservoir, where buzzing watercraft and armadas of anglers await. The route's final stretch follows the lakeshore, offering views up the canyon. Foothills climb to mountains, rising in layers to the horizon. From here to the headwaters—40 miles southeast as the crow flies—the river drains a vast and still wild (if heavily logged) watershed.

The final mile gets some pedestrian traffic from the nearby boat launch, so keep an eye out. The boat launch, about halfway around the lake, is just past the gate marking the end of Faraday Road's car-free stretch and the end of this ride. Turn around at the gate and retrace

Heavy traffic: a midsummer weekend on the Faraday Road

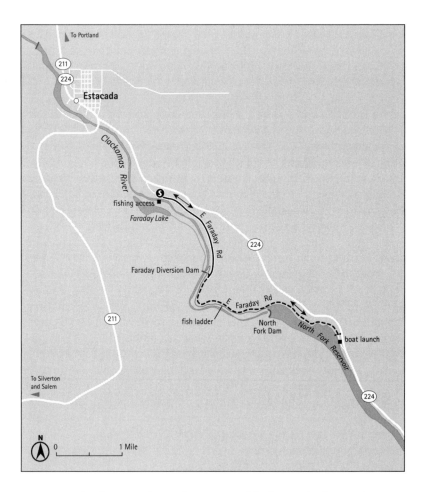

your route back to Faraday Lake. (You could, alternatively, continue on the road 0.3 mile to its end at OR 224, where long and beautiful forest rides beckon, and/or you could also return to your starting point via the broad-shouldered highway, though you'd have to climb a big hill.)

MILEAGE LOG

0.0 Begin at parking area for Faraday Lake fishing access. Continue east on E. Faraday Rd.

1.6 Faraday Diversion Dam at right. Fish ladder begins here; automobile traffic restricted past here.

3.1 North Fork Dam.

4.4 Gate just before boat-launch parking area. Retrace route to return.

40 Eagle Fern Park

DIFFICULTY: Very challenging
DISTANCE: 28.5-mile loop
ELEVATION GAIN: 2300 feet

Getting There: From I-84 eastbound, take exit 16 for NE 238th Dr.; go right. After approximately 2.8 miles, bear left onto NE Burnside Rd., which joins US Hwy. 26 (see map for Ride 42). Continue 11 miles into Sandy and go right onto Meinig Ave. (Oregon Rte. 211) at stoplight. Bear left to stay on Meinig Ave.; park entrance immediately at left.

Transit: Take MAX (Blue Line) to Gresham Transit Center and transfer to SAM (Sandy Area Metro) bus. Get off at Pioneer Blvd. (US Hwy 26) and Meinig Ave. stop in Sandy. Meinig Park entrance is few hundred yards south on Meinig Ave.

Here's another ramble through the Mount Hood foothills, full of challenging climbs, views, a forest of old-growth cedars, and—truth be told—a few stretches of white-knuckle riding.

The ride starts in Sandy, gateway to Mount Hood. Strategically situated where the Sandy and Clackamas Rivers bend closest to one another, Sandy was a key stop on the Barlow Road, the Oregon Trail's final leg. For the pioneers, reaching Sandy meant you had survived the snows and mud of Mount Hood. All that remained was a gentle descent to the broad bench of the Clackamas River, easily forded in late summer near its confluence with Eagle Creek.

From Meinig Park in Sandy, go left onto Meinig Avenue. Across Tickle Creek, you begin a long climb through farm country, crossing several of Deep Creek's headwater streams. This is one of those Oregon places where you could be 50 miles or 5 from the nearest shopping mall. It just feels remote.

By the time you reach the crossroad of Dover—recognizable as a place only by its church—the traffic has all but disappeared. The

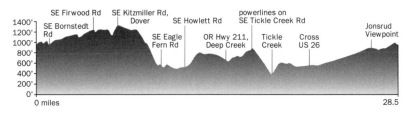

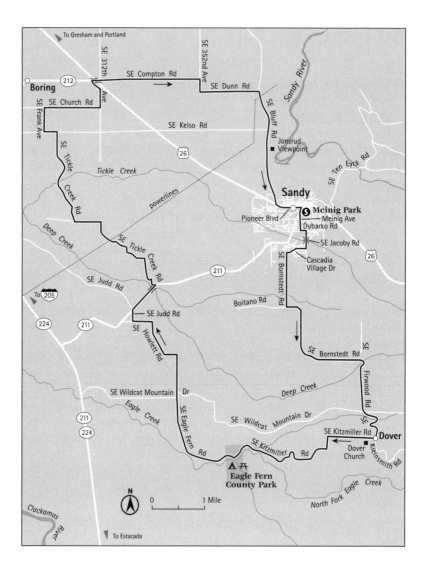

fields give way to forest as you begin a long, winding descent down SE Kitzmiller Road. This thrilling downhill's curves and grade invite you to push your cornering skills. Beware!

The road bottoms at Eagle Fern County Park (restrooms), where ancient cedars tower above Eagle Creek. A picnic area and campground are a few hundred yards to the left on SE Eagle Fern Road; several short hiking trails invite a layover. On warm summer weekends, hordes of

Nature's water park: Eagle Creek in summer

kids play in Eagle Creek's trickle. Use caution around their distracted parents, hunting for scarce roadside parking. (In winter, expect absolute solitude and icy roads in perpetual shade.)

When you're ready to move on, head north on SE Eagle Fern Road (a right turn from Kitzmiller) to begin the long but gradual climb from the canyon. Past SE Wildcat Mountain Drive, you break out of the forest into a landscape of nurseries and ranchettes.

Now comes the aforementioned white knuckling. Hopefully you've been unruffled by traffic so far. Maybe your luck will hold. But now you need to venture onto OR 211 for 0.7 mile. Though it's mostly downhill, a guardrail blocks your escape. Don't try to hug the white line; take the lane and let the cars wait a moment. Across Deep Creek, the road shoots uphill. Fortunately, the guardrail ends just before your left turn onto SE Tickle Creek Road, giving you a chance to stop and collect yourself before carefully crossing the highway.

With the hard part behind you, get ready for a sustained climb up SE Tickle Creek Road. It winds and curves up benchlands, emerging into the open under massive powerlines, matched by an equally massive panorama of Mount Hood, the Clackamas River's broad plain, and the foothills beyond.

You lose a little of your hard-won elevation crossing Tickle Creek's ravine before a final uphill push carries you back into open country on the plains east of Boring. Cross US 26 and follow SE Compton Road as it shoots east toward Sandy.

At Bluff Road the land drops suddenly away to reveal the biggest view yet: the Sandy River flowing through an immense canyon. Picturesque farms line its benchlands; Mount Hood rises above it all. This is a sight best experienced off the bike at the Jonsrud Viewpoint near mile 27. After that, a quick trip through Sandy's downtown brings you back to Meinig Park.

MILEAGE LOG

0.0 Begin in Meinig Park's lower parking area. Go left onto Meinig Ave.

0.3 Left onto Dubarko Rd.

0.4 Right onto SE Jacoby Rd.

0.6 Right onto Cascadia Village Dr.

1.0 Left onto SE Bornstedt Rd., which curves and crosses streams.

4.4 Right onto SE Firwood Rd. across Deep Creek.

5.6 Cross SE Wildcat Mountain Dr. onto SE Kleinsmith Rd.

6.4 Right onto SE Kitzmiller Rd. in Dover. Long downhill.

10.0 Right onto SE Eagle Fern Rd. (**Side trip:** Go left 100 yards to visit Eagle Fern County Park.)

12.0 Continue straight onto SE Howlett Rd.; cross SE Wildcat Mountain Rd. and continue on SE Howlett Rd.

14.3 Right onto SE Judd Rd.

14.5 Right onto OR 211 (caution).

15.2 Left onto SE Tickle Creek Rd. just after crossing Deep Creek.

16.8 Cross under powerlines.

18.7 Cross Tickle Creek.

19.7 Left onto SE Kelso Rd.

19.9 Right onto SE Frank Ave.

20.4 Right onto SE Church Rd. in Boring.

21.5 Left onto SE 312th Ave.

22.0 Left at stop sign, then right onto SE Compton Rd. and over US 26.

24.2 Right onto SE 352nd Ave., which curves left to become SE Dunn Rd.

25.6 Right onto SE Bluff Rd.

27.2 Jonsrud Viewpoint at left.

28.0 Left onto Pioneer Blvd. (eastbound US 26).

28.4 Right onto OR 211 (Meinig Ave.), then immediately left to stay on Meinig Ave.

28.5 Left to end in Meinig Park.

41 Gresham–Fairview Trail

DIFFICULTY: Easy (Loop: Moderate)
TOTAL DISTANCE: 7 miles; option: 18.8-mile loop
TOTAL ELEVATION GAIN: 110 feet; option: 950 feet

Getting There: From I-84 eastbound, take exit 13 and go right onto NE 181st Ave. Continue south 3.5 miles. Go left onto W. Powell Blvd. (US Hwy. 26), right onto W. Powell Loop, and right into Linnemann Station trailhead parking lot.

Transit: Take MAX Blue Line to Ruby Junction–E. 197th Ave. station. Bicycle left onto NW Burnside Ct., left onto NW 11 Mile Ave., right onto SE Burnside St., and left across Burnside at crosswalk to join Gresham–Fairview Trail at mile 2.1.

East Multnomah County has great east-west bikeways, but until recently it lacked a good north-south connector. The Gresham–Fairview Trail has helped meet this need, providing a mostly car-free connection from the Springwater Corridor north to Halsey Street in Fairview. Soon it will connect all the way to Marine Drive, bringing the 40-Mile Loop (see Ride 16) one step closer to completion.

The Gresham–Fairview Trail is more than a connector, though. It's also a scenic ride suitable for beginners—a real boon in this heavily developed and underserved area. The route described here follows the trail from south to north for a 3.5-mile one-way ride, with an optional loop through Fairview and Troutdale to the Sandy River and Columbia Slough.

Begin at Linnemann Station trailhead in Gresham. This was a stop on the old Springwater Line, which ceased passenger rail service way back in 1958. The station survived—the last—until a fire claimed it in 1995. Now its replacement welcomes Greshamites to the Springwater Corridor.

From the station, go left onto the Springwater Corridor. Cross SW Pleasant View Drive at a crosswalk. A few hundred yards later, go left

onto a path for the Gresham–Fairview Trail. It leads to a new pedestrian bridge across W. Powell Boulevard and continues north, skirting Fairview Creek's headwaters at the base of Grant Butte. Until recently, this land was part of a dairy farm, the last holdout of an older Gresham. Now its fate is uncertain, but conservationists hope for a park.

Across NW Division Street, the scenery turns industrial as you pass Vance Pit, a massive gravel quarry owned by Multnomah County, and TriMet's Ruby Junction maintenance yard, home base for MAX trains and nerve center for the entire TriMet system. The MAX tracks force a short detour onto NW Birdsdale Avenue; the trail resumes after NW Burnside Road.

Like many converted railways, the trail feels isolated despite its urban setting. Homes were built facing away from the rail tracks, doing their best to ignore it. You can't help but feel a little like you're snooping—it's hard to resist the temptation to peek through breaks in the vegetation and glimpse Greshamites in their private lives, barbecuing or gardening in their backyards.

The trail ends all too soon at NE Halsey Street. Someday it will continue the final 2 miles north to Marine Drive. For now, retrace your route to return to the Linnemann Station trailhead.

Alternatively, you can continue on the optional loop return for an intentionally meandering ride, with side trips to visit some lesser-known sites in this underappreciated neighborhood. Warning: This loop option includes some unpaved paths, which are likely to be muddy in winter.

From the trail's end at NE Halsey Street, continue through the parking areas for Reynolds Middle School and Salish Ponds Elementary School into Salish Ponds Park. The Salish Ponds are old gravel quarries, now flooded. A soft path circles them, accessing several fishing platforms. The state stocks these ponds, which have proven wildly popular with urban anglers. Follow the trail under Fairview Parkway and along a wild stretch of Fairview Creek to Fairview Community Park.

From the park, NE Park Lane and NE Village Street take you to Fairview's new town center. With its red brick and cozy main street, the "village" feels a bit like a movie-set version of Small Town America. It's very pleasant but slightly surreal. Across NE Halsey Street, continue on Seventh Street to Main Street, which leads east through Fairview's sleepy old town.

Go left onto Fairview Avenue to cross under Interstate 84 and toward the Columbia River. A left turn onto NE Blue Lake Road brings you to Blue Lake Regional Park (see Ride 16). From the park entrance, follow a path west. Beyond the lakes it turns to dirt and passes wetlands, ending

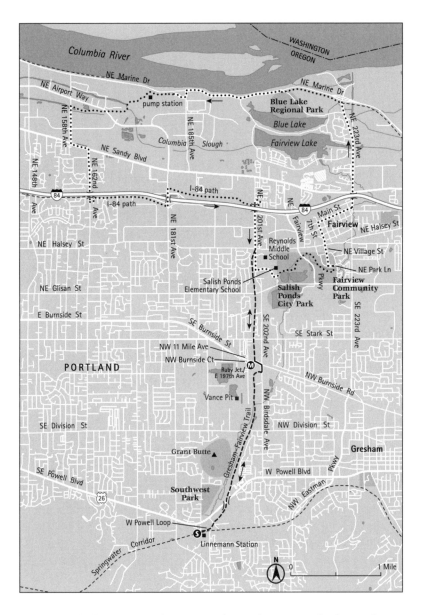

at NE Interlachen Lane. (Plans are in the works to upgrade this trail.) Go right onto Interlachen and then left (carefully!) onto NE Marine Drive.

After a short spell on NE Marine Drive's bike lane, go left onto NE 185th Avenue and immediately right into a parking lot. Hiding at

On the Gresham–Fairview Trail

the back end is what might be the most obscure trail in the city: a short stretch of pavement ending abruptly at a city wellhead. A soft trail continues around the pump house and into the woods.

Follow this trail—it can be sloppy in the rain—along the Columbia Slough, here just a creek fringed by green. At several points you'll need to carry your bike up and down a few steps. Just when you start to think you're on a cyclocross course, the path ends (for no apparent reason) at NE 158th Avenue. Go left here and then jog east a few blocks on NE Sandy Boulevard to NE 162nd Avenue, where you pick up the I-84 bike path eastbound. Exit at NW 201st Avenue to return south to the Gresham–Fairview Trail; retrace it south to the Linnemann Station trailhead to complete the return.

MILEAGE LOG

0.0 Begin at Linnemann Station trailhead for Springwater Corridor in Gresham. Go left onto Springwater Corridor; cross SW Pleasant Dr., then sharp left onto Gresham–Fairview Trail.

0.6 Cross over W. Powell Blvd. via overpass.

1.0 Grant Butte at left.

1.4 Cross SE Division St. at crosswalk and continue on path.

2.1 Left at path's end onto NW Birdsdale Ave. Cross tracks; go left onto SE Burnside St., and then right to continue on path.

3.5 Path ends at NE 201st Ave. and NE Halsey St. in Fairview. Retrace route to return to Linnemann Station trailhead.

Optional loop return:

3.5 Right from path onto NE 201st Ave.

3.7 Left into Reynolds Middle School parking area; follow entrance drive around middle school to Salish Ponds Elementary parking lot. At back end of back parking lot, look for dirt path leading past gate to enter Salish Ponds City Park.

4.3 At second (east) pond, left at trail junction; follow it east into woods. Cross underneath NE Fairview Pkwy. and continue on path along Fairview Creek. Exit path at Fairview Community Park and go left onto NE Park Lane.

5.2 Right onto NE Village St. Cross NE Halsey St. and continue on 7th St.

5.7 Right onto Main St.

6.1 Left onto Fairview Ave. (becomes NE 223rd Ave. after NE Sandy Blvd.).

7.2 Left onto NE Blue Lake Rd.

7.7 Left into Blue Lake Regional Park. Take first left after entrance booth to reach lakeshore, then right to follow shore path; continue past wetlands to exit park right onto NE Interlachen Ln.

8.8 Left onto NE Marine Dr.

9.4 Left from Marine Drive onto NE 185th Drive, then immediately right into first driveway. Continue around building onto path at end of parking area.

9.9 Pavement ends at a pump station. Continue past pump station and go left onto an unpaved trail. Caution: path has several steps.

10.6 Walk bike underneath NE Airport Way and continue on path.

11.1 Left onto NE 158th Avenue.

11.4 Left onto NE Sandy Boulevard, then right at stoplight onto NE 162nd Avenue.

12.2 Cross under I-84 and immediately go left onto path, then right to continue on I-84 bike path.

13.2 Left onto NE 181st Avenue to cross over freeway, then right to resume path.

14.4 Left onto path immediately across NE 201st Avenue overpass. Go left at bottom of ramp onto NE 201st Avenue.

15.0 Right onto Gresham–Fairview Trail across NE Halsey Street.

18.8 End Linnemann Station Trailhead.

42 Oxbow Regional Park

DIFFICULTY: Moderate
DISTANCE: 22.4-mile loop; option: 18.1-mile loop
ELEVATION GAIN: 1300 feet

Getting There: From I-84 eastbound, take exit 14 and go right onto NE Fairview Pkwy. (see map for Ride 41). After nearly 1 mile, go left onto NE Glisan St., then right onto NE 223rd Ave., which becomes NW Eastman Pkwy. After 2.2 miles, go left onto W. Powell Blvd. (US Hwy. 26) and take second right, onto S. Main Ave., to reach Main City Park in Gresham.

Transit: Ride MAX Blue Line to Gresham Central Transit Center station. From platform's east end, bicycle left onto NE Kelley Ave., then immediately right onto NE Eighth St. Go left onto Cleveland Ave. to join the route near mile 1.

Oxbow Regional Park is hands-down one of the greatest parks in the Portland area. It's got ancient forests, mountain biking trails, natural

Bring your swimsuit: the Sandy River at Oxbow Regional Park

history programs, and—best of all—the looping, flooding, wild Sandy River. If the Sandy didn't have to compete with so many other great rivers around here, it would unquestionably be world famous.

Oxbow Park is also surprisingly easy to reach by bike; it's just not so easy to leave. Yes, the park does have a lot to offer, and yes, it does make for a great overnight bike destination. But I'm referring here to the hill you descend to reach the park—the hill you have to climb on your way out. It's not the longest or steepest in this book, but on an otherwise easy ride, it comes as a shock. So I recommend that you pack a good picnic and dawdle as long as possible at the river before tackling the uphill. Or, if you must, skip the park and river altogether. It's still a great tour through some fine East County scenery—and at 18 miles and approximately 700 feet of climbing (minus the park, that is) it should be doable for just about any rider.

Begin at Main City Park in Gresham. Work your way through Gresham's quaint old downtown, then get ready for a slog along NE Division Street through the Gresham familiar to most drivers: big-box stores and fast-food joints.

Relief comes at NE Kane Drive and NE 17th Street, which speed you out of town across that magical Urban Growth Boundary (see "The UGB" sidebar in Ride 23). You arrive a few minutes later into lonesome farm country, surrounded by nurseries as far as the eye can see.

Traffic picks up again on SE Division Drive, which, due to its lack of shoulder, demands some attention. Things quiet down again on SE 302nd Avenue and turn downright peaceful along SE Pipeline Road, where the nurseries are so big they could seemingly meet all of America's landscaping needs. The scenery treads some line between pastoral and industrial; it's a beautiful but relentlessly managed landscape devoid of anything wild. Still, chances are good you'll enjoy the quiet, open road.

At the intersection of SE Oxbow Drive and SE Hosner Road, you descend to the park and its many joys. Before heading into the park, double-check your brakes and then go left. In a little under 2 miles and mere minutes, you arrive at the park entrance.

The mileage log's numbers assume you'll ride to only the park's first

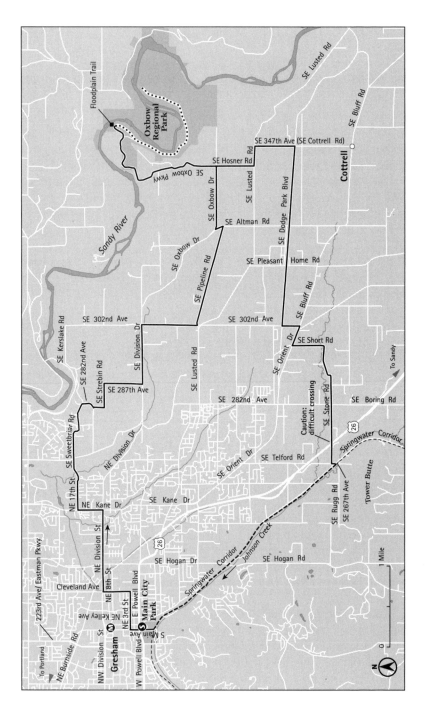

river access point. If you take a side trip to the road's end, add another 3.6 miles to the overall trip distance; you'll pass through an ancient forest, picnic areas, and more river access points. Pack a bathing suit if it's a hot day—there are some great swimming holes. But never, ever, take the Sandy River lightly. Even when it's at low flows, people routinely drown. At higher flows, it's downright treacherous.

Even if you choose not to ride to the road's end, consider a quick hike on the Floodplain Trail. It visits a forest drowned in gray glacial till, evidence of the river's power to literally move mountains.

When it's time to leave, load up on water and limber up those legs. The hill is definitely longer and steeper than it seemed on the way in! Back at the top, continue south on SE Hosner Road to head home. The riding is mostly flat and very rural, passing the crossroads of Pleasant Home and Orient before descending slightly into the Johnson Creek watershed near SE Short Road. SE Stone Road skirts the county line to reach US Highway 26. This is a tough crossing: be patient and wait for a long pause in the traffic. (It will eventually come!)

A short distance beyond the highway, SE Stone Road delivers you to the Springwater Corridor at the foot of Tower Butte. A little over 3 blissful miles later, you return to Gresham's Main City Park.

MILEAGE LOG

0.0 Begin at Gresham's Main City Park. Go right onto S. Main Ave. Cross W. Powell Blvd.

0.2 Right onto NE 3rd St.

0.7 Left onto Cleveland Ave.

1.1 Right onto NE Division St.

2.1 Left onto NE Kane Dr.

2.4 Right onto NE 17th St., which becomes SE Sweetbriar Rd. after crossing SE Troutdale Rd.

3.8 Right onto SE 282nd Ave.

4.0 Left to stay on SE 282nd Ave., which curves left to become SE Strebin Rd.

4.4 Bear right onto SE 287th Ave.

4.9 Left onto SE Division Dr.

5.6 Right onto SE 302nd Ave.

6.4 Left onto SE Pipeline Rd.

7.7 Left onto SE Altman Rd., then sharp right onto SE Oxbow Dr.

8.6 Left onto SE Hosner Rd., which becomes SE Oxbow Pkwy.
(**Option:** Go right onto SE Hosner Rd. to skip the park, continuing at mile 12.9 below.)

10.1 Entrance to Oxbow Regional Park.

10.4 Trailhead for Floodplain Trail.

10.7 River access point; turn around and retrace route out of park. (**Side trip:** Continue to end of park road for additional 3.6 miles round-trip).

12.9 Straight at stop sign onto SE Hosner Rd.

13.4 Left onto SE Lusted Rd.

12.7 Right onto SE 347th Ave. (SE Cottrell Rd.).

14.2 Right onto SE Dodge Park Blvd.

16.4 Left onto SE 302nd Ave.

16.7 Right onto SE Bluff Rd., then continue straight onto SE Orient Dr.

16.9 Left onto SE Short Rd., which curves right to become SE Stone Rd.

18.9 Cross US 26 (caution).

19.1 Left onto SE 267th Ave. Cross SE Telford Rd., then immediately go right onto Springwater Corridor.

22.3 Right onto S. Main Ave.

22.4 End at Gresham's Main City Park.

43 East Buttes

DIFFICULTY: Moderate to Challenging
DISTANCE: 23.5-mile loop
TOTAL ELEVATION GAIN: 1500 feet

Getting There: See Ride 42's directions to Gresham's Main City Park.

Transit: Ride MAX Blue Line to Gresham Central Transit Center station. From platform, bicycle right onto NE Kelley Ave., right onto NE Second St., and left onto N. Main Ave. Cross W. Powell Blvd. at stoplight to reach Main City Park.

This ride features a rolling tour through a landscape in transition, bookended by two of the Springwater Corridor's best stretches. It should appeal equally to plodders and speed demons. When you get to visit places with names like Happy Valley, Sunshine Valley, and Pleasant Valley, what's not to love?

These three vales of suburban bliss owe their bucolic topography to something far less happy, sunny, or pleasant. Geologists know the hills separating these valleys as the Boring Lava Domes. Like their citified

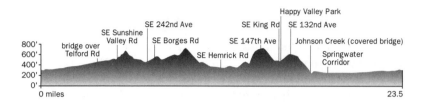

cousins Mount Tabor and Rocky Butte, they were born in fire, from tectonic forces that stretched the earth and opened massive cracks through which lava vented and piled. But "Boring Lava Domes" is a name that doesn't seem to have wide usage. To the extent people pay any notice to these hills at all, they seem to prefer calling them the "East Buttes." There's nothing boring about a lava dome, of course—but presumably neither "lava" nor "boring" help much with home sales.

THE FLOODS

As every Portland cyclist knows, this town is pretty flat—except where it's really, really hilly. This fact can largely be explained by floods. Very large floods.

During the last ice age, about 15,000 years ago, the glaciers covering most of Canada extended icy fingers southward to Puget Sound and the Rockies. One such finger blocked off an entire valley near present-day Missoula, Montana. A lake the size of Lake Erie formed behind this ice dam. Then the dam abruptly burst, unleashing a watery torrent equivalent to 10 times the combined flow of all the world's rivers today.

Over three or four days, the flood swept westward, scouring soil down to bedrock. (The moonscape of eastern Washington's Channeled Scablands is one result.) Rushing toward the ocean, the floods pushed through the Columbia Gorge, backed up into the Willamette Valley, and inundated present-day Portland under as much as *400 feet* of water.

High places made of hard, resistant rock—buttes like Mount Tabor and Rocky Butte, ridges like the Tualatin Hills and Alameda—turned into temporary islands as the surrounding land liquefied and was washed away. The whole process repeated itself dozens of times over several millennia.

A visionary geologist named J. Harlan Bretz first dreamed up this notion in the 1920s. He then endured 40 years of skepticism and outright ridicule until the rest of the scientific community caught up with him. Now they're known as the Bretz—or, more commonly, Missoula—Floods.

Begin in Gresham's Main City Park and follow S. Main Avenue to the Springwater Corridor. Follow the trail eastward, skirting the base of Gresham and Butler buttes. Housing tracts surround you, but you'd never know it from the trail. Soon the land opens up in the Springwater Valley area. Tower Butte rises ahead.

As of this writing, pavement ends after the SE 267th Avenue crossing. (Plans call for paving the trail all the way to Boring by the end of 2012.) The gravel is easy to ride, but if you'd prefer pavement you can continue on SE Telford Road, which parallels the trail in this stretch. The Springwater eventually crosses over Telford on a bridge shortly before it intersects SE Haley Road, which is poorly signed. This is where you leave the Springwater Trail, go right to backtrack a short distance on Telford, and turn uphill on SE Sunshine Valley Road.

Forest closes in around you as the climbing starts—a good warmup for things to come. Cross the saddle between Zion and Tower buttes to descend into Sunshine Valley, where several branches of Sunshine Creek meet. Forest-clad buttes fill the horizon, hiding the cities beyond.

A brief stretch on busy SE 242nd Avenue leads to a difficult intersection at SE Borges Road. Use extreme caution turning left here, as traffic from SE Hogan Road comes quickly around a bend. On Borges Road, things quiet down again. Sunshine Butte, mostly untouched by development, looms to the right; at left, a rectilinear landscape of nurseries spreads out below you.

SE Borges Road passes rural hideaways, tucked in shady dells between Butler Buttes and Damascus Buttes, on a gradual descent to SE Tillstrom Road. Time to pay attention: traffic here and on SE Foster Road is heavy and fast. Fortunately, it doesn't last long. At SE Hemrick Road the quiet returns.

Now begins another climb, around the flank of Scouter Mountain. Several spots along SE Hagen Road afford a good view back across the valley you've just crossed. It's actually two valleys: North of the Tillstrom-Foster intersection, Pleasant Valley spreads from the banks of Kelly Creek, a tributary of Johnson Creek. South of the intersection, the forks of Rock Creek flow through Damascus area south to the Clackamas River.

If the real estate market ever bends to the wishes of urban planners and real estate developers, the valleys at your feet will one day be filled with homes, shopping malls, highways, and "town centers." Metro, the regional government, has the job of deciding where growth will occur in the region. In 1998, it targeted Pleasant Valley, which has since been annexed to Gresham. Metro then expanded the boundaries to include

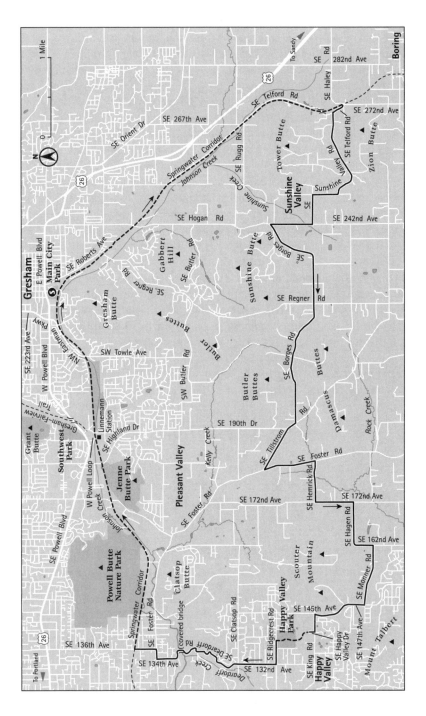

1 Mile

0

N

To Sandy

Boring

SE 282nd Ave

SE Haley Rd

26

SE Telford Rd

SE 267th Ave

SE 272nd Ave

SE Orient Dr

Springwater Corridor

Johnson Creek

SE Rugg Rd

SE Telford Rd

Valley Rd

Zion Butte

Tower Butte

Sunshine Valley

SE Sunshine

26

Gresham

E Powell Blvd

Main City Park

SE Roberts Ave

SE Hogan Rd

Sunshine Creek

SE 242nd Ave

SE Borges Rd

Gabbert Hill

Sunshine Butte

SE 223rd Ave

NW Eastman Pkwy

W Powell Blvd

Gresham Butte

SE Regner Rd

SE Butler Rd

Butler Buttes

SE Regner Rd

SE Borges Rd

Butler Buttes

SW Towle Ave

SW Butler Rd

Buttes

Damascus

Rock Creek

Grant Butte

Southwest Park

Linnemann Station

SE Highland Dr

Butler Buttes

SE 190th Dr

Rd

SE Tillstrom

SE Foster Rd

SE Hemrick Rd

Jenne Butte Park

W Powell Loop

Johnson Creek

Kelly Creek

Pleasant Valley

SE 172nd Ave

SE 172nd Ave

SE Hagen Rd

SE 162nd Ave

SE Powell Blvd

Powell Butte Nature Park

Springwater Corridor

SE Foster Rd

Clatsop Butte

SE Foster Rd

Scouter Mountain

SE Monner Rd

26

SE 136th Ave

SE Foster Rd

covered bridge

SE Deardorff Rd

SE Clatsop Rd

SE Ridgecrest Rd

Happy Valley Park

SE 145th Ave

SE 147th Ave

Mount Talbert

To Portland

SE 134th Ave

Deardorff Creek

SE 132nd Ave

SE King Rd

SE Happy Valley Dr

Happy Valley

Gresham–Fairview Trail

the entire Rock Creek area and beyond, making the tiny crossroads of Damascus a future city. Since then, it's merely been a matter of time until the inevitable development follows. And more time. And some more time....

It may be awhile before the next housing bubble paves Pleasant Valley and Damascus. To get an idea of how it might look, though, ride on. SE Monner Road carries you up and over Scouter Mountain's shoulder into Happy Valley via SE 145th Avenue. Mount Scott, Scouter Mountain, Clatsop Butte, and Mount Talbert surround this little community, lending it an intimacy and sense of place that most new suburbs can only envy. At its center is Happy Valley Park, where ball fields teem with Little League games and trails meander through a large wetland. Go left onto SE King Road and right to enter the park.

At the park's north end, follow SE Ridgecrest Road to SE 132nd Avenue, which leads up and out of Happy Valley and down Mount Scott's north slope along Deardorff Creek, changing names to SE Deardorff Road. Dropping in curves through a cool, deep forest, Deardorff bottoms out at Johnson Creek, crossing via a charming covered bridge. The bridge isn't quite authentic (it was built in 1982 and its cover is purely decorative) but fits the sylvan scene perfectly.

After a short climb north from the creek, the scene changes somewhat dramatically at gritty SE Foster Road, but before you can adjust, you're back on the Springwater Corridor (see Ride 7 for details), cruising past Powell and Jenne buttes on the way back to Gresham.

MILEAGE LOG

0.0 Begin at Main City Park, Gresham. From S. Main Ave., go left onto Springwater Corridor.

3.2 Pavement ends after crossing SE 267th Ave.

4.5 Cross SE Telford Rd. on bridge.

4.8 Right onto SE Haley Rd., then immediate right onto SE Telford Rd.

5.0 Left onto SE Sunshine Valley Rd.

6.9 Right onto SE 242nd Ave.

7.4 Left onto SE Borges Rd. (caution).

10.3 Right onto SE Tillstrom Rd.

11.0 Left onto SE Foster Rd.

11.7 Right onto SE Hemrick Rd.

12.2 Left onto SE 172nd Ave.

12.7 Right onto SE Hagen Rd., which curves left to become SE 162nd Ave.

Too winded to enjoy the view: Hagen Road in Pleasant Valley

13.5 Right onto SE Monner Rd.
14.2 Right onto SE 147th Ave. (becomes SE 145th Ave.).
14.9 Left onto SE King Rd.
15.1 Right onto SE Happy Valley Dr. Go left to far end of parking lot
      and then right onto path leading through Happy Valley Park.
15.9 At north end of park, go left onto SE Ridgecrest Rd.
16.2 Right onto SE 132nd Ave., which becomes SE Deardorff Rd.
17.7 Cross Johnson Creek on covered bridge and continue on
      SE 134th Ave.
18.1 Right onto SE Foster Rd., then immediate left onto SE 136th Ave.
18.5 Right onto Springwater Corridor.
23.4 Left onto S. Main Avenue.
23.5 End at Main City Park, Gresham.

44 Corbett and Crown Point

DIFFICULTY: Challenging
DISTANCE: 18-mile loop
ELEVATION GAIN: 1400 feet

Getting There: From I-84 eastbound, take exit 18 for Lewis and Clark State Park. Go left at stop sign and continue 0.5 mile to second stop sign, where a bridge crosses Sandy River to Troutdale. Park just past this intersection at day-use parking area. (If parking area full, backtrack to Lewis and Clark State Park.)

Transit: Take TriMet bus No. 77 to Glenn Otto Park in Troutdale and bicycle across bridge over Sandy River to day-use parking area.

Corbett and Crown Point are synonymous with the Columbia Gorge and with cycling in Portland. For more than a century, visitors have come from across the globe—on two wheels and four—to visit Crown Point's Vista House, which has probably the most famous view in the Pacific Northwest.

There's more to this ride than the view, though. The Corbett area is bounded to the south and west by the Sandy's deep canyon and to the north by the Gorge's rim. To the east rises Larch Mountain, an ancient volcano cloaked in old-growth forest. From its crater spring Multnomah and Oneonta Creeks, which drop over their famous falls a few miles north in the Gorge. Surrounded by this rugged terrain, Corbett is an island in the sky, an isolated region of rolling hills, wooded valleys, rustic homesteads, and polished estates—in short, a fantastic place to ride.

Keep two things in mind, though. First, you've got to earn this view by climbing up from river level. No individual hill is too brutal, but they add up. Second, shoulders are mostly nonexistent on these roads. The area is well trafficked by cyclists, but motorists distracted by the views—as well as occasional exasperated locals—demand vigilance. Though it's not overly long, it's not a ride for beginners.

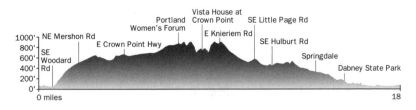

Taking the plunge from Crown Point to the Columbia River, with the Gorge beyond

Begin at Lewis and Clark State Park's day-use parking area next to the bridge spanning the Sandy River into Troutdale. The first few miles on the Historic Columbia River Highway (also called the Crown Point Highway here) are busy, but the shoulder is wide. When you turn left onto SE Woodard Road, things quiet down—just in time for the first big hill. The forest canopy closes in, shutting out the sights and sounds of the metropolis behind you.

Around the 1.5-mile mark, the climbing eases. After a left turn onto NE Ogden Road, vistas gradually open south, revealing a huge territory stretching to the East Buttes (see Ride 43) and beyond. Go right onto NE Mershon Road to drop back into forest and then climb again to eastern views. At the intersection with the Crown Point Highway, go left to pedal a few miles to the town of Corbett on a generous shoulder.

Past Corbett, the road draws closer to the Gorge's edge, finally meeting it at the Portland Women's Forum Viewpoint. It's worth stopping here to take in the panorama: the pastoral highlands of Mount Pleasant on the Washington shore; the river emerging from the Gorge's western gate at Cape Horn; Crown Point jutting out in the middle distance, its Vista House like a lighthouse on a coastal headland; mountains upon mountains stretching east up the Gorge to the horizon.

Not far past the viewpoint, the highway suddenly plunges into the Gorge, dropping through curves carved in the side of a cliff. Three quarters of a mile later, it reaches the Vista House, possibly the world's most famous highway rest stop. It was built in 1918, near the dawn of the automobile age, to serve sightseers on the brand-new Columbia River Highway. Crown Point's famous view up the Gorge is remarkably unchanged since then, thanks to the conservationists and community members who worked to create the Columbia River Gorge National Scenic Area (see Ride 55).

Now you have to climb back up that cliff! It's not really so far back up, but the narrow, curving road can rattle nerves. Back up at the rim, head left onto E. Knieriem Road, which follows Big Creek down a secluded valley. The route then swings west, quiet and remote, to the village of Springdale, where it rejoins the Crown Point Highway and returns to the Sandy River.

After Springdale, the traffic picks up considerably. There's no shoulder here—only stone walls rising straight from the road. Since it's downhill, you can more or less pace the traffic. Still, it's probably not a fun place for inexperienced riders. Once you reach the Sandy, the highway grows a good shoulder. Consider a stop at Dabney State Recreation Area midway through this stretch to visit the Sandy River. The shoulder inexplicably disappears again on the very last stretch before you return to Lewis and Clark State Park.

MILEAGE LOG

0.0   Begin at Lewis and Clark State Park day-use parking area. Go left onto E. Historic Columbia River Hwy. (E. Crown Point Hwy.).

0.7   Left onto SE Woodard Rd. (becomes E. Woodward Rd.).

1.9   Left onto NE Ogden Rd., then right onto NE Mershon Rd.

4.3   Left onto E. Crown Point Hwy. (E. Historic Columbia River Hwy.). Continue through Corbett.

6.9   Portland Women's Forum Viewpoint at left.

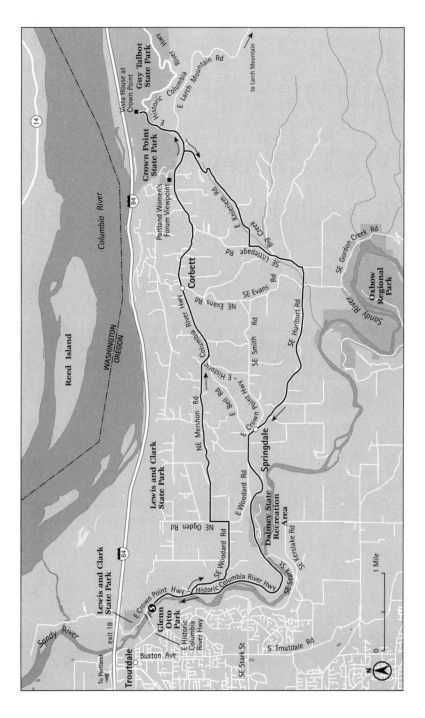

7.3 Continue straight to visit Crown Point.

8.0 Vista House at Crown Point. Retrace route back 1 mile.

9.0 Left onto E. Knieriem Rd.

10.7 Left onto SE Littlepage Rd.

11.4 Right onto SE Hurlburt Rd.

13.7 Continue straight at stop sign onto E. Historic Columbia River Hwy. (E. Crown Point Hwy.).

15.1 Dabney State Recreation Area at left.

18.0 End at Lewis and Clark State Park day-use parking area.

45 Sandy River

DIFFICULTY: Very challenging
DISTANCE: 55.3-mile loop; option: 27.8-mile loop
ELEVATION GAIN: 4700 feet

Getting There: From I-84 eastbound, take exit 18 to Lewis and Clark State Park. Go left onto E. Crown Point Hwy.–E. Historic Columbia River Hwy. and follow it approximately 3 miles to Dabney State Recreation Area at right.

Transit: Take MAX Blue Line to Gresham Central Transit Center and follow Ride 42 to mile 3.8. Continue straight on SE Sweetbriar Rd.; sharp left onto SE Kerslake Rd., then immediate right onto SE Stark St. Cross Sandy River and go right to reach Dabney State Recreation Area (4.5 miles one way).

The rugged Sandy River carries silt-laden water from a glacier high on Mount Hood down a deep canyon to meet the Columbia River at Troutdale. It's a powerful, wild river. Farms and country homes line some

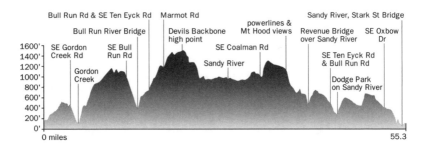

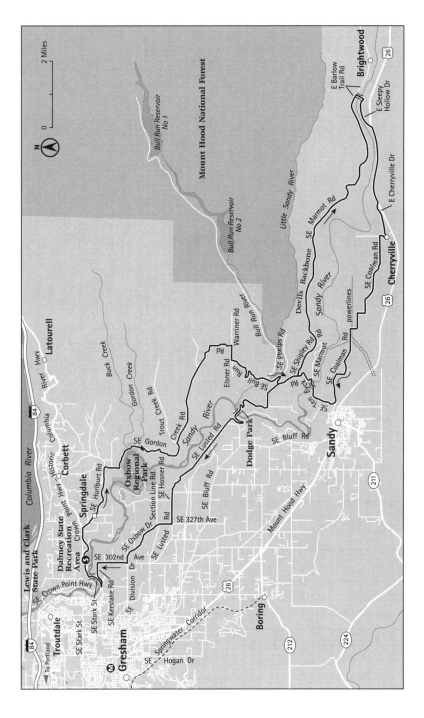

High country and Mount Hood from Marmot Road

stretches, but a dynamic floodplain and high bluffs keep most development at a respectful distance. The country roads following it—often from high above—afford plenty of solitude. And lots of hills. Long hills.

This ride climbs those hills! It's the toughest in this book, hands down.

Begin at Dabney State Recreation Area a few miles upriver from the Sandy's mouth. The climb begins straightaway, on a busy stretch of the Historic Columbia Highway, aka Crown Point Highway. If you're comfortable with the traffic here, you should be fine for the rest of the ride.

Forests give way to fields as you climb away from the river on SE Hurlburt Road. This is secluded country, hemmed in by the river's gorge and the Bull Run watershed—the latter being Portland's water source and closed to the public (see "Taste That Old Growth" sidebar). Outside the little crossroad of Springdale, go right onto SE Gordon Creek Road for a thrilling descent to the Sandy, where the road clings to precipitous slopes above a sweeping river bend. Oxbow Regional Park (Ride 42) lies across the river, beyond the sandbars and rapids.

Gordon Creek Road crosses Buck and Gordon Creeks, then commences a long and rigorous climb, gaining 1000 feet in 5 miles. It will test any rider. And truth be told, there is no grand reward at the top, just a quiet road passing some isolated farms. As soon as you've finished climbing, SE Bull Run Road plunges you right back down into the canyon, giving up most of the elevation you just gained!

At the bottom, cross the Bull Run River for a short but steep climb to SE Ten Eyck Road. Now you're rewarded with ... well, more climbing. In fact, you're about to embark on the biggest climb of the ride—and the book. (Alternatively, if all this is proving to be a bit too much, you can turn right on Ten Eyck Road to shortcut the loop to 27.8 miles.)

~~~~~~

TASTE THAT OLD GROWTH

Next time you stop at a Benson Bubbler—those ornate water fountains gracing street corners downtown—remember that you're drinking some of the purest municipal water in the world. It comes from the Bull Run River, flowing from the slopes of Mount Hood, where it rains 130 inches a year. Portland has drawn its water from there since 1895.

Nearly the entire Bull Run watershed is in the Mount Hood National Forest. Parts of it felt the ax in the early 1900s—and as recently as the 1990s—when job number one for the US Forest Service was cutting trees, water supply be damned. Times have changed, though, and logging has ceased. Half of the forest has never been logged and, thanks to an agreement between the City of Portland and the Forest Service, it never will be.

Logging isn't the only thing prohibited in the watershed. You are, too. The only legal way to access it is on a tour. The Portland Water Bureau (www.port-landonline.com/water) runs them twice a year. The tour's best stop is pristine Bull Run Lake, nestled among ancient trees at the top of the watershed.

~~~~~~

The main route turns left on Ten Eyck Road, then left onto narrow SE Shipley Road, a paved but rough forest lane. It emerges into the open at SE Marmot Road, where a left turn leads you up to expansive views. Marmot Road continues climbing, now more gradually, as the land falls away on both sides. This is the famed Devils Backbone, a ridge pinched between the canyons of the Little Sandy (oddly enough, a tributary of the Bull Run) and the Sandy.

The Devils Backbone was the final travail for emigrants on the

Oregon Trail. After maddening tedium on the High Plains, thirst and fear of Indian raids in the Great Basin, and blizzards in the Blue Mountains, emigrants arrived at The Dalles to a painful choice: Shoot the Columbia's churning rapids, risking life and property in hopes of a speedy arrival to the Willamette Valley? Or take the (relatively) safer but grueling route over Mount Hood?

Those who opted for Mount Hood followed the Barlow Road, a rutted, muddy forest track. West of present-day Government Camp, where the "road" descended a 60-degree grade on Laurel Hill, emigrants had to lower their wagons with winches. They then stumbled up and over the Devils Backbone, gaunt and weary, to cross the Sandy River en route to Oregon City.

Plenty of these pioneers, despite their exhaustion and fear, recorded amazement at the beauty of this land, impossibly green after half a continent of brown and yellow. As you drop down the Devils Backbone around mile 23, with Mount Hood suddenly looming above Zigzag and Hunchback mountains, it's easy to see why.

Marmot Road now descends somewhat anticlimactically to the Sandy River near Brightwood. Across the river, E. Sleepy Hollow Drive leads to several miles of westbound riding on US Highway 26. It's busy, but the shoulder is wide. Where the highway starts to climb above the Sandy's canyon, turn onto unmarked E. Cherryville Drive, which leads to SE Coalman Road, lined with small farms and rural homes. Where the road passes underneath large powerlines, look for Mount Hood— hidden for most of the ride—jutting into the sky.

After a long climb, Coalman Road descends almost to the town of Sandy; at SE Ten Eyck Road, cross the Sandy River at Revenue Bridge and climb through curves back toward Bull Run Road (the intersection you reached at mile 15.1). Continue past this intersection on Ten Eyck, whch curves right to become SE Lusted Road.

A steep, twisting descent brings you to Dodge Park at the confluence of the Sandy and Bull Run Rivers. Despite being a dozen miles east of city limits, this is a City of Portland park. Portland's drinking water crosses the Sandy River here in a huge pipe, pushed up and out of the canyon by hydraulic force. Having bought the land for the pipes, the city decided to make the most of its riverfront real estate and established Dodge Park. In the early 1900s, Portlanders came by the thousands on pleasant summer weekends to picnic and swim, brought here by an electric trolley from East Portland. Things are a lot quieter now, but Dodge Park remains a favorite among fishermen and boaters.

Across the Sandy you face another stiff climb, up SE Lusted Road to farm country east of Gresham. The freeways and big-box stores lurk just over the western horizon, out of sight. On SE 327th Avenue and then SE Oxbow Drive, you parallel the Sandy's canyon (Oxbow Regional Park is at right; see Ride 42). Then, at SE 302nd Avenue, you plunge down to the river one final time, crossing the Sandy via Stark Street to go right onto the Historic Columbia Highway. Dabney State Park is just 0.25 mile down the road at right.

MILEAGE LOG

0.0   Begin at Dabney State Park. Right onto E. Crown Point Hwy. (E. Historic Columbia River Hwy.; caution).

1.5   Continue straight onto SE Hurlburt Rd. in Springdale.

3.6   Right at flashing red light onto SE Gordon Creek Rd.

4.9   Cross Buck Creek; cross Gordon Creek in 0.3 mile.

7.4   Trout Creek Rd. at left; continue straight.

12.0   Road curves right to become SE Bull Run Rd.

14.5   Cross Bull Run River.

15.1   Left at top of hill onto SE Ten Eyck Rd. (**Option:** Go right here to shorten loop and rejoin route at mile 42.6.)

15.8   Left onto SE Shipley Rd.

17.2   Continue straight, at stop sign, onto SE Marmot Rd., climbing Devils Backbone, then descending to Sandy River.

27.1   Right onto E. Barlow Trail Rd. to cross Sandy River, then right onto E. Sleepy Hollow Dr.

28.3   Right onto US 26.

30.9   Right onto unmarked E. Cherryville Dr. (just past E. Sylvan Dr.).

32.1   Right onto SE Baty Rd.

32.3   Left onto SE Coalman Rd.

35.9   Cross under powerlines; views of Mount Hood.

38.9   Right onto SE Ten Eyck Rd.

40.2   Cross Revenue Bridge over Sandy River.

42.6   At SE Bull Run Rd., continue straight on SE Ten Eyck Rd. (**Option:** Shortcut rejoins main route here.)

42.8   Ten Eyck Rd. curves right to become SE Lusted Rd.

44.7   Cross Sandy River at Dodge Park; continue on SE Lusted Rd.

50.1   Right onto SE 327th Ave. (SE Altman Rd.).

50.6 At stop sign, continue onto SE Oxbow Dr., which becomes
      SE Division Dr.

52.4 Right onto SE 302nd Ave., which curves left to become
      SE Kerslake Rd.

54.2 Sharp right (downhill) onto SE Stark St.

54.8 Cross Sandy River; go right onto E. Crown Point Hwy.
      (E. Historic Columbia River Hwy.).

55.3 End at Dabney State Park.

ACROSS THE COLUMBIA

The mighty Columbia is a formidable physical barrier—and to some extent a cultural one as well. Yet as the Portland region's Washington neighbors know, there is great bicycling to be had across the river. This chapter offers a few highlights, taking in urban greenways, secluded timber country, and Columbia River scenery.

46 Fort Vancouver and Burnt Bridge Creek Greenway

DIFFICULTY: Easy
DISTANCE: 23.1-mile loop
ELEVATION GAIN: 750 feet

Getting There: From I-5 northbound, take exit 1B toward City Center–Convention Center. Turn left onto E. Sixth St., then left again onto Columbia St. Follow it under the freeway approximately 0.5 mile to Waterfront Park on the right.

Transit: Take MAX Yellow Line to Expo Center station. Bicycle across I-5 bridge (see "Crossing the Interstate 5 Bridge" sidebar in Ride 47). At bottom of exit ramp, go left onto SE Columbia Way. Waterfront Park is immediately at right.

Mindless sprawl? A refuge of sanity from the liberal crazies across the river? It depends on your perspective, of course, but most will agree

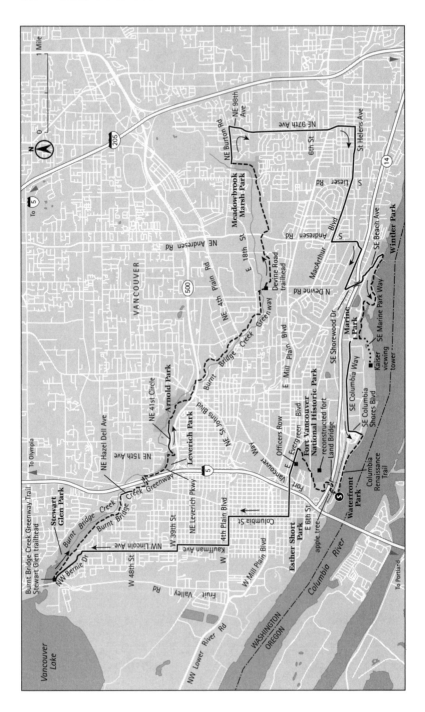

that things are different over in Vancouver, Washington. A lot more than a river divides it from Portland: cross-border debates rage over land use, taxes, (potential) bridge tolls, and light rail—to name only a few. Any Portlander paying attention might detect a hint of resentment emanating from the Washington shore. But that would require paying attention. Ask a Portlander how much he or she knows of Vancouver, and you'll likely tap a deep well of ignorance.

This is a shame, since ties of commerce, family, and work tightly bind Portland and Vancouver. And those who do know Vancouver treasure its fine parks and greenways. This ride showcases some of the best.

Begin at Waterfront Park, on the Columbia River in downtown Vancouver. From the park, cross SE Columbia Way and pass through a tunnel under the railroad. The tunnel leads to an old apple tree, planted by Hudson's Bay Company employees and now reputed to be the Northwest's first—the seed from which Washington's booming apple industry grew.

Go right at the tree to cross a new bridge over Washington Route 14. Called the "Land Bridge," it was built in 2008 as part of the Confluence Project (www.confluenceproject.org), brainchild of architect Maya Linn. Famed designer of the national Vietnam Veterans Memorial in Washington, DC, Linn has spent the last decade creating public artworks along the Columbia River. Functional, beautiful, and tinged with loss, these works reflect on the profound social and environmental change in and along the river since Lewis and Clark's journey of discovery in 1804–06.

Across the bridge, you arrive at Fort Vancouver National Historic Park. Though sandwiched between two freeways and an airfield, this just happens to be the most important site in the Euro-American history of the Pacific Northwest. It was the Hudson's Bay Company's main fur-trading post, serving for a time as the Northwest Territory's unofficial capital. It all but disappeared under 20th-century urbanization before the National Park Service acquired the site in the late 1940s. It's since been partially reconstructed. *If you visit only one cultural site in this entire book, visit this park!* It tells an incredible story (see "Fort Vancouver" sidebar).

From the bridge, follow a path past the reconstructed fort, its wooden palisades rising above orchards. Continue uphill toward 19th-century US Army barracks and the park's interpretive center. Go left at path's end onto E. Evergreen Boulevard to continue along Officers Row, a string of elegant 19th-century homes. Continue across Interstate 5 into downtown Vancouver.

Officers Row, Fort Vancouver National Historic Park

After 50 or so years of freeway-induced torpor, downtown Vancouver is coming back to life. In the first decade of the 21st century, the area around Esther Short Park sprouted a major new hotel and condominiums to rival Portland's Pearl District. Buoyed by this success, planners and developers dreamed up an entire high-rise riverfront city—Vancouver's answer to Portland's South Waterfront neighborhood—to be built on vacant land between downtown and the port. Then came the Great Recession of 2009. All that's come of the vision as of this writing are graffiti-tagged artist's renderings affixed to a chain-link fence, which surrounds the rubble-strewn vacant lot. Someday, maybe, the good times will return.

In downtown, go right onto Columbia Street, then jog left a few blocks to continue north on Kaufmann and NW Lincoln Avenues. The route gradually climbs through older neighborhoods and then drops abruptly to Fruit Valley Road.

Go right here to begin the Burnt Bridge Creek Greenway, surely one of the best bike paths in the entire region. It traces an 8-mile green swath across the city, meandering among wetlands, forests, and fields. Some sections delve so completely into nature you almost feel disoriented upon reemerging into the suburban fabric of homes, boulevards, and businesses. Heartening signs of habitat restoration are everywhere along Burnt Bridge Creek, which, long abused and neglected, truly needs it.

Large parks line the greenway. The first, Stewart Glen, is an extensive system of wetland and meadows walled off from its urban surroundings by steep bluffs. In Leverich Park, near the halfway point, Burnt Bridge Creek courses through a narrow, wooded valley. At Arnold Park, the creek arcs through a wide floodplain edged with forest. Near the greenway's east end, Meadowbrook Marsh Park offers eastern mountain vistas. Every one of these places is worth a picnic.

The greenway currently ends at NE Burton Road, deep in East Vancouver. Go right onto NE 98th Avenue to climb up and out of Burnt Bridge drainage and begin a long suburban descent to the Columbia River at Wintler Park. From Wintler's inviting beach, the Columbia River Renaissance Trail leads west, past luxury condos and a wetland. It ends near the old Kaiser Shipyards, where a short detour visits an observation tower and interpretive display. (These yards built a big chunk of America's World War II naval fleet.)

Beyond the shipyards, follow SE Columbia Way west to the Columbia Shores condominium development—oddly marooned between freeway and shipyards—where the Renaissance Trail resumes. Assuming you're not pedaling into a head wind (common on summer afternoons), it's a quick trip back to Waterfront Park.

MILEAGE LOG

0.0 Begin at Waterfront Park. Cross SE Columbia Way, following signs through railroad tunnel to Old Apple Tree Park. Follow path east to cross over SR 14 via the Land Bridge into Fort Vancouver National Historic Park; continue through park on path.

0.7 Left onto E. 5th St., then immediate left to resume path.

1.1 Left onto path along Officers Row (E. Evergreen Blvd.). Exit path onto street at roundabout and continue straight (west) to cross over I-5.

2.0 Right onto Columbia St.

2.8 Left onto W. 4th Plain Blvd.

3.2 Right onto Kauffman Ave.

3.8 Left onto W. 39th St., then right onto NW Lincoln Ave.

5.1 Left onto NW Bernie Dr.

5.7 Right onto NW Fruit Valley Rd.; entrance to Burnt Bridge Greenway Trail at Stewart Glen Park immediately on right.

7.1 Right at path's end onto NE Hazel Dell Ave.

7.3 Left to resume path (this turn easy to miss). Cross I-5 on overpass, then go right at intersection to stay on greenway.

7.9 Right onto NE Leverich Pkwy., then left to resume greenway at Leverich Park.

8.4　Cross NE 15th Ave. and continue east on NE 41st Circle. Greenway resumes at street end in Arnold Park.

9.4　Right onto sidewalk at NE St. Johns Blvd. Cross at crosswalk to continue east on greenway.

10.7　Cross E. 4th Plain Blvd. at stoplight and continue on greenway.

11.1　Cross E. 18th St. at crosswalk and continue across creek on greenway.

11.5　Right onto N. Devine Rd., then left to continue on greenway. Devine Road trailhead at right.

12.4　Cross NE Andresen Rd. at crosswalk and continue on greenway.

13.6　Right at end of greenway in Meadowbrook Marsh Park onto NE Burton Rd.

14.0　Right onto NE 98th Ave., which, after stoplight at E. Mill Plain Blvd., becomes NE 97th Ave. for a mile or so.

15.7　Right onto St. Helens Ave.

16.4　Cross S. Lieser Rd. at flashing red light to continue west on MacArthur Blvd.

17.3　Left onto S. Andresen Rd.

17.8　Right onto E. Evergreen Blvd.

18.4　Sharp left at four-way stop onto SE Shorewood Dr. Follow signs for SR 14 eastbound. Cross SR 14 overpass and go right onto SE Beach Dr.

19.3　Sharp right at street end, at Wintler Park entrance, onto Columbia River Renaissance Trail.

20.7　Left onto SE Columbia Way at end of path. (**Option:** left onto SE Marine Park Way to visit Kaiser viewing tower.)

21.9　Left onto SE Columbia Shores Blvd. Continue straight through parking lot to resume Renaissance Trail.

23.1　End at Waterfront Park.

FORT VANCOUVER

The Native people of the Pacific Northwest have lived here for millennia, but to Euro-Americans it's still a pretty new place. As early as the 1790s, Boston sea captains and British explorers sailed the coast. Then Lewis and Clark followed Native American guides to the ocean in 1804. Early fur traders set up shop in Astoria around 1812. But not until the Hudson's Bay Company built Fort Vancouver in 1824 did anything resembling a settlement exist here.

In 1824, this land was still up for grabs. A young United States was rapidly acquiring territory east of the Rockies. The Russians held a tenuous grip on

Alaska. The Spanish clung to California and New Mexico. The British held Canada and dreamed of retaking the United States. The one place no one yet owned was that "far corner"—to use Stewart Holbrook's phrase—the Pacific Northwest.

If anyone could be said to rule the territory, it was the Hudson's Bay Company. One of the world's oldest corporations (still in business today as the Bay), it was chartered by the British government in 1670 to exploit North America's "soft gold"—furs. The company operated from Montreal to the Pacific, building forts where local natives traded furs for European goods. With Fort Vancouver, the company hoped to tap all of the fur-rich Columbia Basin. It also hoped to keep foreign powers—especially the United States—out.

Built on a level plain with a commanding view over the Columbia and Willamette Rivers, Fort Vancouver proved a highly strategic site. Nearly all the furs harvested in the Northwest moved through here.

It was an incredibly polyglot place. Local Native Americans came to trade; many settled near the fort, intermarrying with native Hawaiians brought as laborers by fur traders traversing the Pacific. Many of the company's employees were French Canadians who grew up in the Quebec fur trade. When their bodies broke after hard years gathering furs, many retired to farms in the Willamette Valley.

Fort Vancouver's boss, a longtime Hudson's Bay hand named John McLoughlin, kept the peace. He earned the title "Father of Oregon" by wisely aiding the Oregon Trail migrants who stumbled, often starving, down from Mount Hood to Fort Vancouver after a transcontinental trek. McLoughlin could have ignored their requests and let them struggle; they were, after all, foreign intruders in territory claimed by Britain. Instead McLoughlin lent them seed, farm tools, clothes, and other essentials, then gently steered them south to the Willamette Valley.

Though a loyal employee, McLoughlin knew his good deeds were speeding the Hudson's Bay Company's exit from the territory, as Americans entered in ever-greater numbers. Feeling the balance of power tilt toward the United States, and sensing the fur trade's days were numbered, McLoughlin retired from the company and settled in the recently established territorial capital of Oregon City (you can visit his house on Ride 32).

The flood of American migrants soon overwhelmed the Hudson's Bay Company, forcing a gradual retreat northward. Long before Fort Vancouver officially closed in 1860, the area was effectively American—and officially so after the Oregon Treaty established the 49th parallel as the international border in 1846. The US Army established a barracks next door to the old trading fort, which gradually returned to the earth.

As Vancouver developed into a modern American city, disfigured by free-ways and suburban sprawl, most signs of its origins disappeared. That finally changed in the late 1960s, when archaeologists rediscovered the fort's foundations. Some of the buildings have since been reconstructed. The fort is now a national park, celebrating and interpreting two centuries of Pacific Northwest—and world—history.

47 Vancouver Lake

DIFFICULTY: Easy to Moderate
DISTANCE: 26.8 miles
ELEVATION GAIN: 200 feet

Getting There: See Ride 46's directions to Waterfront Park in Vancouver.

Here's a straightforward and flat out-and-back tour visiting Vancouver Lake and the Columbia River. There's no real destination: just follow NW Lower River Road west from Vancouver as far as you care to go. The road runs a little over 11 miles before falling—literally—into the Columbia River.

Begin at Waterfront Park in downtown Vancouver. Go left onto SE Columbia Way and then right onto W. Third Street. Check out the Remembrance Wall murals lining Third Street; they honor veterans from World War II to Vietnam. Continue to Esther Street and through a roundabout. At right are the 1867 Slocum House (home to a community theater) and Esther Short Park, which the city claims to be the oldest public square in the Pacific Northwest. It was dedicated in 1855.

The route now meanders through downtown to W. Mill Plain Boulevard, which crosses railroad tracks via an overpass and leads you to NW Lower River Road. The road soon skirts Vancouver Lake, hidden behind its riparian woods.

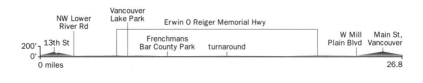

Vancouver Lake is essentially a giant puddle on the Columbia's floodplain. It averages less than 3 feet deep, 15 at most. Surrounding it is a lacustrine expanse where the boundary between land and water shifts with the seasons. Stately cottonwoods and ash trees line board-flat fields, half-drowned and given over to the birds. The whole place is quiet and surprisingly wild.

Where Lower River Road turns westward, continue straight a short distance on the NW Erwin O. Reiger Memorial Highway and then go right onto a path. It ends at a beach and picnic area in Vancouver Lake Park, where the massive lake finally reveals itself. When you're done visiting, backtrack on the path and cross Reiger Highway to pick up a second path heading west along a canal.

The canal is actually a "flushing channel," built in 1983 to improve the flow of water into and out of the lake. Once upon a time, Vancouver Lake was deeper, clean, and full of fish. Then came the Columbia River dams, which shut off floodwaters that had historically refreshed the lake. During World War II an aluminum plant was built directly

Approaching storm, Frenchmans Bar County Park

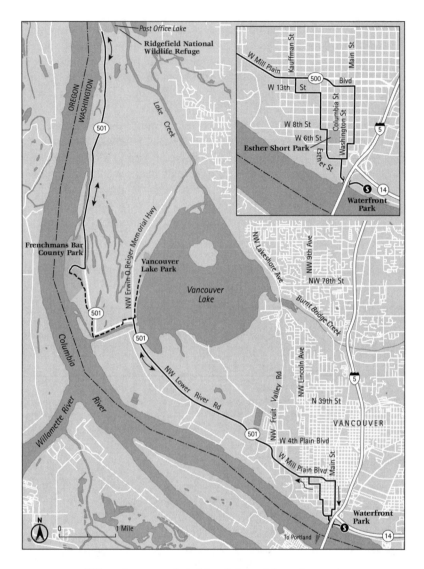

upstream, filling the now-shrinking lake with toxic nasties. Postwar residential development added great quantities of sewage to the beleaguered water body, feeding algal blooms. By the late 1960s, it was dying.

Engineers came to the rescue, dredging the lake and building the flushing channel to improve water flow to and from the Columbia River. Though Burnt Bridge Creek flows into Vancouver Lake, the lake gets most of its water directly from the Columbia River, which flows into it via the lake's outlet stream, Lake Creek. This happens when the tide—perceptible even here, 100 river miles inland—overcomes the Columbia's current and pushes the great river back on itself. The lake remains polluted, but the flushing channel has at least prevented Vancouver Lake from becoming Vancouver Swamp.

CROSSING THE INTERSTATE 5 BRIDGE

The relationship between Portland and Vancouver is complicated. So is the 2.3-mile bike route connecting them via the Interstate 5 bridge over the Columbia River.

From the Expo Center MAX station (see map for Ride 13), head north to NE Marine Drive on a path. It crosses Marine Drive at a stoplight and continues east under I-5. The path then loops partway around the freeway on-ramp to reach a junction. Go left here, then immediately right, onto a path ascending to the first bridge section.

Cross this first bridge to Hayden Island, where the path bends right to briefly follow N. Tomahawk Island Drive. Cross this road at the first crosswalk and continue north; the path now briefly parallels N. Hayden Island Drive before crossing it, via two crosswalks. Now you are on the inside of the looping, cloverleaf-style freeway on-ramp. The path hits a T intersection here; go left (a right leads under the freeway) and up onto the second bridge section.

Follow this narrow but adequate path across the Columbia's main channel. Crosswinds can make it exciting. Immediately across the river, the path loops down off the bridge to intersect SE Columbia Way in Vancouver.

After almost a mile along the channel, the path heads northward to Frenchmans Bar County Park, where you can watch mighty freighters ply the great river, stacked with automobiles and containers from Asia. Fishermen lounge around the long beach, their salmon rods anchored in the sand. Paved paths circle through the park, leading nowhere in particular.

Exit the park via its entrance road (not the path) and go left to continue on NW Lower River Road, now even quieter after shedding its traffic at Frenchmans Bar. The remaining 4 miles pass a secluded houseboat community, a sand and gravel operation, and a handful of lonely farms. The road draws ever closer to the river, eventually narrowing to one lane. Then—poof—it's gone, ending at Ridgefield National Wildlife Refuge. Time to turn around.

The road was built to reach Ridgefield, but the Columbia River had different plans. It shifted course and took a bite from the land, leaving the road to crumble on a precipice. At the desolate turnaround, you might feel tempted to continue past the barrier on that narrow bit of remaining asphalt. You might think it will lead you on a car-free adventure through the wildlife refuge. If you don't mind plunging into the swirling Columbia from a 20-foot bank or bushwhacking through miles of swamp, give it a try. Otherwise, enjoy the gloomy spectacle of nature upending humanity's works—then return the way you came.

Back in Vancouver, W. Mill Plain Boulevard crosses just before the railroad overpass, consider moving from the road to the barrier-separated sidewalk. This way you can mosey across the overpass and enjoy views of the massive grain terminals lining the river. Then continue on Mill Plain to Main Street and go right to cruise Vancouver's old commercial district. It leads back to Columbia Street, which in turn carries you under Interstate 5 and back to Waterfront Park.

MILEAGE LOG

0.0   Begin at Waterfront Park. Go left onto SE Columbia Way, which crosses under I-5 and becomes Columbia St.

0.4   Left onto W. 3rd St., then right onto Esther St.

0.6   Left onto W. 8th St. at Esther Short Park, then right onto Franklin St.

1.0   Left onto W. 13th St., then right onto Kauffman Ave.

1.3   Left onto W. Mill Plain Blvd.

2.2   Continue straight through stoplight onto W. Fourth Plain Blvd., which becomes NW Lower River Rd.

5.6   Continue straight at intersection onto NW Erwin O. Reiger Memorial Hwy. Go right onto bike path just beyond intersection.

6.4   Path ends at Vancouver Lake Park (beach, restrooms). Retrace route back to beginning of path.

7.1   Cross NW Erwin O. Reiger Memorial Hwy. and continue west on path toward Frenchmans Bar.

9.3   Path ends in Frenchmans Bar County Park. Go left onto park road to visit beach, then follow park road east to park entrance.

9.6   Left onto NW Lower River Rd.

13.8   Lower River Road dead-ends at Post Office Lake in Ridgefield National Wildlife Refuge. Retrace route to NW Erwin O. Reiger Memorial Hwy.

20.5   Right onto NW Erwin O. Reiger Memorial Hwy. Continue through intersection onto NW Lower River Rd.

24.2 Intersection of W. Mill Plain Blvd, and Thompson Rd. Enter barrier-separated sidewalk along W. Mill Plain for better views from overpass immediately ahead. Continue on Mill Plain Blvd.

25.3 Right onto Main St.

25.9 Right onto W. 6th St.

26.0 Left onto Columbia St., which crosses under I-5 to become SE Columbia Way.

26.8 End at Waterfront Park.

48 Salmon Creek

DIFFICULTY: Easy (Loop: Moderate)
DISTANCE: 6.4 miles; option: 20.8-mile loop
ELEVATION GAIN: 75 feet; option 1100 feet

Getting There: From I-5 northbound, take exit 5, NE 99th St. in Washington State. Go right onto NE 99th St., then left onto NE Hwy. 99. After approximately 1 mile, go left onto NE 117th St. Cross under freeway and turn right into parking area for Klineline Pond in Salmon Creek Regional Park. If parking area is full, continue west on NE 117th St. to next right, which leads to additional parking. Parking fee at either location.

Transit: Take C-TRAN bus (multiple routes) to 99th St. Transit Center. Ride north on NE 7th Ave., go left onto NE 99th St., right onto NE Hazel Dell Ave., right onto NE 117th Ave., and left into park entrance. Continue through parking area to join path.

Here's another one of the region's best greenway trails, a 3.2-mile paved path following the meandering lower Salmon Creek. As an out-and-back, it makes a great family ride. It can also form the beginning of a moderate loop through the countryside north of Vancouver, with rolling hills, sweeping Columbia River views, and a tour of Washington State University's new Vancouver campus. Ambitious riders could even connect it with Ride 49 for a yet longer tour.

Begin at Salmon Creek Regional Park, at the parking area for Klineline Pond. The pond, an old gravel quarry, is often overrun with swimmers in summer. It can be a madhouse or a giant party, depending on your attitude. (A footpath from the main pond leads underneath Interstate 5 to another, quieter pond, where you can poke

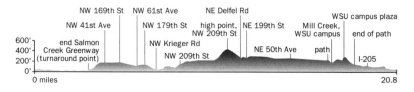

around the creek and assorted swimming holes away from the main crowd.)

The greenway trail begins at the far (west) end of the main parking area. It heads west, skirting a second parking area and some baseball fields to reach a junction. Go right here and continue along a wetland. The path reaches Salmon Creek's bank around mile 1 and stays near it for the next 1.5 miles. Subdivisions line bluffs above the creek, but down here it feels surprisingly wild.

At mile 1.8 the greenway curves left to intersect a spur trail at the base of steep, forested bluffs. Go right at this intersection to continue west on the main path, which hugs the edge of the floodplain, away from Salmon Creek. The final mile has more limited views of the creek, which slows and broadens into a wetland. During the rainy months it can spread to fill the entire valley bottom, looking more like a lake.

The greenway ends at NW 36th Avenue, short of the creek's confluence with Lake Creek and the Columbia River. Retrace your route back to Klineline Pond.

Alternatively, to return via a 20.8-mile loop, go right at the greenway's end onto NW 36th Avenue. After a short but tough climb up NW Seward Road, you arrive on high ground dividing Salmon and Whipple Creeks. The Tualatin Mountains rise above Sauvie Island across the Columbia as you follow the bluffs above Lake Creek and Ridgefield National Wildlife Refuge. At right, vineyards blanket hills topped by mansions. At NW 209th Street, the route strikes eastward, climbing gradually toward the freeway. Views stretch east across plains to the hills, crowned by Silver Star Mountain.

Over the freeway, continue east a few miles and go right onto NE 50th Avenue to reach Washington State University's Vancouver campus. Go right onto a bike path paralleling NE 159th Street and follow it across Mill Creek. Beyond, the trees part to reveal the new campus, gleaming on the slopes of Mount Vista. The path crosses the campus ring road and continues up through switchbacks to the central campus plaza, passing the student union, library, classrooms, and a fountain. It's a beautiful campus with a great vantage; views stretch south clear to Mount Hood.

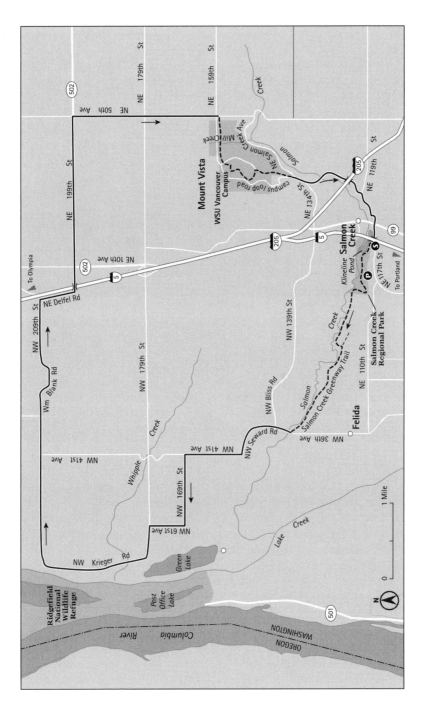

On the Salmon Creek Greenway

From the central plaza, continue past the fountain and go left onto a service road. (If you reach the parking area, you've gone too far.) This road curves left and downhill, then intersects a path. Make a sharp right onto the path and follow it downhill to NE Salmon Creek Avenue, which returns you to the Klineline Pond parking area.

MILEAGE LOG

0.0 Begin at Salmon Creek Greenway trailhead in Salmon Creek Regional Park, at Klineline Pond parking area. Join greenway trail at far (west) end of parking area.

0.5 Right at path junction beyond baseball fields.

1.8 Right at junction to continue on greenway.

3.2 Salmon Creek Greenway ends. Retrace route to return.

Optional loop return:

3.2   Right onto NW 36th Ave. Cross Salmon Creek and continue on NW Seward Rd., which curves right to become NW 41st Ave. 1 mile farther.

4.9   Left onto NW 169th St.

5.9   Right onto NW 61st Ave.

6.4   Left onto NW 179th St., which curves right to become NW Krieger Rd. in 0.4 mile.

8.4   Krieger curves right to become NW 209th St.

11.9 NW 209th curves right to become NE Delfel Rd.

12.4 Left onto NE 199th St. Cross freeway on overpass and continue through stoplight at NE 10th Ave.

14.8 Right onto NE 50th Ave.

16.8 Right onto path paralleling NE 159th St. Enter Washington State University campus.

17.4 Cross campus loop road and continue uphill through main campus area.

17.8 Continue past fountain in central campus area and go left onto service road. Take first right onto path heading downhill.

18.6 Right onto NE Salmon Creek Ave. at path's end.

19.0 Left at stoplight to stay on NE Salmon Creek Ave. Cross under I-205.

19.9 Right onto NE 119th St. (becomes NE 117th St.). Cross NE Hwy. 99 and continue under I-5.

20.7 Right into Klineline Pond parking area at Salmon Creek Regional Park.

20.8 End at Salmon Creek Greenway trailhead.

49 Ridgefield and La Center

DIFFICULTY: Moderate
DISTANCE: 23.3-mile loop
ELEVATION GAIN: 1900 feet

Getting There: From I-5 northbound in Washington State, take exit 14, Pioneer St.–SR 501, toward Ridgefield. Go left onto Pioneer St. (Washington Rte. 501), cross over freeway, continue straight through roundabout, and follow Pioneer St. into Ridgefield, approximately 3 miles from freeway exit. Plentiful street parking.

Transit: Take C-TRAN bus (multiple routes) to 99th Street Transit Center and catch the Ridgefield Connector Bus (weekdays only) to Ridgefield City Center and beginning of ride.

This ride tours northwestern Clark County on a loop connecting Ridgefield and La Center. It begins at the Columbia River and crosses a rolling plain toward the Mount St. Helens foothills, visiting sleepy towns and the still-wild East Fork of the Lewis River. This is farm country, southwest Washington's answer to the Willamette Valley.

Begin in downtown Ridgefield, a small town gradually becoming a bedroom community for Vancouver. Fortunately, it lies just far enough from Interstate 5 to preserve a genuine small-town charm. That charm is on full display during the Fourth of July, when Ridgefield looks about as much like a Norman Rockwell painting as any town could.

From the center of town, head north on N. Main Avenue. The city limits are quickly reached and soon you're in the countryside. Don't start cranking just yet, though. Ridgefield National Wildlife Refuge, a mile down the road, is not to be missed.

The refuge—more than 5000 acres of floodplains and wetlands along the Columbia River—owes its existence to Alaska's 1964 Good Friday earthquake. The massive quake and its ensuing tsunami killed hundreds of people and destroyed several coastal towns. It also drowned millions of acres of Alaskan wetlands that had been home to migratory waterfowl. The US Fish and Wildlife Service responded by establishing Ridgefield and three additional refuges in the Willamette Valley (including Basket Slough; see Ride 35) to protect the birds' wintering grounds.

The Ridgefield refuge has a lot more to it than birds, though. For millennia, a settlement of Chinook Indians stood here, graced by the long, low plank houses typical of Lower Columbia River tribes. When Lewis and Clark passed by the settlement, called Cathlapotle, on their way to the Pacific in 1805, the explorers estimated the population at upward of 1000 people. By the time Ridgefield's earliest white settlers showed up, however, Cathlapotle was nearly abandoned, its people nearly extirpated by infectious disease brought to the region by early European traders.

A replica of Cathlapotle's vanished plank houses, constructed at the site in 2005, now commemorates the village's vibrant history and tragic end. You can visit it by following a trail several hundred yards

East Fork Lewis River at Daybreak Park

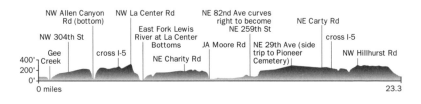

from the refuge's Carty Unit parking area, across a pedestrian bridge spanning the railroad tracks. The house, set among oaks on a hill above the refuge's wetlands, is worth the quick detour from your ride. If you visit on a summer weekend, you can tour the house's interior (www.ridgefieldfriends.org/plankhouse.php).

Now the real riding begins. From the refuge, continue north on NW 71st Avenue, which despite the name is a quiet country road. From here on out you'll be on roads much like this, passing rural residences set a few acres apart. The mix of homes is classic Washington: backwoods compounds (junked cars, curtained windows, vaguely threatening dogs) mingle with tidy old farmsteads and tasteless new McMansions. It's fascinating.

After a sharp dip down into Allen Canyon (where Clark County has recently purchased the lake in the valley bottom—Mud Lake—as a park), the route heads east. As you cross I-5, look for Mount St. Helens and Mount Adams looming ahead. After a short climb, you descend to the La Center Bottoms, where the East Fork Lewis River widens into a floodplain teeming with wildlife. Across the river, a right turn leads you to La Center's main drag.

So what's with that name? Late 19th-century town boosters—not known for their subtlety—sought a name reflecting their ambition to make the town the "center" of commerce in northern Clark County. Apparently they felt "La Center" sounded a little more sophisticated— it's French, right?—than "the Center." But before you snicker too loudly, keep in mind that the town's original name was Podunk!

In truth—and despite the good people of La Center's best efforts—the town has been more Podunk than a Center until quite recently. As neighboring communities flourished through the early 20th century, La Center couldn't seem to find any mojo. The town's population declined even as the county's population grew by leaps and bounds. By the 1980s, La Center had fewer than 500 souls and was on the verge of bankruptcy.

Desperate for revenue, the town looked to a tried-and-true economic development tool: gambling. Not everyone loves the tacky card rooms that now dot the town, but none can doubt that they saved the

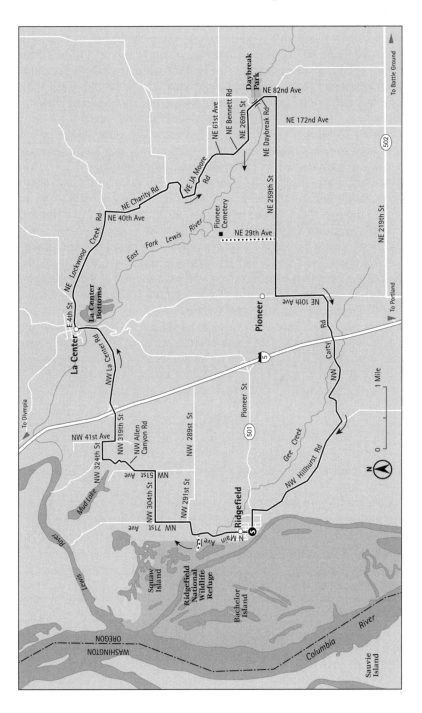

To Battle Ground

Daybreak Park

NE 82nd Ave

NE 172nd Ave

502

NE 269th St

NE Bennett Rd

NE 61st Ave

NE Daybreak Rd

NE LA Moore Rd

NE 259th St

NE 219th St

NE Charity Rd

NE 40th Ave

NE Lockwood Creek Rd

Pioneer Cemetery

NE 29th Ave

East Fork Lewis River

La Center Bottoms

La Center

E 4th St

Pioneer

NE 10th Ave

To Portland

NW La Center Rd

NW Carty Rd

5

1 Mile

NW 41st Ave

NW 319th St

NW Allen Canyon Rd

NW 289st St

Pioneer St

501

To Olympia

NW 324th St

NW 51st Ave

NW 304th St

NW 291st St

Gee Creek

NW Hillhurst Rd

0

N

Mud Lake

NW 71st Ave

Ridgefield

N Main Ave

River

Lewis

Squaw Island

Ridgefield National Wildlife Refuge

Bachelor Island

Columbia River

WASHINGTON
OREGON

Sauvie Island

town. Turning itself into a little Reno, La Center managed to quintuple its population and can at last dream big. It's currently annexing a huge swath of land so it can sprawl westward to I-5. The future isn't entirely bright, though. The area's original inhabitants, the Cowlitz tribe, have at long last received government approval to build a giant casino on the freeway just west of La Center, threatening the town's cash cow.

From La Center, head east on NE Lockwood Creek Road. Beyond the school, library, and town hall, a right turn onto NE 40th Avenue leads you back into the countryside and down to the river. Old farms, some fallen into ruin, line the road. The air of decrepitude may stem from the devastation wrought on this stretch of river by decades of gravel mining. Massive pits, many now filled with floodwaters, lie just out of sight from the road. Mining has dramatically altered the floodplain, triggering erosion that has devastated salmon habitat, threatened nearby homes, and put drinking water sources at risk. Local residents and conservationists have fought for a decade to prevent further mining and accelerate the difficult task of restoring this badly damaged reach.

All signs of eco-catastrophe disappear just a short distance upstream, though, where you cross the river to arrive at Daybreak Park (restrooms). This busy wayside—haunt of inner tubers, picnicking families, and skulking fishermen—spans a 0.25-mile stretch of river, perfect for wading and swimming mid- to late summer's low water.

Beyond the park, follow NE 259th Street up a short but stiff climb out of the floodplain. Follow it west across the gradually rising farmland. A detour to the right on NE 29th Avenue leads 1 mile north to an obscure, unmarked, and slightly spooky old pioneer cemetery, half-overgrown and seemingly lost in time. The main ride continues west on NE 259th Avenue and then cuts south at NE 10th Street to skirt the encroaching sprawl.

A right turn on NW Carty Road leads you back over the freeway and across Gee Creek, through one last blissful stretch of countryside as yet untouched by the subdivisions creeping down S. Hillhurst Road—your route back into Ridgefield.

MILEAGE LOG

0.0 Begin at Pioneer Street (SR 501) and N. Main Ave. Go right onto N. Main Ave.

0.7 Cross Gee Creek.

1.1 Entrance to Ridgefield National Wildlife Refuge, Carty Unit, at left. Just beyond, N. Main curves right to become NW 291st St.

1.3 Left onto NW 71st Ave.

1.9 Right onto NW 304th St.

2.8 Left onto NW 51st Ave.

3.2 Bear right onto NW Allen Canyon Rd. Steep drop down into canyon.

4.0 Continue straight at stop sign onto NW 324th St. Curves right to become NW 41st Ave., then left to become NW 319th St.

5.0 Cross I-5 (Mount St. Helens and Mount Adams views from overpass) and continue on NW La Center Rd.

6.8 Cross East Fork Lewis River at La Center Bottoms.

7.0 Right onto E. 4th St. in La Center. Becomes NE Lockwood Creek Rd. upon leaving town.

9.2 Right onto NE 40th Ave., which becomes NE Charity Rd.

10.6 Bear right onto NE J. A. Moore Rd. Steep downhill. Becomes NE 61st Ave., then NE Bennett Rd., then NE 269th St., then NE Daybreak Rd.

13.4 Right to stay on Daybreak Rd. and cross bridge over East Fork Lewis River. Entrance to Daybreak County Park several hundred yards beyond, at left. Road becomes NE 82nd Ave. after park.

13.8 NE 82nd Ave. curves right to become NE 259th St. and begins climbing

14.3 Right to stay on NE 259th St. near top of climb.

16.3 Cross NE 29th Ave. (**Side trip:** Go right onto NE 29th Ave. for 1 mile to visit Pioneer Cemetery.)

17.3 Left onto NE 10th Ave.

18.2 Bear right onto NW Carty Rd.

19.0 Cross I-5 on overpass.

20.6 Right onto NW Hillhurst Rd.

22.9 Left onto Pioneer St. (SR 501).

23.3 End at N. Main Ave. and Pioneer St. in Ridgefield.

50 Woodland Dike

DIFFICULTY: Easy to Moderate
DISTANCE: 14.8-mile loop
ELEVATION GAIN: 75 feet

Getting There: From I-5 northbound in Washington State, take exit 21 for Woodland. Go left onto Washington Rte. 503 and cross under I-5. Go left onto Lakeshore Dr., then immediately left into Woodland Information Center and Park and Ride parking lot.

Disclosure: Until researching this book, I thought of Woodland as little more than the freeway exit for Mount St. Helens. Turns out there's more to this community, though—including the mellow, scenic riding to be had along Woodland's Dike Road. Like Lower River Road in Ride 47, Dike Road offers a close-up of the Columbia River on a quiet, flat route.

As with that ride, you'll likely be amazed at how soon the freeway's drone dissipates in the silence of vast lowlands, full of farmland and birds. The river is simply so huge, and its floodplain so broad, that even on a short ride it's possible to feel as though you've left the town far behind. The river forms a world unto itself.

Begin at Woodland's Park and Ride, where a humble mobile home serves as the town's visitor center. From here, follow Lakeshore Drive south past Horseshoe Lake, formerly a sweeping arc of the Lewis River. The builders of Interstate 5, finding this river bend inconvenient, rammed the road right through it. The result is this artificial oxbow lake. Opposite Lakeshore Drive, I-5 thunders. This is admittedly not the most auspicious beginning for a ride, but persevere!

The road soon curves away from the freeway, changing names to Pinkerton Drive. Quick turns on S. Pekin and Whalen roads lead you across railroad tracks and into the quiet. Go left onto Kuhnis Road and follow it south past fields to the Lewis River, held back from the land by a tall levee. Dike Road follows the levee. Perched between the wide, slow river and the cultivated lowlands, you can almost imagine yourself somewhere in Holland. Minus the windmills, that is. (But if you were in Holland, you wouldn't see anglers pulling giant salmon out of the river, either. So call it even.)

Near mile 5, the road curves right to leave the Lewis River, mere yards from its mouth. A short distance later, Dike Road reaches the Columbia River. A denuded stretch of riverfront, cluttered with rusting bulldozers and backhoes, serves as a proving ground for rookie heavy equipment operators. Just downstream, a remnant wetland offers a scrap of habitat to a lucky few salmon.

Farther along, a couple of gated, terra-cotta-roofed compounds pretend they're somewhere in California or the Mediterranean. One of them sits immediately across the road from a tattered apartment building housing migrant farm workers. There could hardly be a blunter reminder of the feudal conditions that persist for the people who help make our food so cheap and so easily wasted. Beyond, you pass an RV campground, a gravel quarry, and Lions Day Park. Across the river in Oregon, houses climb the hillsides in St. Helens and Columbia City. The wide, wild Columbia rolls slowly toward the sea.

Around mile 10 the route leaves the river and turns inland. Passing more fields, you cross the plain toward timbered hills rising above the broad Lewis River valley. Just before you reach the freeway and a Walmart, turn right onto S. Burke Road to linger in the hinterlands, cruising through a jumbled landscape of homes, light industrial buildings, farms, and wooded swales.

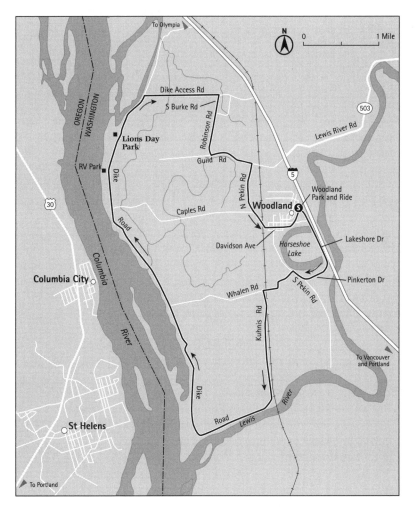

Lonely road along the Lewis River

A few miles later, N. Pekin Road leads back across the railroad tracks and into town along Davidson Avenue. There's not much left to this old main street: some vacant lots, a few old buildings, and a mural harkening back to Woodland's logging heyday. The freeway seems to have treated Woodland like it did the Lewis River: an obstacle to move aside. So show this town some love. Before you get back on that freeway, buy lunch at a local shop and enjoy a picnic at the handsome new plaza overlooking Horseshoe Lake, where Davidson curves to become Goerig Street. The Park and Ride is just 0.25 mile down the road.

MILEAGE LOG

0.0 Begin at Woodland Information Center and Park and Ride. Go left onto Lakeshore Dr.

1.0 Road curves right to become Pinkerton Dr.

1.3 Curve right onto S. Pekin Rd., then left onto Whalen Rd.

2.1 Cross rail tracks and go left onto Kuhnis Rd.

3.7 Kuhnis curves right to become Dike Rd.

5.0 Dike Rd. curves right to follow Columbia.

9.6 Lions Day Park (boat launch, beach access) at left.

10.3 Curve right onto Dike Access Rd.

11.5 Right onto S. Burke Rd., which becomes Robinson Rd.

12.4 Left onto Guild Rd.

13.1 Right onto N. Pekin Rd.

14.1 Pekin curves left to cross railroad tracks and becomes Davidson Ave., which curves left to become Goerig St.

14.8 Right onto Lakeshore Dr., then immediate left to end at Woodland Park and Ride.

51 Cedar Creek

DIFFICULTY: Challenging
DISTANCE: 27.9-mile loop
ELEVATION GAIN: 2000 feet

Getting There: See Ride 50's directions to Woodland Information Center and Park and Ride parking lot.

This ride ventures up the Lewis River valley in northern Clark County, visiting the lower reaches of lovely Cedar Creek. The loop is scenic from start to finish, with some moderate climbs and mostly mellow traffic. Midway, you visit a historic gristmill on Cedar Creek. This is a pastoral corner of the Mount St. Helens foothills too many people have never seen—so venture north, Portlanders!

Begin at the Park and Ride in Woodland, where a humble trailer does duty as the visitors center. Cross under Interstate 5 to the east side of town and follow E. CC Street across the Lewis River. The freeway exit, gas stations, trailer park, and wastewater treatment plant now disappear as NW Hayes Road leads up the valley. The road—busy but wide-shouldered—skirts the wooded slopes of Goose Hill before climbing into more open farmland.

Around mile 5.5 the road's shoulder abruptly disappears—right at the base of a big hill. Ride with caution. Atop the hill, Hayes Road follows a bluff high above the Lewis River. Mount St. Helens foothills, ravaged by logging, fill the horizon.

Just before the road begins another climb, veer left onto NE Etna Road and follow it down through a tunnel of trees. On sunny days, the Lewis River's emerald water gleams through small breaks in the forest. The descent ends at a bridge over Cedar Creek where it meets the Lewis River. Just before the bridge, look left for a boat launch. In spring

and fall, watch for coho and chinook salmon. Informal trails from the boat ramp lead a short distance east to the mouth of Cedar Creek. At low water you can explore up the creek's densely vegetated canyon (respecting private property, of course).

Now get ready for a long but mostly gradual climb through forest and fields back up to the highlands. Near mile 11 you can glimpse Merwin Dam at left, the lowest of three large hydro projects that have turned 30 miles of Lewis River into slack water. Originally built to tame spring floods, Merwin cranks out 136 megawatts of electricity, nearly enough to power every household in Clark County. (The dams higher up are even bigger.)

The dams also did a number on the river's formerly abundant salmon runs. Earlier attempts to retrofit the dams for fish passage met with limited success. Now the dams' owner, Pacific Power and Light, is throwing more than $100 million at the problem. That sum will buy, among other things, a giant floating building to collect juvenile salmon for transport by truck around the dams.

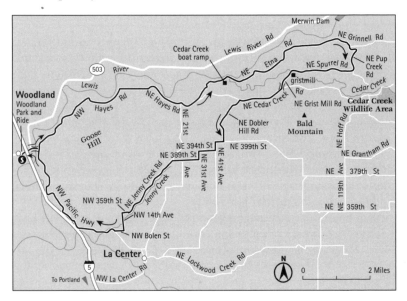

The gristmill, Cedar Creek

After mile 11 Etna Road becomes NE Grinnell Road and climbs to a saddle. Follow the main road as it curves right to become NE Pup Creek Road, which descends a shady ravine to NE Spurrel Road. Go right here. Views open again, now south across pastures and the green strip of Cedar Creek toward Bald Mountain.

On Spurrel Road, look for a small sign indicating the sharp left turn onto NE Grist Mill Road. It leads steeply downhill and soon reaches the Cedar Creek Gristmill. Built in 1876, the mill ground grain for settlers from across northern Clark County. Over the years it's also served as a smithy, a machine shop, a residence, and even a dance hall. In the 1980s a group of volunteers restored the mill; now they run it as a museum, milling grain on original equipment. They sell it hot off the wheel—the freshest flour you'll ever buy.

From the mill, continue over Cedar Creek on a covered bridge to climb a short but steep hill. Go right onto NE Cedar Creek Road, a moderately busy thoroughfare with little by way of a shoulder. The traffic mostly disappears at Dobler Hill Road. That's a good thing, since the hill slows your progress to a crawl. Though not really so big, it feels like it takes an eternity to climb. The payoff is evident on top, though, with views south across most of Clark County and an epic descent down secluded Jenny Creek Road.

The ride's final leg follows NW Pacific Highway, the old regional thoroughfare made obsolete by I-5. This is another busy-ish road. It also lacks a shoulder but has enough twists and curves to slow traffic somewhat. At points, you're directly above I-5, but you'd hardly know it. After 4 miles of mostly downhill cruising, head left to cross the Lewis River and return to your starting point.

MILEAGE LOG

0.0 Begin at Woodland Information Center and Park and Ride. Go right onto Lakeshore Dr., then right onto Goerig St. Continue under I-5 and make first right onto E. CC St. Cross Lewis River.

0.5 Left onto NW Hayes Rd.

6.3 Veer left (downhill) onto NE Etna Rd.

6.7 Left at fork to stay on Etna.

7.5 Cedar Creek boat ramp at left.

11.4 Etna becomes NE Grinnell Rd.

11.7 Grinnell curves right to become NE Pup Creek Rd.

12.6 Right onto NE Spurrel Rd.

14.7 Sharp left onto NE Grist Mill Rd. Steep downhill to Cedar Creek Gristmill at left. Cross creek and continue uphill.

15.5 Right onto NE Cedar Creek Rd.

16.8 Left onto NE Dobler Hill Rd.

18.3 Right onto NE 399th St., which curves left to become NE 41st Ave.

18.8 Right onto NE 394th St., which curves left to become NE 31st Ave. and then right to become NE 389th St.

20.3 Left onto NE Jenny Creek Rd.

22.3 Jenny Creek becomes NW 359th St.

22.6 NW 359th curves left to become NW 14th Ave., which curves right to become NW Bolen St.

23.4 Right onto NW Pacific Hwy. Watch for uneven pavement in first 0.25 mile.

27.4 Left onto NW Hayes Rd. Cross bridge to E. CC St., then left onto Lewis River Rd. (SR 503). Pass under I-5.

27.9 Left onto Lakeshore Dr., then immediately left to end at Woodland Information Center and Park and Ride.

52 Moulton Falls

DIFFICULTY: Easy
DISTANCE: 5.2 miles
ELEVATION GAIN: 100 feet

Getting There: From I-5 northbound in Washington State, take exit 9 and go east on NE 219th St. (Washington Rte. 502) almost 5 miles, then go left onto NW 10th Ave. in Battle Ground. This becomes NE Lewisville Hwy. (SR 503). Follow it north approximately 5.5 miles across East Fork Lewis River and go right onto NE Rock Creek Rd., which becomes NE 152nd Ave. and then NE Lucia Falls Rd. After 5 miles, go right onto NE Hantwick Rd. to trailhead parking area on left. (See map for Ride 53.)

This is one of my favorite paths, a forested trail following Murphy Grade along the East Fork Lewis River. It's part of the Foothills Loop (Ride 53), but I include it here as a separate ride because it's a great family outing, suitable for riders of all levels.

Begin at the Hantwick Road trailhead, where a 0.5-mile stretch of pavement leads from the parking area eastward into the forest. It slopes down to river level, passing a small pond, and turns to smooth gravel.

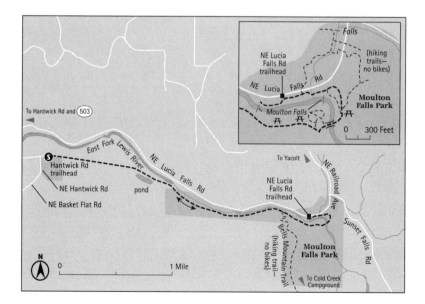

Cottonwoods and ash trees fill the river's floodplain below steep, fir-clad hills. You immediately feel you could be deep in the wilderness. Only birdsongs and the river's rush—and the occasional whistle of the old Chelatchie Prairie train, now carrying tourists on scenic excursions—interrupt the stillness.

The trail poses few challenges, though it's always a good idea to keep an eye out for equestrian users and give them a wide berth. Views get better as you continue, now along the riverbank. Around mile 2.3 a pedestrian bridge crosses the river, affording views up and down one of the East Fork's many pools. Depending on the water flow, look for intrepid kayakers or foolhardy swimmers passing beneath you.

Moulton Falls, no mountain bike required

Across the bridge, go left at the trail intersection to head briefly downriver (on the far bank) for a close-up view of Moulton Falls. Then choose one of the secluded picnic areas on either side of the bridge to soak up the ambience. A trail opposite NE Lucia Falls Road leads a short distance to another falls on Big Tree Creek.

Several unofficial trails lead down from the pedestrian bridge to the riverbank. At low water, you can easily pick your way (on foot) upstream for more solitude. Use caution around the water, though, since this river is a lot more powerful than it looks. And take care not disturb the fragile vegetation along the riverbank.

When you're ready to head back, simply retrace your route to the Hantwick Road trailhead.

MILEAGE LOG

0.0 Begin at Hantwick Rd. trailhead. Follow path eastward.
0.5 Pond at right.
2.1 Bells Mountain hiking trail at right.
2.3 Pedestrian bridge over East Fork Lewis River. Go left at junction immediately beyond. (Right-hand trail leads to main parking area, off Sunset Falls Rd.)
2.4 Upper Moulton Falls.
2.5 Big Tree Creek Falls trail at right (crosses road).
2.6 Lower Moulton Falls at NE Lucia Falls Rd. trailhead. Retrace route to return.

53 Foothills Loop

DIFFICULTY: Challenging to Very Challenging
DISTANCE: 38.8-mile loop
ELEVATION GAIN: 2500 feet

Getting There: From I-5 northbound in Washington State, take exit 9 and go east on NE 219th St. (Washington Rte. 502) into Battle Ground and go left onto NW 10th Ave., which becomes NE Lewisville Hwy. (SR 503). Cross East Fork Lewis River and go right into Lewisville County Park. Day-use fee.

Transit: Take MAX Yellow Line to Delta Park station, then ride C-TRAN bus No. 47 to Community Center (Fairgrounds Park) stop in Battle Ground and join the route at mile 35.4.

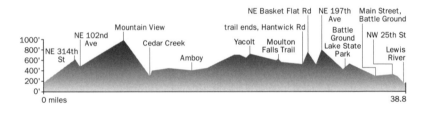

In northeastern Clark County, Mount St. Helens's foothills rise above rugged and isolated country. The Lewis River, with its huge dams and reservoirs, hems the area in on the north; vast timberlands in the national forest stretch to the east. With Interstate 5 far to the west, this area isn't on the way to anywhere. That's exactly why you should visit.

That's not the only reason, though. There's also the still-wild East Fork of the Lewis River, a beautiful river with several regional parks. This ride visits two of those parks—Lewisville and Moulton Falls— on a challenging loop, linking several small towns via miles of rural roads. With several big climbs and occasional stretches of busy road (no shoulder, of course), this is not a beginner's ride. But it's very scenic—a standout among the rides in this guide.

Begin at Lewisville County Park north of Battle Ground, a 154-acre forest on the East Fork. This is the county's oldest regional park, dating back to the 1930s. (A 2.5-mile trail loops among its towering firs and river beaches, making for a great post-ride ramble.) From the park's main entrance, go right onto the Lewisville Highway and start uphill. This is a very fast, often busy road, but the shoulder is wide.

After less than 0.5 mile, cross the highway with extreme caution to head west on NE 269th Street, which curves right to become NE 122nd Avenue. For the next 8 miles, you climb gradually but continuously to almost 1000 feet above sea level. Views stretch far to the south; on a clear day you can see downtown Portland.

The scenic (and literal) high point comes around mile 8.4, at the aptly named crossroad of Mountain View. Where NE 119th Avenue meets NE Grantham Road, a 19th-century cemetery and rustic chapel preside over the highlands dividing the East and North Forks of the Lewis River. Here—if the clouds cooperate—your long climb ends at a stunning view of Mount St. Helens. From this vantage high above the valley floor, you can better appreciate the volcano's immensity.

Now comes a screaming downhill to Cedar Creek. From NE Munch Road, go right onto NE Cedar Creek Road. At right is the Cedar Creek State Wildlife Recreation Area, a unit of the Washington Department

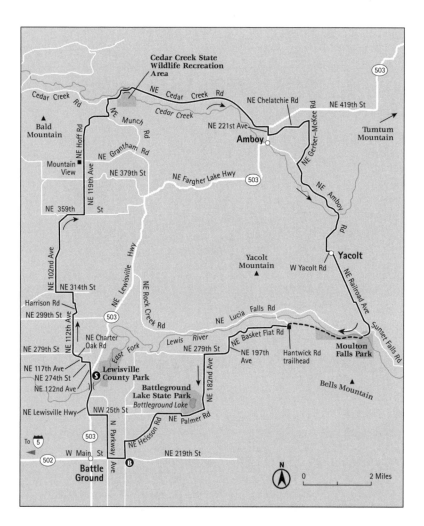

of Fish and Wildlife's Mount St. Helens Wildlife Area. This area is protected for band-tailed pigeon, which you're unlikely to spot. Still, it's worth a stop at the parking area (just before the Cedar Creek bridge) to ramble in the woods.

After 5 somewhat busy miles on Cedar Creek Road, go right onto NE 221st Avenue to reach the little town of Amboy, basically a general store and a school. Go left onto NE Chelatchie Road to loop through Chelatchie Prairie, a wide and flat valley ringed by hills. Across the prairie, Tumtum Mountain rises 1500 feet in a nearly perfect cone. This is the far corner of Clark County: from here, Gifford Pinchot

Tumtum Mountain and Chelatchie Prairie at Clark County's far corner

National Forest stretches east through 50 miles of rugged terrain to Mount Adams.

The route heads south over a small saddle and down to Yacolt, a tidy little town on another prairie. Yacolt's name is known far and wide for the eponymous fire that raged here in 1902. It's not clear where or how the blaze began, but in the absence of any organized firefighting system, it spread unchecked. Flames reached the edge of Yacolt, turning the hills above town into a moonscape. Residents fled in panic as the town nearly ignited. Just in time, a providential wind shifted the fire northward.

In the space of three days the blaze torched more than 200,000 acres of forest, $500 million of today's dollars in timber. Ash coated Portland a half inch deep and turned day to dusk in Seattle. It was the largest and most destructive forest fire in Washington's history. It prompted state leaders to establish a fire warden and launch the policy of fire suppression that, a century later, has unfortunately created forests poised to burn even more destructively.

From Yacolt's main street, go right onto NE Railroad Avenue and head south out of town. The road follows the Chelatchie Prairie Railroad, which once carried timber to Vancouver but now carries tourists to nearby Moulton Falls Park. With some luck and a lot of money, a bike path will someday accompany the tracks. Plans call for it to run all the way from Chelatchie Prairie to Vancouver.

In 2.5 miles down the road reach Moulton Falls Park, where the East Fork cascades over rock ledges. A trailhead just past the intersection with NE Sunset Falls Road leads you to an unpaved but very rideable trail (see Ride 52) along the river's south bank. At the trail's end, follow narrow NE Basket Flat Road up and over the shoulder of Bells Mountain where you break out of the forest to return to the plains.

Go left onto busy NE 182nd Avenue, which leads past the entrance to Battle Ground Lake State Park, where a little pond fills a tiny old caldera. (Think Crater Lake but smaller. A lot smaller. And no Wizard Island.) It's a charming and intimate spot, worth the quick side trip if the crowds aren't too big.

Beyond the park you reach Battle Ground, northeastern Clark County's metropolis. Pass the skate park and go right onto Main Street to get a taste of the town, then head right onto N. Parkway Avenue to leave town and return to the Lewisville Highway. Almost immediately it dips down to the East Fork, crosses the river, and returns you to Lewisville County Park.

MILEAGE LOG

0.0 Begin at Lewisville County Park. Go right onto Lewisville Hwy. (SR 503).

0.4 Left onto NE 269th St., which curves right to become NE 122nd Ave., NE 274th St., NE 117th Ave., NE Charter Oak Rd., and NE 112th Ave.

2.4 Cross NE 299th St. and continue north on Harrison Rd.

3.3 Left onto NE 314th St.

3.8 Right onto NE 102nd Ave.

6.2 Road curves right to become NE 359th St.

6.8 Follow road left onto NE 119th Ave.

8.4 Intersection with NE Grantham Rd. at Mountain View. NE 119th Ave. becomes NE Hoff Rd.

10.2 Left onto NE Munch Rd.

10.8 Right onto NE Cedar Creek Rd.

11.3 Entrance to Cedar Creek State Wildlife Recreation Area at right, just before bridge over creek.

15.8 Right onto NE 221st Ave. into Amboy.

16.0 Left onto NE Chelatchie Rd.

17.4 Right onto NE Gerber-McKee Rd. at Chelatchie Prairie.

18.8 Left onto NE Amboy Rd.

22.0 Left onto W. Yacolt Rd. in Yacolt, then right onto N. Railroad Ave.

24.8 Immediately past intersection with Sunset Falls Rd., go left into Sunset parking area for Moulton Falls Park. Continue on path and across East Fork Lewis River.

27.6 Path ends at Hantwick Road trailhead. Go left onto NE Hantwick Rd., which curves right to become NE Basket Flat Rd.

29.6 Road curves left to become NE 197th Ave., then right to become NE 279th St.

30.9 Left onto NE 182nd Ave.

32.4 Entrance to Battle Ground State Park at right. NE 182nd Ave. curves right to become NE Palmer Rd.

33.5 Follow road left to NE Heisson Rd.

34.9 Left onto NE Grace Rd.

35.4 Right onto W. Main St. in Battle Ground.

35.9 Right onto N. Parkway Ave.

37.3 Left onto NW 25th St.

37.9 Right onto NE Lewisville Hwy. (SR 503). Cross bridge over East Fork Lewis River.

38.8 Right to end at Lewisville County Park.

54 Camas and Washougal

DIFFICULTY: Moderate
DISTANCE: 23.2-mile loop—Camas loop 11.2 miles, Washougal loop
   12 miles
ELEVATION GAIN: 1250 feet; Camas loop 650 feet, Washougal loop
   600 feet

Getting There: From I-205 northbound take first exit in Washington State, exit 27, to follow Washington Rte. 14 eastbound. After 5.5 miles, take exit 12 onto SR 14 Business Loop and continue on NW Sixth Ave. into Camas. After 1.3 miles, go left onto NE Garfield St., which curves left to NE 14th Ave.; go right onto NE Everett St. (SR 500). Follow it 1 mile to Lacamas Park trailhead parking area on the right, just past intersection with NW Lake Rd. and before bridge over Lacamas Lake.

   Transit: Take MAX Yellow Line to Delta Park station, then take C-TRAN bus No. 41 to NE Third Ave.–Dallas St. stop in Camas. Bicycle up NE Dallas St. to Crown Park. Go right onto NE 15th St. and then left onto NE Everett St. to join Camas Loop near mile 10.3 (1.5 miles one way).

Camas and Washougal sit astride the Washougal River near its mouth. Behind them, the land steps up to Yacolt State Forest and the Mount St. Helens country beyond. On a winter day, when winds off the Columbia pin mist to the foothills, these towns capture the gloomy beauty of the Pacific Northwest as well as any place could.

   The ride visits both towns via connected loops, each beginning and ending at Lacamas Park, a forest enclave in the heart of Camas. Note: Both follow a mix of roads and paths, some gravel but suitable for road bikes.

   For the Camas loop, go left from the parking area onto NE Everett Street, then right onto NW Lake Road to reach the Lacamas Heritage Trail, a gravel path following Lacamas Lake's south shore. It's narrow

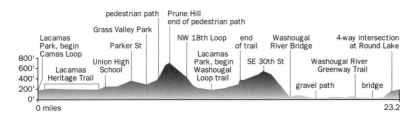

and curvy, so keep your speed down and watch for joggers. The solitary Victorian mansion on the far shore once belonged to Henry Pittock, the Portland publishing magnate. (Visit his opulent Portland home on Ride 4.) It neatly juxtaposes the newer mansions immediately behind you.

At trail's end, go left onto NE Goodwin Road and left again onto NW Friberg-Shrunk Street. It leads past colossal Union High School, plusher than many college campuses. Now you're pushing deep into the heart of suburbia, where friendly people walking their dogs offer directions to the bewildered cyclist. A left onto NW Lake Road and a right on NW Parker Street carry you past several of Camas's tech companies; they've helped this mill town reinvent itself as another Silicon Forest.

At NE 38th Avenue, go left to reach Grass Valley Park, where a paved path leads up Prune Hill. Near the top it gets so steep you'll probably have to push the bike. Beware of slick moss.

The path disappears for a few blocks near the top of Prune Hill, then resumes for a final tree-lined climb to big views at NW 28th Avenue. Go left here to cruise down toward Camas's old downtown. It's fast and very scenic, overlooking the sprawling paper mill and the mighty Columbia. A final quiet mile on Everett returns you to Lacamas Park.

Now for the Washougal loop. From the parking area, follow the paved trail into Lacamas Park. Beyond the picnic area and bathrooms, it follows the wooded shore of Round Lake. The trail turns to packed gravel and then abruptly ends at an old fish screen and dam. You can see where the trail resumes a hundred yards distant; to get there, carry your bike along the awkwardly narrow (but safe) top of the dam. Once across, continue a short distance farther along Round Lake to a junction, where a right turn leads you to the park's maintenance access road (packed gravel, closed to cars). Follow it gradually uphill through the forest to arrive at SE Crown Road. Go left onto Crown Road, then right onto SE 23rd Street. Small farms line the road, their old farmhouses and half-abandoned orchards holding off the subdivisions and mansions for a few years more. A low hill soon blocks your view of the city you just left. To the north, timbered foothills rise above the Little Washougal River.

Several turns and several miles later, SE Woodburn Road carries you down to Washougal. The route continues down to the Columbia River. Here, at the end of S. 27th Street, go right onto a path leading along a levee. (You might consider a side trip left to visit Cottonwood Beach, where William Clark camped. Now it's a summer sunbathing destination.) After 0.75 mile, look for a path at right leading under Washington Route 14 through a tunnel. It leads past the Two Rivers Heritage Museum (a block to the left and worth a visit) into the old town center.

For a place with so much history, Washougal looks pretty sad these days. Despite a recent makeover, the commercial strip along B Street is moribund. Continue west to the Washougal River Greenway, a secluded riverfront path. It's probably the tour's highlight: a 1-mile ramble alongside and over the river, through forest and wetlands.

Autumn on the Columbia River dike path near Cottonwood Beach, Washougal

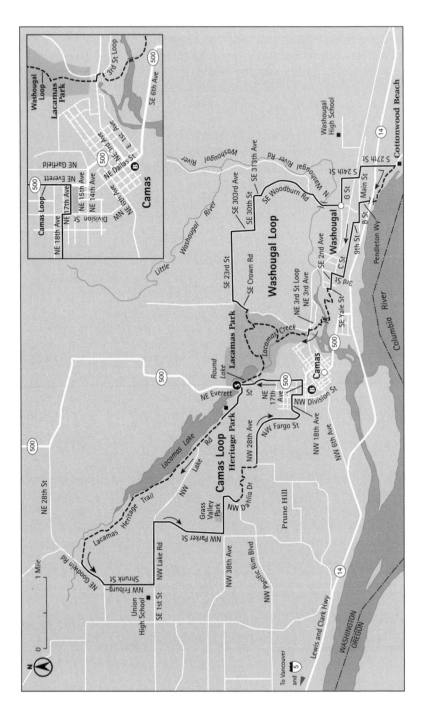

The path ends at NE Third Street Loop. Turn left and at busy NE Third Avenue, turn left again. Go left and cross Lacamas Creek, then immediately go right into an easy-to-miss trailhead. At the back of the small parking lot, a gravel path leads up the creek and into Lacamas Park. Follow it up a forested canyon to a bridge over Lacamas Creek, which slides over tiered ledges in a long, elegant cascade. It's a fantastically scenic spot, intimate and wild, a sylvan hideaway within walking distance of town. Continue across the bridge and up the ever-climbing main trail. It leads you to the maintenance access road; go left to retrace the initial mile and a half of your route back to the parking area.

MILEAGE LOG

Camas Loop:

  0.0 Begin at Lacamas Park. Left onto NE Everett St., then immediate right onto NW Lake Rd.

  0.4 Right into Heritage Park. Go left onto Lacamas Heritage Trail (bike path) at crosswalk.

  0.7 Trail turns to packed gravel and follows shore of Lacamas Lake.

  1.9 Private boat launch. Trail continues 100 feet up the road.

  3.9 End of Lacamas Heritage Trail. Go left from trailhead onto NE Goodwin Rd. Caution.

  4.3 Left onto NW Friberg-Shrunk St. Union High School at right.

  5.1 Left onto NW Lake Rd.

  6.0 Right onto NW Parker St. Use bike lane or bike path on opposite side of street.

  7.0 Left onto NW 38th Ave. Use pedestrian path on north side. Grass Valley Park at left.

  7.6 Right onto NW Dahlia Dr.

  7.8 Left onto pedestrian path at crosswalk. *Very* steep uphill!

  8.2 Path continues across NW Valley St.

  8.3 Right onto tree-lined path heading uphill.

  8.5 At end of path, go left onto NW 28th Ave., which becomes NW Fargo St.

  9.6 Sharp curve to left; Fargo becomes NW 18th Loop, then NW 18th Ave.

 10.0 Right onto NW Division St., then left onto NE 17th Ave.

 10.3 Left onto NE Everett St.

 11.2 Return to Lacamas Park.

Washougal Loop:

  0.0 Begin at Lacamas Park. Enter park on paved path and continue past bathrooms. Path turns to gravel and then ends at fish screen and dam. Carry bike across dam and continue on main trail as it circles Round Lake.

0.6 At trail junction on the south end of Round Lake, go right, following sign for Lower Falls. Keep left to stay on main trail (the access road). Follow it all the way to park exit at SE Crown Road.

1.6 Left onto SE Crown Road.

1.8 Right onto SE 23rd St.

2.8 Road curves right to become SE 303rd Ave.

3.1 Road curves left to become SE 30th St.

3.6 Road curves right to become SE 313th Ave., then SE Woodburn Rd. (steep downhill).

4.8 Right onto N. Washougal River Rd. Cross bridge.

5.1 Left onto G St.

5.5 Right onto S. 24th St.

5.8 Left onto Main St., then first right onto S. 27th St.

6.4 At the end of S. 27th (before it bears left), continue straight onto gravel path and go right. (**Side trip:** Go left to visit Cottonwood Beach.)

7.1 Right onto ramp (adjacent to stairs) to exit path. Proceed through tunnel and continue on Pendleton Way. (**Side trip:** Go left 1 block to visit Two Rivers Heritage Museum.)

7.4 Left onto Main St.–B St. in "downtown" Washougal.

7.8 Right onto 9th St., then immediate left onto C St.

8.5 Right onto 3rd St.

8.7 Left onto SE 2nd Ave.

8.9 Right onto SE Yale St.

9.0 Go left onto Washougal River Greenway Trail (begins at SE Yale and 2nd).

10.1 Greenway Trail ends at NE 3rd St. Loop. Go left, cross NE 3rd Ave. at crosswalk, and continue west (left) on sidewalk over Lacamas Creek Bridge.

10.4 Go right into Lacamas Park trailhead parking area. Continue north, uphill, on gravel trail.

11.1 Cross Lacamas Creek on bridge (caution) and continue straight on main trail. After a steep up and then downhill, trail curves left and climbs steadily.

11.5 Left at T intersection onto access road. From here, retrace route to Round Lake, cross dam, and continue to parking area.

13.0 End at Lacamas Park parking area on NE Everett Street.

55 Cape Horn

DIFFICULTY: Challenging
DISTANCE: 18.4-mile loop
ELEVATION GAIN: 1750 feet

Getting There: From I-205 northbound, take first exit in Washington State, exit 27, to follow Washington Rte. 14 eastbound. After 10.5 miles, turn left at stoplight onto 32nd St. in Washougal. After 0.6 mile turn right onto J St. and find Washougal High School on left in 0.25 mile. Park here.

Transit: Take MAX Yellow Line to Delta Park station, then take C-TRAN bus No. 41 to stop at B St. and 32nd Ave. in Washougal. Bicycle up 32nd Ave. and go right on J St. to reach Washougal High School (about 2 miles round-trip).

The Columbia Gorge is one of America's treasures, a sublime landscape of mountains, waterfalls, and the great river of the Northwest. But beautiful though it is, the Gorge can be difficult to experience by bike if you're not an advanced rider comfortable with busy roads and stiff winds. This ride is an exception, getting you to the Gorge's western entrance via back roads. It climbs from near river level in Washougal to the edge of Cape Horn, an enormous basalt cliff where a new overlook offers an iconic Gorge view.

Begin at Washougal High School and head east on J Street. The climbing begins past a golf course. Get used to it—this hill lasts about 4 miles! After the first mile, though, you leave Washougal's residential fringe to enter secluded and relatively level country.

From here the ride heads east along a gradually rising plateau. The land drops steeply south to the Columbia and north to the Washougal River, offering vistas in both directions. It's a mix of old homesteads, newer hobby farms, and the occasional McMansion. You'll also pass

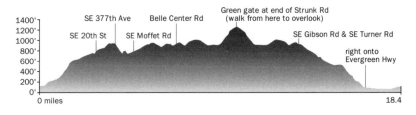

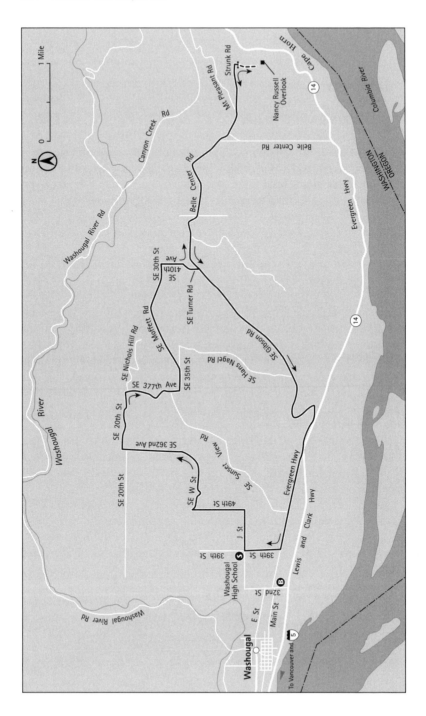

a few sketchy rural compounds (moss-laden old cottage, junked cars, creepy *Twin Peaks* vibe).

Topography prevents most of these roads from leading anywhere in particular, so the traffic is mostly local and light. After a mercifully level stretch along Belle Center Road, a final climb commences up Mount Pleasant Road to the top of Cape Horn. The road ends at a small parking area, where a gravel path begins beyond a gate.

The path—once called Rim Drive—could symbolize the story of the Gorge, in particular how it came to pass that this incredible landscape has remained largely free of sprawl.

People who love the Gorge sought for a century to protect it from spoliation, but the effort took on new life—and new urgency—in the early 1980s. The completion of Interstate 205 put both sides of the Gorge within easy reach of Portlanders, raising the specter of intensified bedroom community developments. A small group of citizens, led by a Portland homemaker named Nancy Russell, took action. Despite a lack of political experience or connections, they managed to write and pass the Columbia River Gorge National Scenic Area Act, which established strict zoning to protect the Gorge's scenic integrity. It was the only major piece of environmental legislation to emerge from the Reagan era.

Exhibit A in the argument for why the Gorge needed protection can be found atop Cape Horn, at Rim Drive. In the early 1980s, a developer laid out a subdivision here, directly above the river. If built upon, the lots would have created a line of mansions atop Cape Horn, immediately across the Columbia from Oregon's famed Crown Point. To avert aesthetic disaster, Nancy Russell and her husband, Bruce, took out a bank loan to help the Trust for Public Land acquire the lots, which were eventually conveyed to the US Forest Service.

One lot got away, though, and eventually a home was built on it—a massive bunker of a mansion visible from miles away. But after a protracted effort, the Trust for Public Land and Nancy's own group, the Friends of the Columbia Gorge, managed to buy it too. The Friends then carefully deconstructed the home. In its place, in 2011, they built an overlook dedicated to Nancy Russell.

The overlook, a simple circular stone plaza, is the true destination of this ride, about a 0.5-mile walk from the gate. The view is simply spectacular, taking in Archer and Hamilton mountains on the Washington side and Angels Rest, Nesmith Point, Larch Mountain, and points beyond on the Oregon side. It's the same view drivers see on Washington Route 14 directly below—and yet so different. Above the

The Columbia Gorge from the Nancy Russell Overlook at Cape Horn

highway's dull roar, you're alone with the wind, with the time you need to truly comprehend the Gorge's immensity.

When you're done, backtrack to SE Gibson Road. (Other routes back necessitate riding on SR 14 or Washougal River Road, which are for experts—or masochists—only.) The long descent down Gibson, through oak grasslands and orchards, may be the most scenic stretch of the entire ride. Wild views of the Columbia River and Oregon's cliffs accompany you all the way down.

At the bottom, continue straight through a stop sign to follow the Evergreen Highway west into Washougal. A right turn on 39th Street and a final climb return you to your starting point at the high school.

MILEAGE LOG

0.0 Begin at Washougal High School parking lot. Turn left to proceed east on J St.

0.5 Street curves left to become 49th St.

1.2 Street curves right to become SE W St., then SE St. Clair Rd., then SE 362nd Ave.

2.9 Right onto SE 20th St.

3.8 Right onto SE 377th Ave.

4.6 Left at stop sign onto SE 35th St.

4.9 Bear left onto SE Moffett Rd.

6.2 Road curves left to become SE 30th St.

6.4 Road curves right to become SE 410th Ave.

6.7 Road curves right to become SE Turner Rd.

6.9 Sharp left onto SE Gibson Rd.

7.0 Road curves right to become Belle Center Rd.

9.1 Continue straight onto Mount Pleasant Rd.

9.5 Right onto Strunk Rd.

10.0 Road ends at parking area and green gate. Continue on foot past gate on a gravel path 0.5 mile to Nancy Russell Overlook. Return to gate and ride back to SE SE Gibson Rd. (mile 6.9 above).

13.2 SE Turner Rd. at right; continue straight on SE Gibson Rd.

16.5 Bear right onto Evergreen Hwy.

17.9 Right onto 39th St.

18.4 End at J St. at Washougal High School.

RECOMMENDED RESOURCES

Information

Bike Portland. Portland's most influential and informative bike blog; essential reading: www.bikeportland.org.

City of Portland. Probably the best assemblage of information, maps, links, and wonky bike planning: www.gettingaroundportland.org.

Metro. The regional government's website has information on bicycling, public transit, planning and sustainability, and natural areas conservation: www.oregonmetro.gov.

Ride Oregon Ride. Ride suggestions, events calendar, bike shop listings, and much more; put together by the State of Oregon's tourism agency, Travel Oregon: www.rideoregonride.com.

Organizations

Bicycle Transportation Alliance. Influential bike advocacy organization, working for safer streets and improved bike infrastructure: www.bta4bikes.org.

Community Cycling Center. Nonprofit helping broaden access to bikes and bicycling: www.communitycyclingcenter.org.

Northwest Bicycle Safety Council. Nonprofit focused on safety education, especially for kids and senior citizens: www.nwbicyclesafety council.org.

Oregon Bicycle Racing Association. Organizes and sanctions racing events: www.obra.org.

Portland Velo. West Side road riding club: www.portlandvelo.net.

Portland Wheelmen Touring Club. Portland's oldest and biggest club, with an emphasis on recreational rides: www.pwtc.com.

SHIFT. Devoted to making bicycling fun, with events like Breakfast on the Bridges, Pedalpalooza, and the Midnight Mystery Ride: www.shift2bikes.org.

Vancouver Bicycle Club. Vancouver's leading bike club, with organized rides most days: www.vbc-usa.com.

Events

Cirque du Cycling. Part bike race, part street fair, completely Portland: www.cyclingcircus.com.

Union Street Bridge, Salem

Cycle Oregon. "The Best Bike Ride in America," an annual weeklong ride visiting scenic corners of Oregon, complete with catered meals, camping, hot showers, and 2000 of your closest friends; a classic event that routinely sells out: www.cycleoregon.com.

Harvest Century. Last big ride of the season; supports Community Vision, a nonprofit working with the disabled: www.harvestcentury.org.

Pedalpalooza. SHIFT's big summer bash, a loosely organized three-week June festival celebrating all things bike; events include the World Naked Bike Ride (complete with police escort) and the Multnomah County Bike Fair (bike jousting, general hipsterism): www.shift2bikes .org/pedalpalooza.

Portland Century. Popular supported ride looping Portland and the Sandy River: http://portlandcentury.com.

Providence Bridge Pedal. The blockbuster event on Portland's busy bike calendar; several bridges, including the soaring Fremont, close to traffic for an August morning as thousands of bicyclists stream across— awesome views and huge (huge!) crowds: www.bridgepedal.com.

Ride Around Clark County. Grand tour of that mysterious land across the Columbia, organized by Vancouver Bike Club: http://vbc -usa.com/racc.

River City Bicycles Cross Crusade. Highly popular cyclocross racing series: www.crosscrusade.com.

Seattle to Portland. A mammoth (10,000-plus participants) supported ride benefiting Seattle's Cascade Bicycle Club: http://shop .cascade.org/contents/events/stp.

Sunday Parkways. Several Sundays each summer, the city closes streets to cars along a designated neighborhood loop. A huge party ensues. It's Portland's best bike event—or best event, period: www .portlandsundayparkways.org.

Worst Day of the Year Ride. Celebrates winter riding with an easy lap around Portland and catered stops for food and beer; benefits the Community Cycling Center: http://worstdayride.com.

Maps

Bike It! Clackamas County's official bike map, available at local bike shops and directly from the county: www.clackamas.us/transporta-tion/bikes/map.htm. The county also offers ride suggestions: www .mthoodterritory.com/biking.jsp.

Bike There! Metro's map covers the entire region, with insets for urban centers; the one must-have map: www.oregonmetro.gov /bikethere.

Ride the City: Portland. Online route planner: www.ridethecity .com/portland.

Vancouver and Clark County, Washington. The official bike map: www.cityofvancouver.us/bike.

Washington County. The county's official map, with ride suggestions: www.visitwashingtoncountyoregon.com/bikemap.

Suggested Reading

Abbott. Carl. *Portland in Three Centuries: The Place and the People.* Corvallis: Oregon State University Press, 2011. A concise and engaging history from the dean of Portland historians.

Bell, Trudy, and Roxana Bell. *Bicycling with Children: Everything a Parent Needs to Know About Bikes and Kids—From Toddler to Teen.* Seattle: The Mountaineers Books, 1999.

Foster, Laura. *Portland City Walks: Twenty Explorations In and Around Town.* Portland: Timber Press, 2008.

_____. *Portland Hill Walks: Twenty Explorations in Parks and Neighborhoods.* Portland: Timber Press, 2005. Excellent guides brimming with local history, geography, and culture—the kind of stuff worth discovering on foot or bike.

Granton, Shawn, and Nate Beaty. *Zinester's Guide to Portland.* Portland: Microcosm Publishing, 2005. A pocket- (or pannier-) friendly guide to all things Portland, by and largely for locals.

Houck, Michael. *Wild in the City: Exploring the Intertwine: The Portland–Vancouver Region's Network of Parks, Trails, and Natural Areas.* Corvallis: Oregon State University Press, 2011. A comprehensive guide to the region's natural heritage, packed with stories and information about the ongoing effort to make this great place even better.

Houle, Marcy Cottrell, and Eric Goetze. *One City's Wilderness: Portland's Forest Park.* Corvallis: Oregon State University Press, 2010. The definitive guide to Forest Park's human and natural history, with trail descriptions and maps.

Hurst, Robert. *The Cyclist's Manifesto: The Case for Riding on Two Wheels Instead of Four.* Guilford, CT: Falcon Guides, 2009. A former bike messenger argues—with wit and humor—why we can't afford not to drive less and ride more.

Mapes, Jeff. *Pedaling Revolution: How Cyclists Are Changing American Cities.* Corvallis: Oregon State University Press, 2009. A reporter for *The Oregonian* offers national and local perspectives on the urban bike revolution.

Moore, Jim. *75 Classic Rides Oregon: The Best Road Biking Routes.* Seattle: The Mountaineers Books, 2012. Get out of town!

Oates, David. *City Limits: Walking Portland's Boundary.* Corvallis: Oregon State University Press, 2006. A writer spends two years walking the Urban Growth Boundary, meeting people living along and affected by it, and meditating on the meaning of community.

INDEX

ABOUT THE AUTHOR

Raised in Alaska, Owen Wozniak has lived and cycled in Portland for the last decade. As a project manager at the Trust for Public Land, a national nonprofit conservation organization, he works across the Portland region and beyond to protect natural places for people to enjoy (learn more at www.tpl.org).

A member of the Mazamas, Owen is a has-been mountaineer and current avid skier. His main pastime right now involves keeping up with his one-year-old son. He looks forward to joining Portland's growing ranks of cargo bike–riding parents.

Owen's previous books for The Mountaineers Books include *50 Hikes in Alaska's Chugach State Park.*

The author and his son enjoy a break during a ride, with Lee relishing a (temporary) victory in his battle against the dreaded helmet.